Day Tripping:

Kayak Wisconsin

Lake Michigan Water Trail

Sturgeon Bay to Chicago

Babs Smith

Book cover photo:
Milwaukee Skyline, paddling past Milwaukee's Art Museum,
the Burke Brise Soleil

Back cover photo:
Rick with Wisconsin's Tall Ship: the Denis Sullivan

Photos by:
Babs Smith
Rick and Chris Malchow
Mike Smith
Jeff Fitch
Ava and Lilly Bellis

Graphic Design:
Ryan Malchow

Editor:
Gerry LaBonte

*A portion of the cost of this book is donated
to protecting Lake Michigan*

CONTENTS

Sturgeon Bay to Chicago

The Rivers

Sturgeon Bay to Chicago

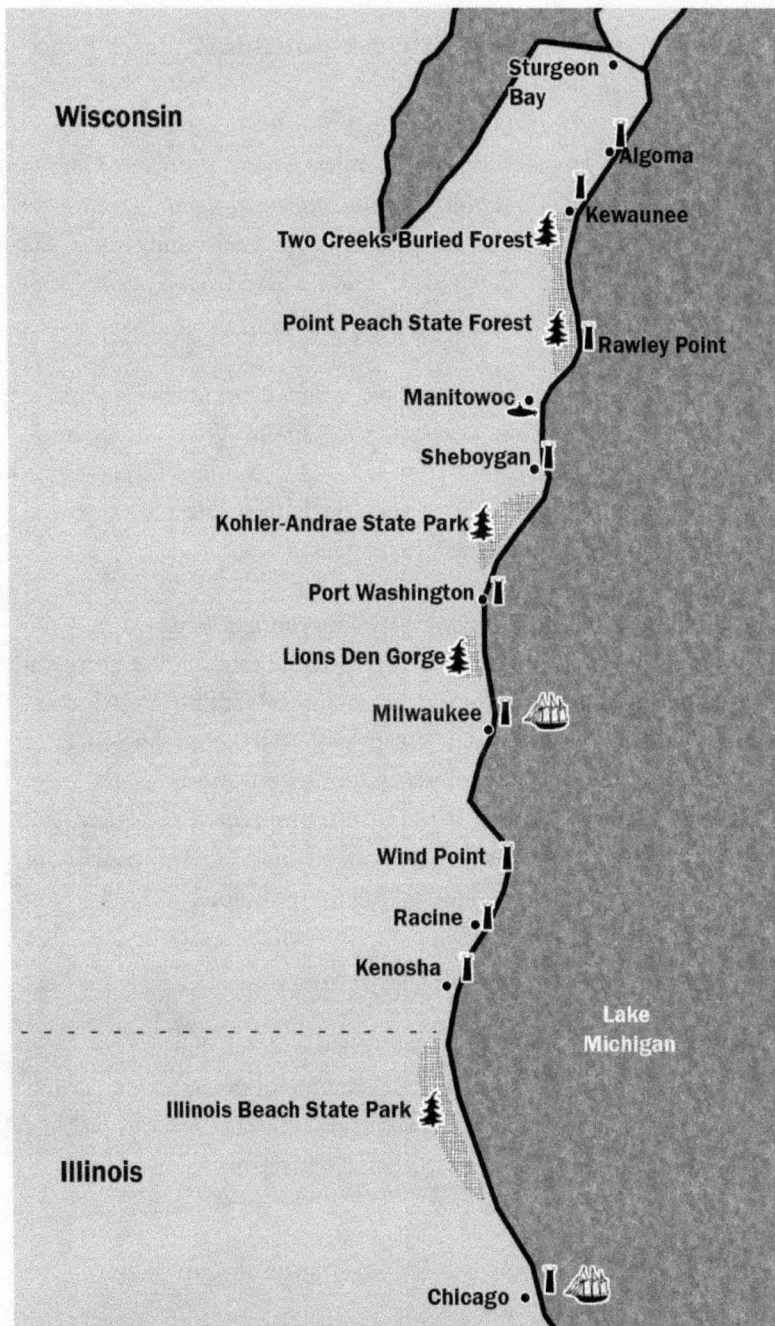

Wisconsin

Sturgeon Bay

Algoma

Kewaunee

Two Creeks Buried Forest

Point Peach State Forest

Rawley Point

Manitowoc

Sheboygan

Kohler-Andrae State Park

Port Washington

Lions Den Gorge

Milwaukee

Wind Point

Racine

Kenosha

Lake Michigan

Illinois Beach State Park

Illinois

Chicago

Our Adventure Continues!

We did it! We kayaked over 300 miles around the Door County Peninsula, Wisconsin's thumb. From Green Bay up and around the peninsula, through Deaths Door, and back south along the Lake Michigan coast line to Kewaunee! Paddle lift! Check out my first book for these adventures.

Now what? Took us a little time, and then we got it. The shoreline didn't end! So. . . we can keep paddling south. We continue to do day paddles, trying for about 10 miles a day. But don't fret—again in this book, there are all the possible launch sites, so you can customize the paddles to your preferences.

This journey starts in Sturgeon Bay, appropriate because it is the beginning of the Schooner Coast. We paddle through the Sturgeon Bay Shipping Channel, and turn south. Paddling to Algoma, Kewaunee, Two Rivers, and to Manitowoc. All part of the Schooner Coast. But. . .on we travel south, following Wisconsin's Lake Michigan Water Trail and Wisconsin's proposed Lake Michigan National Marine Sanctuary: to Sheboygan, Port Washington, Milwaukee, Racine, Kenosha, and finally to Illinois! But why stop there? We choose to make Chicago our final destination. Yup, it's not part of Wisconsin, but who can resist?

Such fun to explore the cities with urban paddles, but the between sections are the true slice of Wisconsin with all the nature areas and state parks to discover. This book offers the best of both worlds, quiet natural solitude, and busy urban enthusiasm!

i

Sturgeon Bay to Chicago

At times, the Lake is serene, and other times boisterous and wavy. A few times, we choose to not attempt Lake Michigan and her whitecaps. These days, we choose to sightsee the rivers. Thus, I include the kayak-able rivers in this book: Algoma's Anhapee River, the Kewaunee River, Two Rivers West and East Twin Rivers, Manitowoc River, Sheboygan River, the Milwaukee River, the Root River in Racine, Kenosha's Pike River, and the memorable Chicago River.

Whichever paddle you choose to enjoy, we pray for your safety, and that you have a unique unforgettable fantastically fun experience! Hopefully, our story and information, guides you to enjoy the incredible beauty of Wisconsin's Lake Michigan Water Trail, Schooner Coast, and Marine Sanctuary. From her beautiful beaches, soaring bluffs, lovely lighthouses, underwater shipwrecks, parks, and cities, have fun and enjoy exploring!

Safety and Stuff

One thing we've learned the longer we paddle, safety is paramount. You'd think as we develop our skills, we wouldn't be as concerned. But. . .what we've learned is, you can't have fun if you aren't safe.

Know your skills: We are talking about paddling the big pond, Lake Michigan. This is a big lake, with big water. It is important to realize that the weather, wind, and waves can change during your paddling. You must be ready for big waves even if the lake is quiet and smooth when you start.

A PFD: Personal Floatation Device: Please wear it all the time, as the weather may have different plans than you have.

Sea Kayaks: To paddle Lake Michigan, we highly recommend sea kayaks or at least "transitional kayaks". They are longer and slimmer than recreation kayaks, which means you don't have to paddle so hard. But that is not the reason sea kayaks are preferred. Sea kayaks are made for big water. . .and Lake Michigan certainly qualifies as a big pond! Sea kayaks are more maneuverable, turn easier, and have closed hatch space—which means they float better, which can be pretty important if you tip over. And tipping over is always a possibility.

Rudder or Skeg? A rudder or skeg can help steer in wind and waves, something Lake Michigan often has. A rudder can be turned to help your boat turn or correct being pushed in a direction by the weather. A skeg, is a kayak's centerboard such as big ships have. It does not turn, but can help you track straighter. Both can be helpful in wind and waves, but don't do anything if the lake is calm. Your choice, rudder, skeg or none! Either way, it doesn't replace learning the skills of kayaking and paddling. Therefore, what I really recommend is taking a class on how to control your kayak and paddle more efficiently and safer for your body and arms.

A good paddle is really helpful. Just like runners buy running shoes, and bikers buy specialized bikes. Kayakers depend on their paddle. A traditional Euro blade offers a bigger surface on the paddle for more power in each stroke, whereas a Greenland blade is long and narrow, which pulls less water with each stroke (so you'll do more strokes than with the Euro blade), but it is less strenuous. Kind of even steven? So, it is a preference thing. An ergonomic paddle is crooked to place your hands in a better position which may help limit shoulder and hand and wrist pain. Bottom line, your paddle should be light—so you don't get as sore and tired. Floatable is helpful as a sinking paddle is not much help. . . Recommend that your paddle not be metal, just in case a storm brews up—don't be a lightning rod!

Know and practice rescues. During an emergency is NOT the time to try to figure out or remember how to do a rescue. Do you know how to get back into your kayak if you tip over? How to get a boat load of water out of your cock pit? How to rescue your buddies? If not, there are classes you can take, such as at your local YMCA. Then practice at least one time a year—more often is obviously better and can be a lot of fun too especially on a hot summer day.

A kayak skirt is needed on Lake Michigan, or any of the Great Lakes. A boat full of water makes the boat easier to tip over. Wear the skirt. . .if it starts out nice, you can have one that zips down and keep cool, but can zip up if the weather rises up. Please don't keep your skirt in your hatches, they are just not accessible when needed.

Rick's 3 essentials: We now carry safety gear at all times. This includes Rick's 3 essentials:
 -flashlight: preferably LED- it's amazing how many times you stop and play and end up pulling the kayak's out in the dark, Rick also swears by a headband light so two hands are free.
 -lighter: in case safety (like being stranded on shore when weather has become stormy) dictates a fire. A lighter is also very nice for HOT food! If you are a klutz, like me, then you could switch to matches instead, just keep them in a dry bag.
-pocket knife: you never know when you'll need it, and you tend to need it a lot more than you expect.
You can always color coordinate the 3 essentials to your boat color as Rick does. He always has his 3 essentials in his pocket, he is never sure which pocket, but always in his least likely pocket.

Toilet paper: Essential—every trip needs it. Works as Kleenex (tissue if you are not from Wisconsin) in a pinch too!

Carry a first aid kit. Ours keeps growing every time we wish we had something. Our first aid kit includes aspirin/ibuprofen, band aids for little hurts, bandages and tape for bigger hurts, coban wrap –better known in Wisconsin as "vet wrap" available at Fleet Farm type stores, which substitutes for tape or splints if needed, and holds band aids on better for blisters on hands. Chris always has her bee sting rescue pen (which thank God we have not needed yet—knock on wood!), Babs carries Benadryl Itch stopping cream (after a discovery that she is allergic to "no see' em" or gnats when camping on an island), and Rick has a tennis elbow splint (in case that decides to flare up). Then you might as long bring along an Icy Hot type of gel which does seem to help relieve achy muscles.

Running lights that hook onto the kayak when it starts getting dark, 'cause you played so long in the surf! You kind of want other boats to be able to see you in the dark. . . Here's the scoop on where to place them: red light on the port (left) side, a green light on the starboard (right) side. Best if they are kept in an accessible place (i.e.: not in your hatches) because you can't always find a good place to land when it starts getting dark.

A GPS: waterproof and made for boating, and extra batteries, not much help when it clunks out. It is amazing how many arguments we have had over where we are and where is that take out spot—sure looks different from the water than when standing on shore. . .

A flare to alert rescue help: If something bad does happen, it would be helpful to have a rescue team find you. An emergency radio would be helpful too: not cheap, but it allows you to send a signal for help if needed.

Always carry food. Dry food in case you can't make it back to where you started because of weather changes (mother nature likes to keep us guessing you know). You can always land, hunker down and eat. Eating is nice and when using up energy paddling, you tend to do a lot of it.

Water: more than you think you will need. And a water pump that can change questionable water into drinking water and/or tablets that can also do that if your water pump dies on the trip, been there, done that. . .

A tarp: We have found by cold experience that kayak skirts do NOT make a good umbrella (they do have a hole in them you know), so we now always have at least one tarp. Dry is always a plus if a storm suddenly pops up.

Dry clothes in a dry bag: Dry clothes are always better if they stay dry! If you tip over or roll, the rest of the trip can be agonizingly cold. Better to land and switch to dry clothes. Fleece or the old-time favorite wool (much of which is now not so itchy) keeps you warm even when wet. Bring a fleece or wool blanket for the same reason also. Spending a night cold makes for a very long night!

A wet suit? An absolute necessity in Spring and Autumn if you are kayaking Lake Michigan. Many experienced kayakers never venture onto Lake Michigan without wearing a wet or a dry suit, it's your call.

Plan ahead and know the weather. Rick is our "weather man". He researches the forecast the day before, day of, and then we all listen to the emergency radio's forecast on shore before embarking. Even then we have been surprised by a change in the wind direction, strength of the wind, or storms that suddenly decide to blow in.

One nice thing about paddling Lake Michigan, is that rivers flow into the lake! Eyes on the water is better than any weather report. They don't always seem to match. That means, when you are standing on the shore looking at the lake and are unsure about paddling out onto the lake, listen to your heart. Perhaps, making a new plan is in order, and kayak a river instead! Therefore, I have included in this book the rivers that flow into Lake Michigan and that can be an alternative paddle. Or just paddle them because they are fun!

Anything we missed? Not trying to scare you, but paddling should be fun and not a life-threatening experience. So, knowing what you are doing and how you would handle issues helps keep it fun!

Oh yeah, and a swim suit. We love swimming and stop several times on the shore during a paddling day to enjoy the lake. I now wear a swim suit under my clothes instead of a bra and underwear, so I'm ready anytime for a swim!

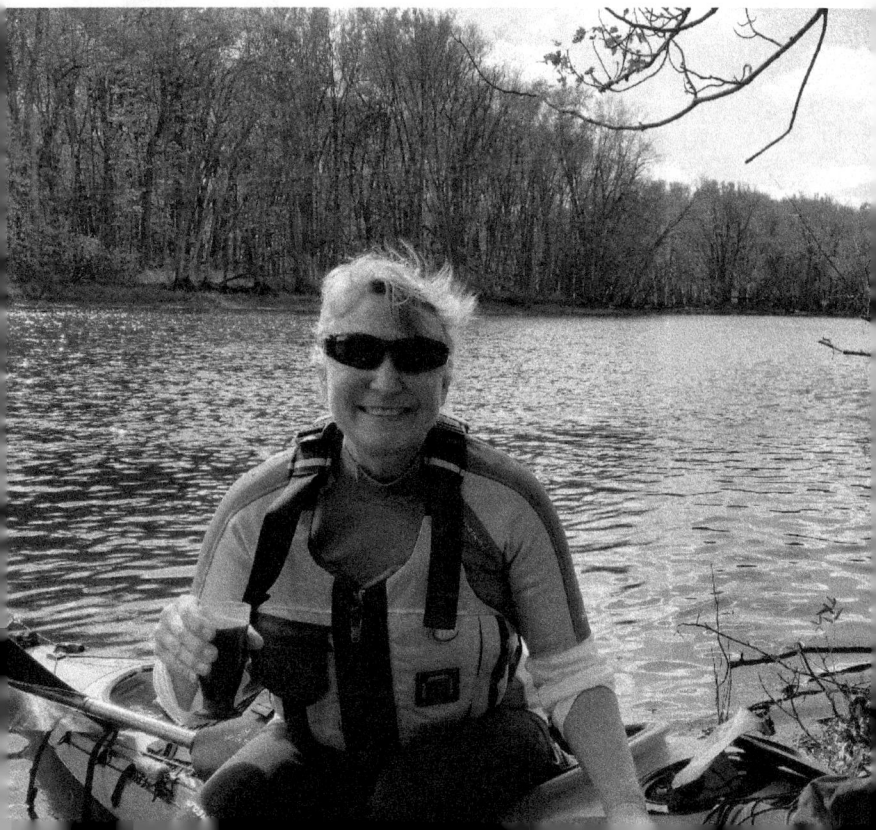

Kayak Wisconsin, Lake Michigan Water Trail

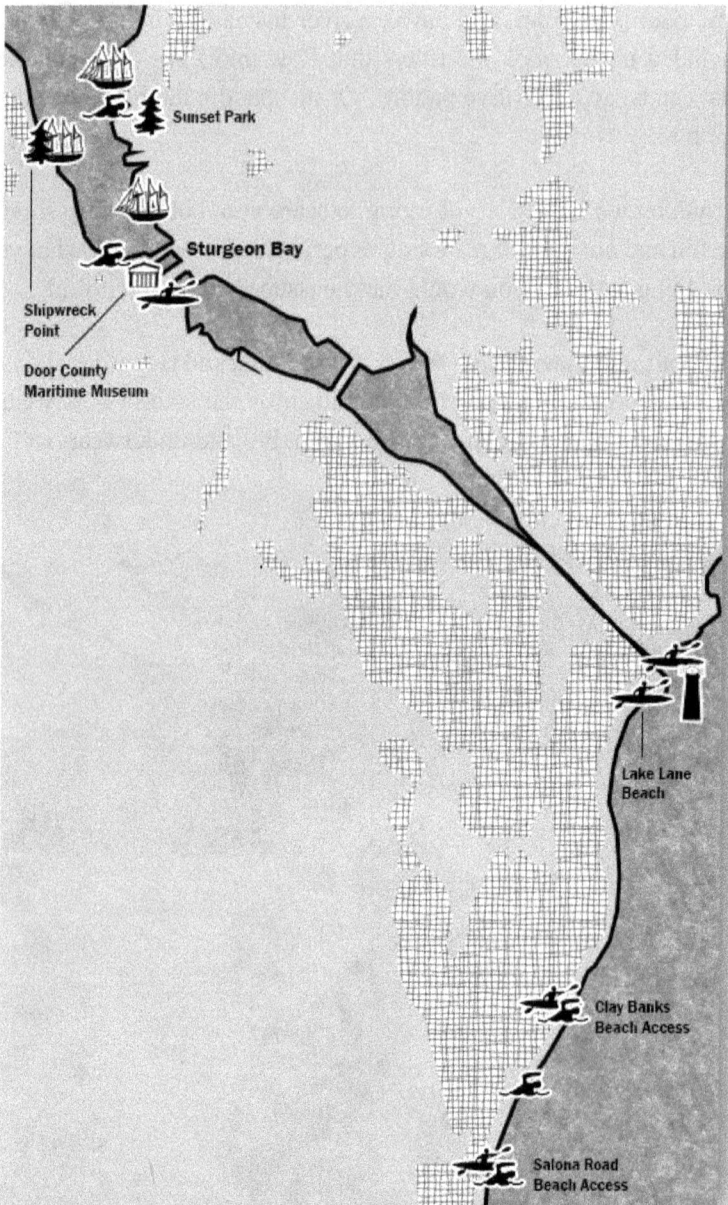

Sunset Park

Sturgeon Bay

Shipwreck
Point

Door County
Maritime Museum

Lake Lane
Beach

Clay Banks
Beach Access

Salona Road
Beach Access

Leg 1

The Schooner Coast Begins

Sturgeon Bay through the channel to Salona Road Beach

With Shipbuilding, Shipwrecks, and Lighthouses

9 miles

Shipwrecks, shipbuilding, and lighthouses too! Great paddle to begin our Schooner Coast tour, and the Lake Michigan Water Trail. Start in downtown Sturgeon Bay and see schooner shipwrecks, and sail on past ships being built at Sturgeon Bay Shipbuilding. Stop and enjoy the Sturgeon Bay Maritime Museum to discover the stories and artifacts. Paddle through the Sturgeon Bay shipping canal and enjoy the two lighthouses. Then settle in and enjoy the sandy coastline with beaches to enjoy. This paddle has it!

You could divide this paddle into two days, one for touring downtown Sturgeon Bay, the beginning of the Schooner Coast for a 6-mile paddle to Lake Lane Beach on Lake Michigan. The second paddle a relaxing coastline bathing beauty journey 3.5 miles south down to Salona Road beach.

We launch on an incredible calm, warm summer day at Sunset Park beach—a very peaceful entry spot. It is a big park on 3rd Avenue in Sturgeon Bay with a nice boat launch, a super sandy beach. This park is named for its famous sunsets, so you might be enticed to stay and enjoy it.

The shipwrecks begin already! As you paddle out of the ramp harbor, go west to where the poor steam barge Joys lies off shore from Sunset Park. The Joys was built in Milwaukee, and worked in the lumber industry, earning the title of the "greyhound of lumber". In 1898 while docked in Sturgeon Bay, she caught fire and with great effort was towed away from land and the Joys burned and sank. She now solemnly lies broken in about 10 feet of water about 300 feet off shore of the western edge of Sunset Park.

Next to Sunset Park is the Bay Shipbuilding Company. They have been building ships in Sturgeon Bay since 1918. Bay Shipbuilding was patriotic and quite active in the World War II effort for the US Army from 1940-1945. The company continues to build, and you can get quite close to the ships being built from the water line.

While you are looking up at the huge ships being built, look down too as there are more shipwrecks under the bay. The Adriatic, a schooner, was sadly abandoned and sank right underneath the shipbuilding pier. She lies in about 15 feet of water just northwest of the historic Michigan Street bridge.

Now set your course directly across the bay to "Shipwreck Point". Shipwreck Point or old Bullhead Pier was an old dock but now is a small park. Most importantly, there are three, count them THREE shipwrecks here. The Empire State was built in 1862 as a wooden passenger propeller steamer, once the "finest craft on the lakes". Unfortunately, toward the end of her career, she was used as a barge carrying stone, and finally in her old age she settled to the bottom of the bay at Bullhead Point's wharf in 1916. She lies closest to the end of the old wharf.

The Ida Corning is the middle shipwreck. She was built in 1881, as a two masted schooner and spent most of her career in the lumber trade. She was abandoned at Bullhead Wharf after the 1929 stock market crash, and finally scuttled and burned in 1931.

Closest to shore is the Oak Leaf, another schooner. Her crew was commanded by Captain Morrison, a one-armed man, no he wasn't a pirate, but it does demonstrate the dangers of being a seafarer. One deck hand fell overboard and drowned in Sturgeon Bay. As was the fate of the other shipwrecks here, Oak Leaf was abandoned at the wharf after the 1929 stock market crash.

On we paddle for about a mile along the mainland side of Sturgeon Bay. The public beach and park are Otumba Park. It is a small park with a wonderful sandy beach and is a kayak launch site that could be an alternative launch spot and is a great spot for a picnic rest.

Now we are in downtown Sturgeon Bay as we float under the historic Michigan Street Bridge. It is a bascule drawbridge steel overhead truss type bridge that is the only example of its type in Wisconsin and was perfect for windy Sturgeon Bay. The Michigan Street Bridge was initially the only bridge across the bay! It is on the National Register of Historic Places and has inspired a Steel Bridge songfest in Sturgeon Bay.

Land the kayaks between the two bridges at the Door County Maritime Museum boat ramp. The Maritime Museum is the official start of the Schooner Coast and gives a wonderful overview of Sturgeon Bay shipbuilding, the many lighthouses still keeping us safe, and the stories of the shipwrecks of Lake Michigan. The story of Sturgeon Bay shipbuilding begins with the Native American dug out or birch bark canoes, and continues with Sturgeon Bay becoming such a huge commercial shipbuilding area. Hear the story of Sturgeon Bay's own "Rosie the Riveter", a true-life woman welder who helped build ships for our country during World War II. Door County has the third largest concentration of lighthouses in the United States and you can discover the harrowing stories of the lonely light house keepers. Blast the ship's horn and turn the steamship wheel or raise the periscope and spy on the boats and folks along Sturgeon Bay's waterfront.

Tour the big red historic tug boat, John Purves. She started her career as a floating radio station for the US Navy. When she was honorably discharged from the Navy, she came to the Great Lakes towing barges. She was called back into service for World War II as a supply boat for the troops. When WWII ended, she came back home to the Great Lakes and back to towing and rescues.

Want more? Take a cruise on the Big Red Boat, the Fred A Busse. This restored fireboat is at the Sturgeon Bay city dock next to the Maritime Museum. She was built in 1937 and is similar to boats built in Sturgeon Bay. She spent her working life in Chicago as a fireboat. Now retired, she is waiting to entertain you.

Back in our tiny ships, glide under Oregon Street Bridge, built to replace the old historic Michigan Street Bridge. It is a drawbridge that is sure to open for the big kayaks coming through. . .umm, perhaps you shouldn't wait for that.

Right after the bridge is the Sawyer Park Boat Launch. The park does require a launch fee because it is a big park which has a six-lane ramp, restrooms with showers, fish cleaning stations, picnic area with grills, and a gazebo. In the Dock master's shanty, there is a special t.v. that provides up-to-the-minute weather maps and conditions, very helpful on windy days!

After the two downtown bridges comes the extremely tall Bayview Bridge. It is as much fun to float under the bridge and look up as it is to walk across the bridge and look down. The "by-pass" bridge was built in 1978 and was a real relief from the traffic jams that used to clog the Michigan Street Bridge. Although it is 228 feet long and really high, it isn't always lofty enough, so it is also a drawbridge that opens for those even taller ships, sailboats or schooners.

Every several years the Tall Ship Festival parades through Sturgeon Bay. This is an awesome opportunity to kayak and see the flotilla of schooners up close and personal. The tall ship's parade may include the four masted schooner from Chicago, the Windy. Or Michigan's the Madeline, a reconstruction of a mid-19th century

Great Lakes Schooner. The original Madeline sailed the Great Lakes 140 years ago. One of the Madeline's original crew members grandchild owned the Edmund Fitzgerald—of Lake Superior shipwreck fame and the Gordon Lightfoot's song. . .the legend lives on from the Chippewa on down. . .

Milwaukee's own SV Denis Sullivan is Wisconsin's Tall Ship and often joins the Tall Ship Festival. She is a recreation of a typical 19th century 3 masted Great Lakes Schooner and shows off her special "raffee". The triangle upper sail was unique to Great Lakes Schooners. She is a beautiful schooner with lots of billowing sails!

Even if you miss the Tall Ships, never fear, you can pleasantly paddle past yachts and sailboats. It is leisurely fun to explore Sturgeon Bay's waterfront. The city of Sturgeon Bay is located at the natural end of Sturgeon Bay, before they cut it in half to create the Sturgeon Bay channel. OK, the 1890 channel was fairly needed since it is a long way to go around the entire Door Peninsula! Cruising through the 1.3-mile Sturgeon Bay ship canal is not for the faint of heart. Charter fishing boats and recreational yachts head down the channel creating a parade of ships. They make big wakes that challenge paddling in the narrow channel, especially as not only is there the boat wakes to attend to, but the waves bounce off the channel wall and attack again.

The reward comes as you approach Lake Michigan as on the left, port side of the boat, you will glimpse the Sturgeon Bay Ship Canal Lighthouse. This 1898 lighthouse has unique circular custom curved glass and diamond astragals on the windows of the lantern room. The lighthouse is quite striking with its white coat of paint and red roof against the brilliant blue sky. Originally, the lighthouse was only the round staircase tower, but howling winds would move the lighthouse so much, it was blowing out the light—fairly important for a light house. They fixed the problem by adding the crisscrossing steel supports. This white light house still has its third order Fresnel lens that can be seen 18 miles away.

The grounds of the white Sturgeon Bay channel lighthouse are a very active coast guard station and Homeland Security Station. Built in 1886 for law enforcement on the water and search and rescues. The coast guard handles approximately two hundred rescues a year. . .please don't be one of them. Use marine radio channel 22A for information, and for distress calling, use marine radio channel 16. Hope you never need it.

The Coast guard station has a sandy beach inside the pier wall. Although there are signs saying "private property, no access", the beach is a designated kayak launch site and it is OK to use the parking lot and carry in/out kayaks. Take time to stretch the legs and stroll down the 1000-foot pier (yup, it's public) and get a close

look at the vivid red Sturgeon Bay pier head lighthouse. It is even older than the channel lighthouse. The red lighthouse still shines its smaller fixed red Fresnel lens in the circular tower.

Paddle across the shipping canal very carefully as this is a very busy channel. Head through the opening of the south jetty and arrive at Lake Lane Beach at the Sturgeon Bay Ship Canal Nature Preserve. This is a public beach area with beautiful white sand surrounded by rolling sand dunes, ancient shorelines swale ridges with towering white pines, hemlocks and maple trees. The preserve is home to bald eagles and osprey and is a resting spot for migrating birds. The beach is a quiet spot with room to drink in the view of Lake Michigan's glittering horizon.

Glide along the Lake Michigan coast south along the sandy shoreline of this gentle bay and past Rocky Point. There is a section of shoreline without homes called Clay Banks Beach with access points off of Lake Michigan Drive just north of Hornspier Road. Look for the thin sand trails leading to the water's edge. The beach accesses are hard to pick out without a GPS to guide you, but that alone makes them worthwhile spots to find and enjoy!

Hornspier Road is a historic pioneer sailing village. Around the Civil War years, W.H. Horn built, aw—you guessed it, a pier. A very long pier to avoid the shallow reefs. The town was a bustling lumber town, but the dock and warehouse burned in 1871. Now all that is left is a small clearing in the woods near the lake.

Continue past Clay Banks Creek running south of Horsnpier Road. The clear water creek with a sandy bottom produces brook stickleback that bass and northern pike like to feed on. Shortly after, comes one of our favorite beaches take out spot. At the end of Salona Road is a little beach access point. Salona was another old town, but besides the fact it had a post office, not much else is known. Why would they leave? Even on a hot summer day, we were the only ones on the whole beach for our lunch and swim. Add a few palm trees and you have a Jamaican paradise. Relax on our beach blanket, swim, wiggled our toes in the sand, and enjoy the brilliant end of our sun filled day.

Logistics:

Sunset Park, Sturgeon Bay:
44.8449, -87.3860. 747 N. 35d Avenue. Restrooms, no fee.

Otumba Park, Sturgeon Bay:
44.8309, -87.3897. 32 N. Joliet Avenue. No fee.

Sawyer Park Boat Launch, Sturgeon Bay:
44.8232, -87.3799. At the intersection of Neenah Ave and Oak St. Parking lot, restrooms, fee.

Maritime Museum Boat Launch, Sturgeon Bay:
44.8306, -87.3832. 120 N. Madison Avenue.
Turn into the Maritime Museum parking lot before the bridge.

Coast Guard Station and Sturgeon Bay Lighthouse and North Pierhead Lighthouse:
44.7944, -87.3127. 2501 Canal Road, Sturgeon Bay. Launch inside the pierhead. No fee, but no public restrooms either.

Lake Lane Beach and Sturgeon Bay Nature Preserve:
44.7916, -87.3150. 5200 Lake Lane, Sturgeon Bay. At the end of Lake Lane, a little parking lot at the end of Lake Lane. No fee!

Clay Banks beach access:
44.7622, -87.3254. Off Lake Michigan Drive.
Only off-street parking and no sign. No fee or restrooms.

Clay Banks beach access:
44.7559, -87.3308. Off Lake Michigan Drive just north of Hornspier Road. Street parking, no sign. No fee or restrooms.

Salona Road public beach access:
44.7481, -87.3357. Michigan. At the end of Salona Road. There is only off-street parking. No fee, no restrooms.

Location of Shipwrecks:

Joys: 44.8488, -87.3890. Lies about 300 feet off shore of the western edge of Sunset Park. Sunset Park is at 747 N. 3rd Avenue.

Adriatic: 44.8366, -87.3834. Lies in 15 feet of water at the Sturgeon Bay Shipbuilding Company dock, just northwest of the historic Michigan St. Bridge.

Empire State, Ida Corning and the Oak Leaf: 44.8415, -87.3955. Off eastern side of Bullhead Point. Bullhead Point, now sometimes called Shipwreck Point, is on the south side of Sturgeon Bay off North Duluth Ave.

Kayak Wisconsin, Lake Michigan Water Trail

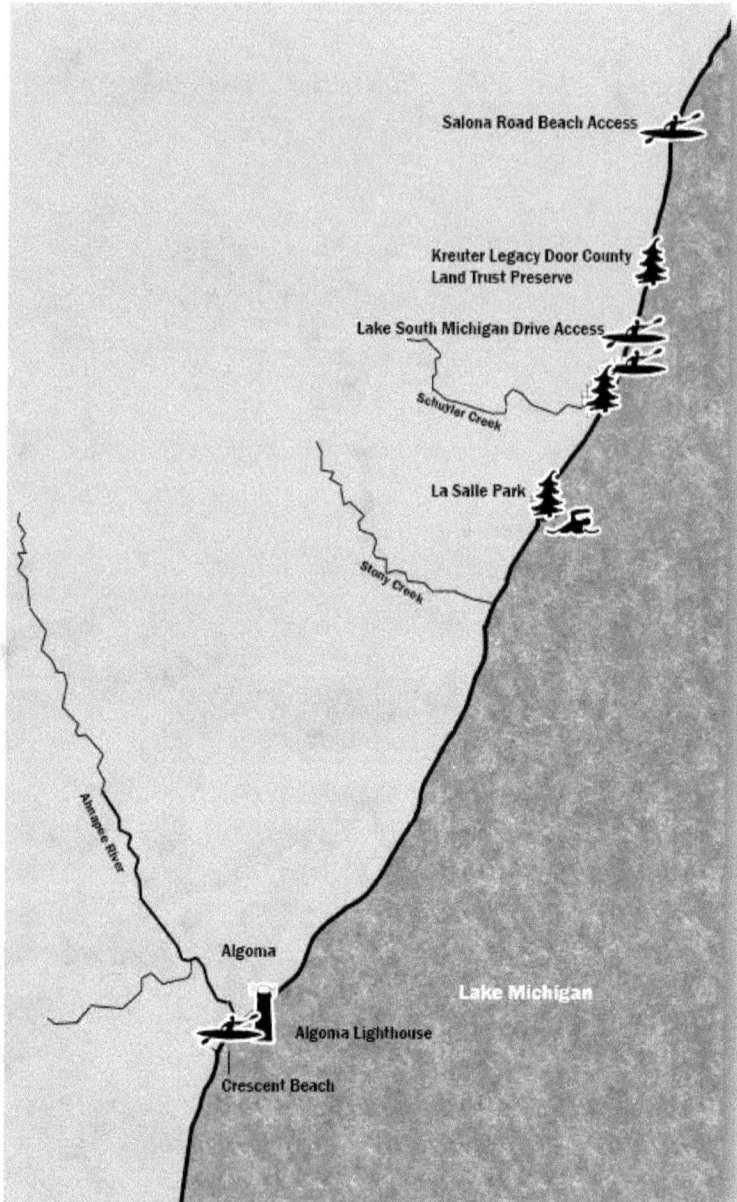

Leg 2

High Banks

Salona Road to Algoma

*With lost ghost towns, lost shipwrecks,
and a beautiful tri-level shoreline*

11.5 miles

"High Banks" is the nautical term the schooner sailors used to describe this undeveloped three-tiered shoreline. The top tier of deep forest green woodlands is separated from the middle level of grassy upland by steep sandy banks jutting down to the pebble and boulder beaches flowing out into Lake Michigan with its hidden rock shelves, sunken boulders—and hidden lost sunken ships. Thirteen unlucky ships are waiting to be discovered.

You may want to divide the paddle into two-day trips using La Salle County Park as your center launch. That gives you an easy 4.5-mile paddle from Salona Road Beach to La Salle County Park, and a second day cruise from La Salle County Park to Algoma's Crescent Beach for a 7.5-mile paddle.

We drive up to Salona Road, get out, load up the kayaks and just stop. Stop and gaze around. Love this beach, perhaps we should just throw down the beach blanket and loaf around for all day. Our gaze drifts north. Imagine a 1000-foot pier jutting out into Lake Michigan, with large schooners moored with tall rigging and three masts. Notice the hustle and bustle as sailors unload the supplies and load up lumber, railroad ties and telegraph poles. Follow the line of the pier to the busy pioneer sailing village with fifteen buildings including warehouses, a post office, and a dance hall. During the Civil War W. H. Horn built this pier, it was destroyed in the October 1871 Chicago and Peshtigo fire that jumped over to Door County. The pier was rebuilt, but by the turn of the century as the lumber faded, so did Horns Pier—fading into a lost ghost town with no trace. The Sea Bird Schooner sprung a leak by Horn's Pier and its wheat grain swelled so much it broke apart and sank. She's our first shipwreck to search for. . .let's get kayaking!

We head south, and almost immediately the terrain switches from sandy beach to pebble beach and the banks begin to grow. Pass by Cedar Creek which is a possible old pier location.

Kreuter Legacy Preserve, a Door County Land Trust nature area offers a beautiful stopping spot to explore this High Bank region. The high banks are actually the remnants of the long-ago glacial shoreline beach, now raised high above the water. At the Preserve,

you'll see the windswept high clay and sandy bank covered with dense forest of cedars, maple, and basswood with fields of milkweed and goldenrod below and bench overlooking the view of the lake. There is 3000 feet of the public sandy shoreline with Woodward Creek rambling over rocks into Lake Michigan. The Glenham schooner floundered ashore in 1872 and the crewmen were saved by a local man. The LaPetite schooner capsized near here in 1903 and broke apart with debris washing up on this beach by the mouth of Woodward Creek.

Lake Michigan Drive follows the undeveloped shoreline and there are two public accesses off the road to launch kayaks or just for a rest break. Soon you will see Schuyler Creek and the State Fishery Area with about a 1000-feet of shoreline that is yours to explore and swim as this is also known as Clay Banks Beach #1. The mouth of Schuyler Creek was the location of Tufts Pier which was a very active shipping port in the lumber years. Three shipwrecks were lost here. The S. L. Noble, a flat-bottomed schooner was pounded to pieces in a gale, while the Ida Bloom drifted ashore and broke apart. Also, the Granite State steam barge became stranded by the creek in a fall snowstorm.

Just south of Tufts Pier was the town of Clay Banks with its own huge 1600-foot long pier located at Bear Creek. Now Bear Creek is a nice bubbling stream which supports wonderful native brook trout. But back in the olde sailing days, on the banks of Bear Creek, Clay Banks was a thriving village with a sawmill along with the massive pier, three schools, a telegraph station and a post office. It too has its share of shipwrecks. The Sea Star got caught in a storm and smashed into the Pier and sank, and the Roving Star was at the dock when huge waves crashed into her causing her to hit bottom and break in half. Both of the star ships have never been found.

Paddle up to La Salle County Park which show cases the High Banks area, the pebble and boulder beach, wild-flower cliff, grassy parkland, and topped with the frosting of rich forest. A small stream cuts through a sandy ravine on the southern edge of the park. We stop for a picnic here and to enjoy the scenic views. It is a beautiful warm summer day, and we top off our rest break with a delightful swim.

Robert de La Salle, the French explorer, landed on this bank in 1679 and received supplies from the local Pottawatomi during his expedition of the Great Lakes. We are paddling in La Salle's footsteps, err wake, we in kayaks, La Salle and his party in canoes.

We are mighty explorers, so back in our kayaks we go. We head to the next point. We are nearing the area of the pioneer lumber town of Foscoro by the banks of the Stoney Creek. Stoney Creek was dammed to help the logging operations with a large sawmill built across the stream. This was a true town with a telegraph station, post office, a general store, another 1000-foot long pier, and of course the legendary shipwrecks. The Reciprocity schooner came ashore in a big storm and is believed to have broken up near the Stoney Creek Reef. A tug belonging to Captain Fellows broke her mooring, and the John Everson tug capsized and sank off Stoney Creek. And the most famous, the Ottawa schooner went aground off shore on Foscoro Reef with several crewmen dying attempting to reach shore. All the shipwrecks are just waiting for us to find them. Being a hot summer day, we hop into the water off Stoney Creek and swim again.

We plop back into our kayaks nice and cool, and on with our exploring.   We are now cruising into Kewaunee County, Pottawatomi for "river of the lost", but we are not lost—it's a beautiful day for paddling.

Silver Creek is spring fed and is known for runs of trout and salmon as it dapples down to Lake Michigan's shoreline. It is here that we can begin to see the hazy Algoma Lighthouse beckoning us.

Algoma was initially named An-Ne-Pe, "land of the great gray wolf", by the Pottawatomi, and the English and Irish pioneers called the town Ahnapee. A few years later, the city was re-named Algoma, meaning "park of flowers". As we arrive in Algoma, we paddle up close to the red steel cylindrical pier head light that stands 42 feet high with red glass giving the north pier head lighthouse the signature red light that makes it a Great Lakes icon. The 1932 an improvement project updated the harbor piers with design assistance by General Douglas MacArthur, an engineer at the time. The north pier is 1100 feet long and the south pier is over 1500-hundred feet long.

Inside the harbor at the end of the parking lot for the boat launch, is a little park area called Christmas Tree Point. At the end of every shipping season in the 1800's, over 50 schooners took one more sail, transporting Christmas trees to Milwaukee and Chicago. Folks would come to watch the Christmas tree schooners sail on south at this point. The most famous Christmas Tree Schooner of all?   The Rouse Simmons and her Captain Santa. She was a three masted schooner who for decades traipsed the Great Lakes carrying lumber. For Christmas, she decorated with electric Xmas lights strung from bow to stern and carried three to five thousand Christmas trees making her look like a floating forest. But the Christmas Tree Ship had a fateful day in November of 1912—when she vanished. Sadly, remnants of Christmas trees washed ashore for weeks giving an indication of the sad end of the famous ship and her Captain Santa.

We cross the harbor entrance and follow the south pier with its myriad of fisherman on the pier. Algoma is the Midwest's salmon and trout capital which is keeping with its commercial fishing history. Glide up to Crescent Beach, yup, it does form a crescent and is a half a mile-long sandy beach with a boardwalk. We pull up close to the breakwater as it is closest to the parking lot. We share the beach with herring gulls, and an occasional dabbling duck teal and diving grebe.

We never found the 13 unlucky shipwrecks. Tag, you're it, your turn to "turn" famous shipwreck hunter and locate the lost ships and ghost towns. Happy paddling!

Logistics:

Salona Road public beach access, Sturgeon Bay:
44.7481, -87.3357. At the end of Salona Road, south of Sturgeon Bay. There is only off-street parking. No fee, no restrooms.

Legacy Preserve, Sturgeon Bay:
44.7288, -87.3405. 1188 S. Lake Michigan Drive. No kayak launch- it would be a long carry and there is that natural high bank to climb down, but this is an awesome spot to stop while kayaking, or for hiking, and scenic views. There is a parking area.

Beach kayak launch accesses off South Lake Michigan Drive:
44.7146, -87.3468 and 44.7124, -87.3478. Where South Lake Michigan Drive hugs the undeveloped shoreline, there are several kayak launches. Roadside parking or pull off parking, carry down the bank to access the beach. No fee, no restrooms.

Schuyler Creek State Fishery Area, Sturgeon Bay:
44.7108, -87.3506. 820 S. Lake Michigan Drive. Not designated as a kayak launch but would be a great rest break area. Parking area.

La Salle County Park, Algoma:
44.6910, -87.3622. 298 County Road U, Lower La Salle Road. Short carry down steps to the beach. No fee, nice restrooms!

Crescent Beach, Algoma:
44.6063, -87.4357. Lake Street. Crescent Beach is a half mile of sandy beach right on Highway 42 in downtown. The parking lot is at the north end of the beach next to the harbor. Restrooms are at end of Lake Street at the corner of Lake and Navarino Streets.

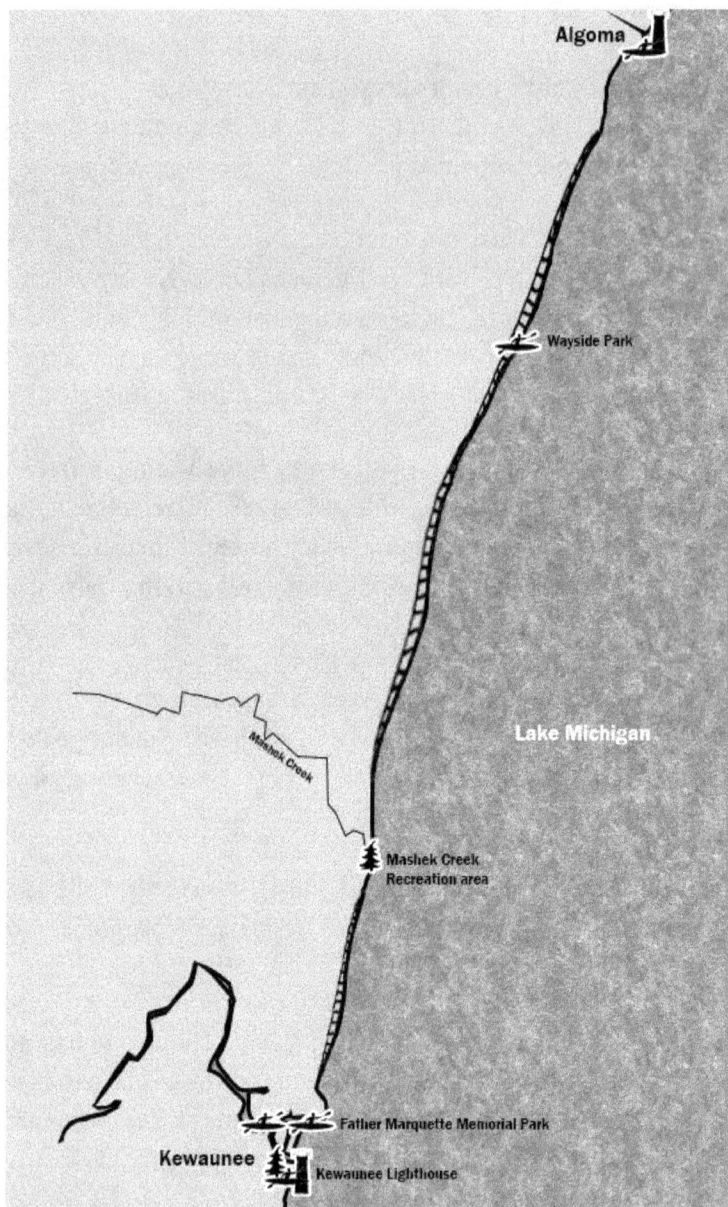

Leg 3

Sandy Bluffs

Algoma to Kewaunee

With sandy bluffs, iconic Algoma and Kewaunee Lighthouses and two beautiful creeks

12 miles

A picturesque paddle with the towering sand bluffs and the crystal clear pristine turquoise water with the rocky lake bed twinkling beneath the waves—which way to look up? Up at the bluffs? Or down into the water? Either way is a delight! Add the two iconic lighthouses in Algoma and Kewaunee, along with the two beautiful babbling brooks; Mashek Creek and Three Mile Creek and this is a paddle worth doing again and again. Picture perfect paddling!

You could shorten this paddle at Wayside Park, 3 miles south of Algoma, but it would be a bit of a climb down to the shoreline on a narrow path.

Beautiful fall breezy day with the wind from the southeast, therefore we choose to paddle up the coast from Kewaunee to Algoma with some awesome gentle surfing. Kewaunee is a historic town, originally a large village of Potawatomi Native Americans in the 1600's that was visited first by the explorer Jean Nicolet in 1634, followed by Father Marquette, and Robert de LaSalle. It grew up to be a lumber town, and now is the spirit of the lakeshore and the heart of Wisconsin's Schooner Coast. We put in at the Kewaunee Marina which does offer a kayak launch, and a campground and showers.

Perhaps La Salle camped right here! As we paddle under the Highway 42 Bridge, on the right south bank is Harbor Park popular for fishing, with a gazebo and boardwalk. The small but mighty Tug Ludington docks here all summer. She was built for World War II and had 50 caliber machine guns mounted above her pilot house. The tug participated in the D Day invasion of Normandy, towing ammunition barges across the English Channel. In 1947, the tug came to Kewaunee to assist with harbor maintenance. Give her a thankful salute for her service as you pass her by.

On the left north bank is Harbor Point Park, a quiet peaceful green grass point with a boardwalk along the large fishing pier built over old wood moorings. At the end of the small breakwater in the harbor, we could turn north to Father Marquette Park memorializing his visit to Kewaunee. It has a beach for launching kayaks well protected by wave action from the breakwater walls. Today, the breakwater walls are lined with pelicans, who allow us to get pretty close to enjoy them. These are American White Pelicans, one of North America's largest birds with nine-foot wingspan and can

weigh up to twenty pounds! They fly with a Z neck pattern that makes them easily distinguishable and often fly in flocks with smooth circular patterns higher and higher. They can look prehistoric with their large bodies and head and heavy yellow bill with the males often sporting a horn nodule on their top bill. Their legs are also yellow orange and when they fly their fringed black wing tips are evident. The pelicans are friendly, have never been aggressive to us, but will either fly away when we get too close, or slowly walk away looking over their shoulder to show their disapproval.

We choose to head towards the end of the harbor to check out the Kewaunee Lighthouse. In the 1850's a pair of piers were built with range lights for the safety of the schooners, with a fog horn house added to the south pier range light. In 1930, the south range light was destroyed when a railroad ferry hit the pier, so a light tower was built atop the fog house. This is what we see today, with the first story covered in white metal plates to support the weight of the tower and lantern room, while the second story is white shingles capped with its bright red roof. The octagonal lantern room sits on a four-sided tower topped with a cast iron railing, which originally had the fifth order Fresnel lens. The poor north pier just has a sad overlooked little red and white striped light.

If you would go around the south point and the Kewaunee lighthouse, back on shore is the Pioneer Park beach with over 500 feet of shoreline, and at the south end of the beach, Selner Park sits atop the beginning of the south sandy bluff with a short path to the beach to launch your kayak.

North, we go, and immediately the sandy bluffs tower on the shoreline. The scalloped edged bluffs rise to sixty to seventy feet and fall steeply down to the pebble beach shoreline. These beautiful bluffs were deposited by the Glacial period 20,000 to 30,000 years ago and were part of the Kewaunee glacial lobe. Lake Michigan itself is a large kettle lake formed as the retreating glacier scoured the land leaving the hole that the melting ice filled in, perhaps that is why its average temperature is about 50 degrees—refreshing!

The Kewaunee bluffs are blonde sand topped with rich forest green grass and woodlands which at times cascade down to water's edge. The light sandy bluffs contrast brilliantly with the twinkling blue waves. Beneath us, the crystal-clear waters shine on the rocky lake bottom, so translucent that we head out further just to see how deep we can go and still see the beautiful bottom! A gregarious grebe dives and ducks under and around our kayaks for a while. He is small brown water bird with a short thick bill with his lobed feet far back on his body, perfect for bobbing around us.

Picture perfect paddling! The long line of steep curving sandy bluffs continues up the coast three miles to Mashek Creek. Here we land for a chance to explore this public area. The shoreline is wooded as Mashek Creek winds its way down the embankment to a pebble beach. This is a needed stopping point for migratory birds, and the creek fosters runs of salmon and trout. The quiet tranquil area gave us a chance to stretch our legs and enjoy the shoreline with the maple, oaks, and white birches leaning over the water's edge. This site is now listed as a kayak and canoe launch site.

It's time to paddle on with the windswept bluffs above us, and the clean clear water below. We are nearing the old forgotten location of the Alaska Pier built in 1860 for the lumber schooners.

Wayside Park greets us with Three Mile Creek at its northern end. We land on the sandy beach and stroll to investigate the shoreline and the bubbling creek as it flows into Lake Michigan with its see-through, cold clean water. The Three Mile Creek winds its way from Krohns Lake west of Lake Michigan to Wayside Park. Guessing it twists and turns three miles, do ya think? Wayside Park also has historical significance with the Casco Pier built in 1860 for the lumber trade somewhere near here, lost and gone again. We throw out the beach blanket and settle in for our picnic lunch. "Wow, the forecast said one to two-foot waves and we haven't even seen a white cap, wait—there's a white cap." Continue to enjoy our relaxed lunch, "boy the waves have picked up, wow now there are a lot of white caps, guess that forecast was right."

During our relaxed shoreline lunch, the winds did begin to gust to 20 miles an hour, and our leisurely paddle has changed in intensity. Now we need to skirt up, and paddle hard off Wayside Park's beach

and casual conversation turns to "great riding the wave" as we maintain our focus for the last three miles of our paddle with regular two-foot waves coming directly from the east onto our starboard side. Soon Algoma's Pier head red Lighthouse beckons us, shall we head for the protected harbor or prove our ability and land on crescent beach (with folks watching from the boardwalk)? Who chose the beach??? Two-foot crashing waves push us to shore threatening to twist us sideways, wait, "that one sounds huge, either we land on this wave or capsize" . . . Land, we did, exciting!

Logistics:

Crescent Beach, Algoma:
44.6063, -87.4357. Lake Street/Highway 42 in downtown. The parking lot is at the north end of the beach next to the harbor. Restrooms are at the north end of Lake Street.

Wayside Park, south of Algoma:
44.5646, -87.4592. Off of Highway 42. Restrooms, tiny path down to beach—would be a difficult kayak/canoe launch.

Mashek Creek Recreation Area:
44.5021, -87.4840. Lakeshore Drive. Small path into the land. No fee, no restrooms, now listed as a kayak/canoe launch.

Father Marquette Memorial Park, Kewaunee:
44.4645, -87.4959. At Hathaway Drive and Lakeshore Drive intersection. Parking lot, restrooms, no fee, protected kayak launch.

Kewaunee Boat Landing, Kewaunee:
44.4637, -87.5045. Peterson Street. The kayak/canoe launch is at the farthest west in the parking lot. Fee, restrooms.

Pioneer Park, Kewaunee:
44.4569, -87.4992. At the end of Kilbourn Street, turnaround at the end of the street. No fee, restrooms nearby.

Selner Park, Kewaunee:
44.4559, -87.4999. Vliet Street, parking lot is at the end of the street. No fee, restrooms nearby.

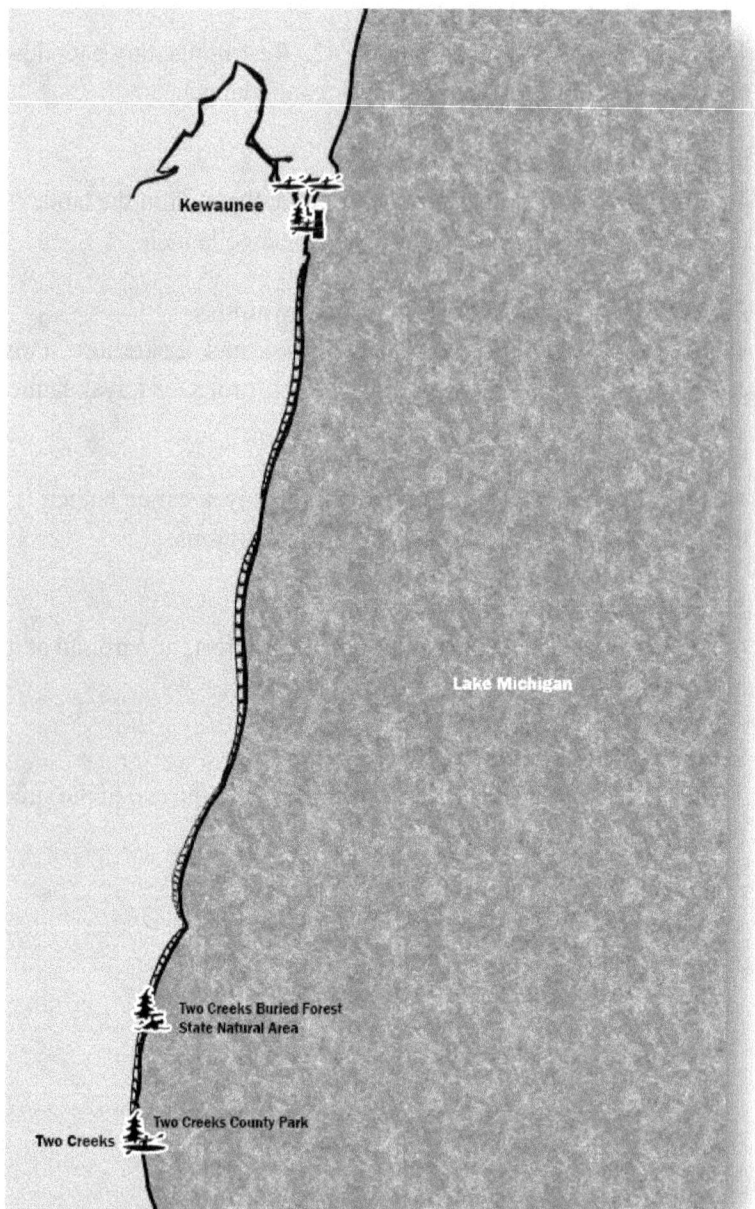

Kewaunee

Lake Michigan

Two Creeks Buried Forest
State Natural Area

Two Creeks County Park

Two Creeks

Leg 4

Two Creeks and the Buried Forest

Two Creeks to Kewaunee

With miles of sandy scalloped slopes

11.5 miles

A geologic wonder to amaze us! Along with the ancient glacial buried forest, you can't beat the crystal-clear water with the sandy bluffs and beaches to explore. This is one interesting paddle!

Explore the bluffs and beaches starting at Two Creeks County Park, and slide into the beach in Kewaunee. Due to the high sandy banks, there are no access points between. Even at the one public area, the Two Creeks Buried Forest, the climb down from the top of the bluff is necessitated with a rope tied to a tree. Try that with a kayak!

We launch at Two Creeks County Park in beautiful summer weather. Light wind of eight to fifteen miles per hour was predicted with one to two-foot waves. Perfect, no problem, I could try out my new kayak in mild waves. Yup, there I stood at the boat launch looking at two-foot white caps whipping the shore. What?? Rick proceeded to explain, that yes, the wind is about 8 to10 miles per hour, but it is coming from the southeast. So? So, that means that it is blowing from Gary Indiana 180 miles away, bringing all of Lake Michigan with it. Ohh. . .perhaps I should have brought my old reliable kayak that I have an understanding with. No, Rick said, this is perfect for practicing, you got this!

Yeah. I wasn't so sure as I launch from shore and a whitecap splashes into my face, then another, then I looked up to a mountain of a wave—at least a three-foot wave that looked like a mountain from my perspective on the water. I crest my mountain like a pro. Ugh, another huge wave. This one I'm sure is a four-foot wave, it curls over into a beautiful surfing curl, right over the front of my kayak and crash lands directly into my cockpit. To my credit, I did not breach, and I handle my new kayak with grace. I pump the wave back out of my kayak and don my kayak skirt, obviously needed today. Chris reports "I'm blind" as she too is attacked by a monster wave and her glasses are dripping wet. Welcome to kayaking on the Great Lakes. On a calm day, this could be a beginner paddle, with moderate wind, not so much.

Two Creeks County Park is a picturesque park perched on the top of the bluff. Only the metal grate and stone boat ramp gently slope down to the beach. The view from the top is exquisite. Perfect for relaxing and enjoying the view—or watching crazies launch their kayaks into crashing waves. They didn't think too hard about naming this park. Yeah, it has two creeks. The first is immediately north of our boat ramp, spilling out onto the sandy beach. The second is just a short stroll north along the beach. Two Creeks has a great beach for skipping stones on a quiet day. Just off shore is the remnant of an old port pier which would be fun to explore, but on our day, the pier posts were spike obstacles to avoid. . .

Much of Two Creeks Park above the sandy bluff is covered with new growth forest. This area was part of the Great Forest Fire of Wisconsin in 1870, the Peshtigo Fire. The fire burnt out much of the virgin tree growth. Two Creeks is also a township of Wisconsin that is mostly rural. Jacque Vieau of the Northwest Fur Company was the first non-Native American to land here in 1795, just south of the creek. He set up a Trading Post in the area.

We putter along the shore line that is a steep sandy slope with short beaches of sand and cobblestone. A few farms and homes are barely perceptible, perched atop the golden cliffs.

Only a mile of paddling, brings us to the Two Creeks Buried Forest. What the heck? A buried forest? Yup, next to the third little creek (maybe, they misnamed their town) is a very unique and special geological site. The area of Two Creeks is imbedded in the Niagara Escarpment. This is America's backbone that arcs from Niagara Falls through the Great Lakes, and down into Wisconsin through Door County, and all the way to Waukesha County. Amazing! In Manitowoc County it is mostly buried under the glacial sediment. The glaciers retreated as the temperature warmed up and a forest of spruce, hemlock and pine grew up 12,000 years ago. Then the darn Valders glacier fought back and advanced again and covered our forest with silt and clay preventing the trees from decomposing. The Red Ice glaciers carried iron particles from northern iron ranges and colored the clay red. As the glacier flattened and buried the forest it created a red clay layer imbedded with logs. Today as Lake Michigan pounds the shore, the wave action exposes the long-buried 12,000-year-old logs and stumps embedded in the twenty-foot high stratum layers of glacial history.

The Two Creeks Buried Forest is a 30-acre natural area with a quarter mile of lake front that is an Ice Age National Scientific Reserve. Pretty special to kayak past, and is the only public access area on our eleven-mile paddle. Therefore, you may want to stop

and search for the buried forest by strolling the beach. This is the best way to explore the protected area as it is a difficult climb down from the top of the bluff. On the summit, there is only a grassy plain, where you "can't see the forest for the lack of trees".

Gib's on the Lake, is a shore line restaurant situated on top of the tower of sand next to the Two Creeks Buried Forest. If you are adventurous, you can climb the cliff at Two Creeks Buried Forest to have lunch made to order with a bonafide beautiful view.

Onward we sway with the waves, cresting and splashing through the rollicking water to Grandmother's house we go, wait—to the old Kewaunee Power Plant we go. It is the big white and blue striped building visible for almost a full mile. This nuclear power plant closed in 2013, and no water is being sucked in from Lake Michigan. The power plant did not close due to any safety concern, but closed totally due to economic issues. It may be closed, but there are still employees working there to maintain safety and to mothball the plant, decommissioning it. It operated for almost 40 years, but now will take 60 years in safe storage to allow the radiation to decay to safe levels to be able to dismantle the equipment and restore the land. I have chatted with the city officials who recommend we do not land on the three quarter of a mile shoreline it dominates.

Four miles inland is the Cold Country Vines and Wines on Nuclear Road. This winery specializes in hand crafted wines from Wisconsin's cold climate, including their ice wine — their treasure of the north. Winter is coming and Ice wine is made from grapes picked on the first frosty day of the coming winter creating a sweet white wine.

The Kewaunee power plant is situated on picturesque Sandy Bay. At t the north end of the property Sandy Bay Creek, a small stream, ripples out into Lake Michigan. Then Lakeview Road dips back towards us to follow us north as we paddle along the sandy bay shoreline. After this, the road sneaks away from us and connects with Lakeshore Road which again sweeps back by the sandy bluff to keep a watchful eye above us.

The top of the bluff is mostly tree lined with cornfields or hay pastures behind. The cliff edge is curvy and zigzags many feet above the sandy shore. Occasionally narrow stairwells cling to the cliffside coming down to the water's edge. There are resting decks amongst the steps. One wonders if folks count each and every step up as they slowly ascend the slopes. Or are these pleasant relaxing decks to enjoy the expansive view across Lake Michigan? The state of Michigan coast is over sixty miles away, so there is no land in sight, just the relaxing lapping of the waves to quell any stress a home owner may have.

Relax and repeat, rhythmic strokes for the eight miles from the power plant to Kewaunee. All the way, are the beautiful bluffs and turquoise blue water. Soon we can see the dyslexic L shaped white Kewaunee light house topped with her red roof. Kewaunee first had range lights back in 1891, and then the fifth order Fresnel lens was moved to the north 1300-foot south pier in the present lighthouse. She is two stories high with the circular cylinder lantern room built out of rings of steel pilings. The lighthouse is on the register of historic places and is in the process of being restored.

The Kewaunee beach continues with the high clay banks and a beautiful sandy shoreline. Greenery tops the bluffs and even in the city it is hard to actually see the houses above the cliffs. As we near the south pier, the City Park beach with its golden sand beckons. Selner Park sits atop the beach with wooden steps to the picnic area. Next door, at the end of Kilbourne Street is Pioneer Park beach and a grassy plain with more picnic areas. After our eleven-mile paddle, it is nice to see the restrooms between the two parks.

If you prefer a gentler take out spot, continue paddling into the harbor, passing close up to the Kewaunee lighthouse and then carefully cross the harbor to the north wall to Father Marquette Memorial Park with its slow water and squishy beach.

Or stay by the south pier wall paddling up river a little, past Harbor Park and the Tug Ludington. She served in World War II with 50 caliber machine guns mounted on her pilot house. The Ludington even helped out the D Day invasion of Normandy by towing ammunition barges across the English Channel. She retired from military service and came to Kewaunee to help with harbor maintenance. Pat her weary side gently as you pass by her.

Across from the tug, is the channel entrance to Salmon Harbor Marina with a private boat launch. After the tug is the Port O Call restaurant with its beautiful river views, and then Lafonds Fish Market with fresh fish and several flavors of smoked fish. Before going under the bridge, is the city of Kewaunee's Marina and campground. After the bridge is the Kewaunee Boat Landing which offers a gentle take out spot with restrooms.

Kewaunee is a small, sleepy picturesque community with the wonderful beach and harbor area to explore. Come back another day, for kayaking the peaceful Kewaunee River, or biking the Ahnapee Trail. The trail head begins by the harbor, under the huge Grandfather Clock. This is the world's largest grandfather clock, at 35 feet tall, you can hardly miss it!

Logistics:

Kewaunee Boat Landing, Kewaunee:
44.4637, -87.5045. Peterson Street. Inside the Kewaunee Harbor on the Kewaunee River. Kayak/canoe launch is at the farthest west in the parking lot. Fee, restrooms.

Father Marquette Memorial Park, Kewaunee:
44.4645, -87.4959. 400 Hathaway Drive. Parking lot, restrooms, no fee, protected kayak/canoe launch.

Pioneer Park, Kewaunee:
44.4569, -87.4992. 90 Kilbourn Street. At the end of Kilbourn Street, turnaround at the end of the street. No fee, restrooms nearby in shelter on Lake Street.

Selner Park, Kewaunee:
44.4559, -87.4999. 616 Lake Street. Parking lot is at the end of Vliet Street. No fee, restrooms in shelter on Lake Street.

Two Creeks Buried Forest State Natural Area, Two Rivers:
44.3273, -87.5437. 18783 Wisconsin Highway 42. Gravel parking area with small sign on Highway 42, on top of the bluff. Maybe there will be a makeshift rope to climb down to shoreline. Easiest accessible by boat.

Two Creeks County Park, Two Creeks:
44.305, -87.5443. 6650 Two Creeks Road. Shelter, no fee.

Kayak Wisconsin, Lake Michigan Water Trail

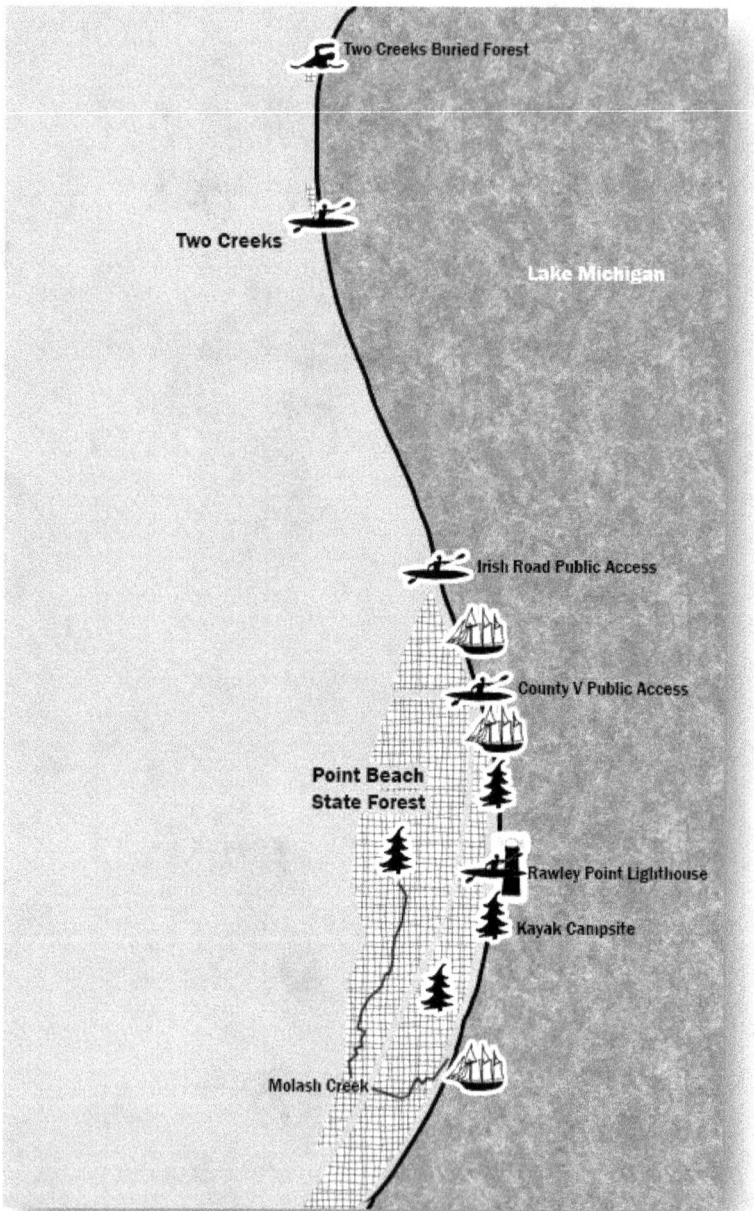

Two Creeks Buried Forest

Two Creeks

Lake Michigan

Irish Road Public Access

County V Public Access

Point Beach
State Forest

Rawley Point Lighthouse

Kayak Campsite

Molash Creek

Leg 5

Point Beach and Forest

Two Creeks County Park to Point Beach State Forest

With park beaches, and 2 possible shipwrecks

8 miles

Home. My home beach. Point Beach State Forest Park, Wisconsin's Cape Cod, without the million tourists (shh, don't tell the New Englander's about this beach.) This is where you should bring out of state guests to show off Wisconsin's "big pond": Lake Michigan. This paddle includes miles of sandy beach, shipwrecks below the waves, and then Two Creeks with its county park.

It may be possible to divide this paddle at Irish Road with a 3-mile paddle of the State Forest and Beach and the Continental and Pathfinder shipwreck. A second paddle from Irish Road to Two Creeks Buried State Forest takes you past a mostly sandy shoreline for a 5-mile paddle with coming ashore at Two Creeks County Park.

We have a slight southerly breeze on our summer day and choose to paddle south to north to use the gentle push of the wind. We put in at Point Beach State Forest Park. As you enter the park curve left to go north and almost immediately the Rawley Point Lighthouse Beach and picnic area parking area is to the right. Rawley Point is the big hump that juts out into Lake Michigan for most of the entire Point Beach State Forest Park area.

Point Beach State Forest Park. . .my home beach, where I grew up with family picnics and body surfing the waves. Here is where our kids grew up. My son's first camping trip was here at 3 months old. Yellow blankee on the beach, crawling and falling face first into the sand, crawling and falling face first into the sand, crawling. . .then came the years of sand sculpturing and swimsuit bottoms heavy with sand. "Don't throw sand at your cousin". Teaching the next generation, the thrill of wave surfing, "here comes a big one!" Slipping away at night for moon bathing with a towel on the beach, gentle lulling of the lapping lake, and the dark night of star gazing. Here is where I come to meditate, and think out frustrations with a forever walk on the beach. Once you stroll a short way from the beach parking, you may run into only a handful of folks on the sandy shore. Perfect get away for blistering hot summer days with the cool breeze off the lake and any time you start getting a bit warm, dive on in, play around, and then back to beach combing.

Short carry of the kayaks from the parking area over the boardwalk dune-scape down to the lake. The sand dune is squeaky as the quartz granules make fun noises as you shuffle your feet through the sand. This is a picture-perfect paradise beach, off white sand and clear water lapping at the shore. Time for a swim? This isn't a day for rushing when you are at Point Beach. Check out to the right, south, where the Rawley Point Lighthouse stands, whitewashed with a cherry red roof. There has been a lighthouse here since 1853 after over 26 ships foundered or stranded on the shoals off this point. This lighthouse beacon is the biggest and brightest on the Great Lakes and can be seen 20 miles away, where as its sister lighthouse, Big Sable Lighthouse fifty miles away in Michigan has a light that can also be seen about 20 miles away, meaning that if you are in the middle of Lake Michigan, you just might be able to see both lights.

Back on our beach, we push off and head north. Such a thrill to be able to see my beach from off shore, great opportunity to fall in love with Wisconsin's Lake Michigan all over again. Enjoy the rippling sand patterns beneath the water, splashing children playing on shore, and folks on beach blankets waving hello. In less than a half-mile is the Lakeshore Picnic area and parking, which would be another wonderful put in spot. We continue paddling past the beach with beach goers skimming stones and in less than another half-mile is the wooden zigzag traversing handicap access to the beach (which kids seem to love also) and right after that is the stone steps leading up to the concession stand. "Can we stop for some ice cream? Can we, can we please?"

The park land continues for another third of a mile with the shoreline a mix of boulders, cobblestone and sand, with few park guests exploring this area. Ahh, smell the mix of woodlands behind the shore of pine, hemlock, birch, maple and cedar trees whispering above the gentle shoreline waves. Several beach homes follow. But notice the one that bumps out and is lined with a pile of rocks. At the northern tip of the bump out, about 420 feet off shore lies the

Continental shipwreck. She was a wooden bulk carrier steamer built in 1882 and in a blinding snowstorm in December of 1904 the captain ran into the sand bar at a high speed, cramming her so successfully into the sand that tug boats could not pull her off. All twenty crew members made it to shore safely with help from local fishermen. The winter weather broke her in two and down she went. She now sleeps in about ten to fifteen feet of water.

Persisting with peaceful paddling for a less than a half mile brings us to Highway V with a winding trail to the water's edge. This is a place for a rest break and swim. It is considered a public access, but the little parking that is available, is across the road. Smoothly we stroke for another half mile with barely discernible beach homes along Sandy Bay Road. Where the road curves toward the lake, about 990 feet off shore lies the large three-masted Pathfinder Schooner shipwreck in about 13 feet of water. She was carrying heavy iron ore and iced up during a snow storm in 1886, filled up with water and sank, and has been covered and uncovered by sand numerous times over the century which has helped preserve her. She is now on the National Register of Historic Places and is part of Wisconsin's proposed National Marine Sanctuary.

Now along the shoreline, we follow Lakeshore Road above the sandy bluff topped with woods and cornfields. The coast continues to be quiet sandy beaches next to the cool aqua turquoise water. Irish Road comes straight down to the water edge through a clearing in the trees and does provide public access and the closest thing to a midpoint as we have on this paddle. Just another mile north and inland is the Cold Country Winery and vineyards which specializes in Ice Wine, sweet wine made from grapes that froze on the vine.

We can see the big building of the Point Beach Nuclear Power Plant which has produced about a sixth of all of Wisconsin's electricity. Onshore there is a visitor and education center for the facility. There is an intake valve off shore that collects the water that is heated and turned to steam and then into electricity. See the little white gulls' way off shore? They are actually the white buoys 800 feet off shore letting you know how far out you need to be—for national security.

Why not keep paddling out to sea? If you paddle about six miles out from the power plant you come to the famed resting place of the Rouse Simmons, the Christmas Tree Ship and her Captain Santa. She was a three-masted schooner who for decades traipsed the Great Lakes carrying lumber to Chicago. Lumber ships often would take one last load of Christmas trees to Chicago each year in late Autumn. The Rouse Simmons was the favorite one. She had electric Christmas lights strung from bow to stern and carried three to five thousand Christmas trees making her look like a floating forest. But on her fateful day in November of 1912 as she passed Kewaunee her flag was hung at half mast, indicating she was in distress. The Two River surfmen rescue team launched a rescue, but when they came to where she was last seen, she had vanished. The crew of ten or twenty joined the approximately 30,000 other souls lost to Lake Michigan. Sadly, remnants of Christmas trees washed ashore for weeks and months. Then two weeks after she disappeared a corked bottle with a message from Captain Santa was found floating. The message said "Friday, everybody goodbye, I guess we are all through…God help us". Twelve years after the Christmas tree ship disappeared, Captain Santa's wallet wrapped in waterproof oilskin was snagged in a fishing net. Through the years ghost sightings of the ship has been reported, but finally in 1971, her final resting place was discovered off this shore 175 feet deep.

Then we are back to the hush of the breeze and tranquil waves rhythmically lapping on the shoreline with the golden sand cliffs topped with trees and farmer's fields. Our trio paddles smoothly for the mile and a half to the Two Creeks County Park. A charming county park at the end of Two Creeks Road with a metal grid boat launch into the lake. There is a trailing trail to the sandy beach on the south side of the boat launch. Towards the north, the park extends for a third of a mile with a sandy bluff overlooking a sand and cobblestone beach with a larger southern and smaller northern creek flowing into the lake. Nice area for a picnic. Out in the lake old pier posts line up sticking out of the water, a testament to past sailing expeditions.

We sit back on the sweet picnic bench perched on top of the sandy bluff, relax and delight in the expansive Lake Michigan view. Sniff the pine filled air, and appreciate this picture-perfect paddling day.

Logistics:

Two Creeks County Park, Two Creeks:
44.305, -87.5443. Two Creeks Road. Shelter, no fee.

Irish Road public access:
44.2549, -87.5197. At the end of Irish Road. Parking on the side of the road. Listed in the Public accesses of Manitowoc County. No restrooms, no fee.

County V public access:
44.2372, -87.5114. At the end of County V, park off the road, no fee, no restrooms.

Rawleys Point Lighthouse beach and launch, Two Rivers:
44.2121, -87.5068. Park Road, Point Beach State Forest, off County Road O. After the park office, turn north to the Lighthouse picnic/ beach parking area. State Park fee is required, pit toilets, short carry to the shoreline.

Shipwreck locations:

Continental: 44.2322, -87.5077. Lies north of Point Beach State Forest Park, just north of beach homes that bump out and lined with a rock pile. At the northern tip of the bump out, about 440 feet off shore lies the Continental shipwreck in 10 to 15 feet of water.

Pathfinder: 44.2458, -87.5114. Lies off shore of Sandy Bay Road, where the road curves toward the lake, about 990 feet off shore in about ten feet of water.

Kayak Wisconsin, Lake Michigan Water Trail

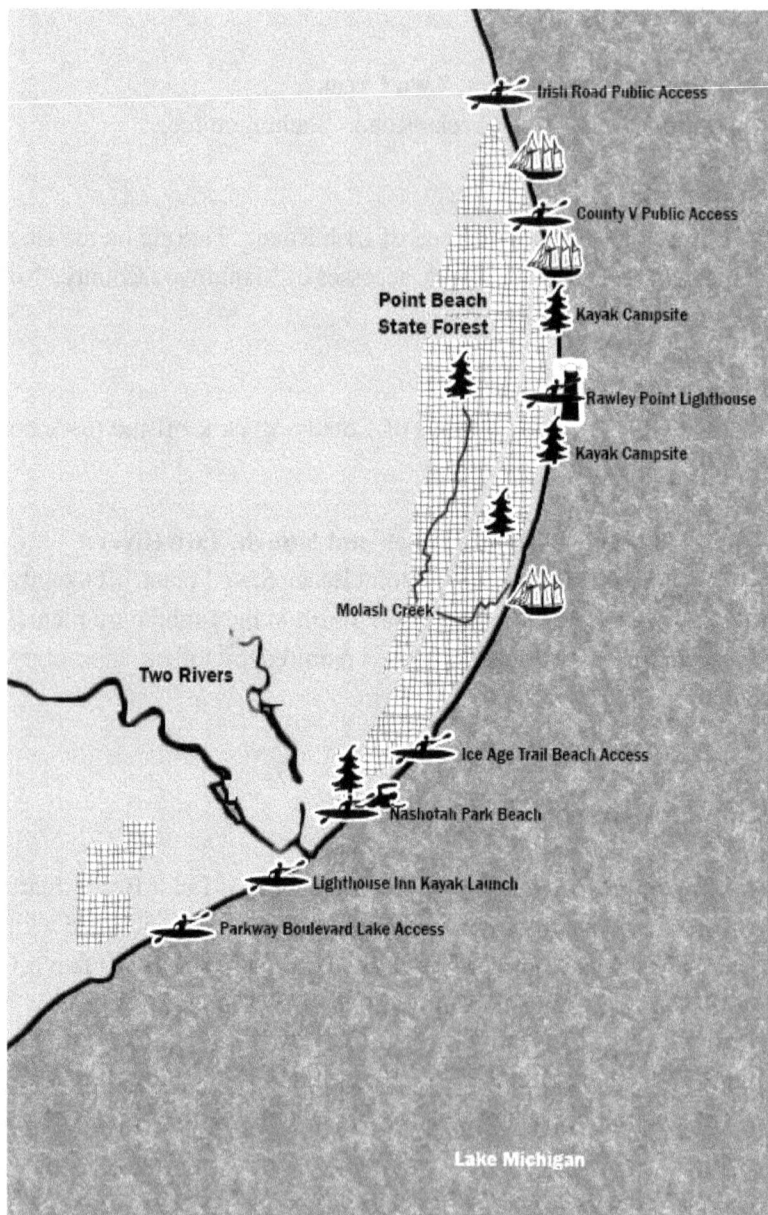

Irish Road Public Access

County V Public Access

Point Beach State Forest

Kayak Campsite

Rawley Point Lighthouse

Kayak Campsite

Molash Creek

Two Rivers

Ice Age Trail Beach Access

Nashotah Park Beach

Lighthouse Inn Kayak Launch

Parkway Boulevard Lake Access

Lake Michigan

Leg 6

Sandy Solitude Shores

Point Beach State Forest to Two Rivers

*With Nashotah Park Kite Festival
and a plethora of shallow shipwrecks*

8 miles

Let's, let's, go fly a kite, up to the highest heights! We planned this paddle for Labor Day weekend to stop at Nashotah Park in Two Rivers for their annual Kite Festival, but any day would be a great time to do this beachy boating with a sandy shore all the way from Point Beach State Forest Park lighthouse to Two River's Nashotah Park's humungous beach. We then continued past the Twin Rivers harbor to one of the boulevard parking areas with beach access to enjoy the town of Two Rivers and her twin rivers. And there are six, count them, six, shallow water shipwrecks to search for, all off shore of Point Beach State Forest!

On a calm day this would be a great paddle for beginners as almost all of it is by a sand beach. If you stay in shallow waters, then if by some means you do capsize, no problem man, just stand up and walk to shore to reenter. Easily shortened paddle by landing at Nashotah Park (but not on a Kite Festival day) for a five-mile paddle. If you wish to lengthen the paddle, you could paddle up the West Twin River six miles to the boat landing before the river dam at West Twin River County Park, or paddle up the East Twin River one mile to friendly and free Paddlers Park at the end of 27th Street.

Hot holiday weekend, perfect paddle for a warm day. We have a measly breeze, so choose to launch in Two Rivers and paddle up to Point Beach State Forest Park. There are a variety of beach access points in south Two Rivers following Highway 42 (Memorial Drive). Parkway Boulevard and Thiede Road have the best lake access, Davis Street, and Woodland Drive may be possible, each adding onto the paddle about a half-mile.

We launch at Parkway Boulevard beach access with a short carry down a few steps and over the small sand dune to the beautiful beach which is part of the Memorial Drive Wayside Beach North. Start this beach day, right and dive on in! The golden sandy bottom had delightful ripple patterns beneath the crystal-clear azure blue lake.

Our chosen day has unforcasted fog that is very stubborn at dissipating, so we have our fog horn whistle at the ready. According to Navigation Rules, "a vessel of less than 12 meters is not obliged to carry a fog horn but if not. . .need to be able to make an efficient signal." While not required, the United States Coast Guard rule states that "a vessel restricted in her ability to maneuver" should "sound at intervals of not more than two minutes three blasts in succession, namely one prolonged followed by two short blasts." We stayed within sight of land, had our GPS on, and did use the horn to alert some jet skiers that we were in shallow water.

Gentle paddling north towards the piers of Two Rivers, in less than one mile is the Lighthouse Inn with their restaurant that is literally on the water's edge. On the Inn's southern shore there is a sandy beach that you could pull up onto shore and stop in for lunch, no outdoor seating, but big beautiful window views of Lake Michigan.

Two Rivers is the fishing and shipping hub of the schooner coast and that is evident as we near the long parallel piers dotted with fishermen and lines. The north pier has a small red and white fog horn light that we appreciate on our foggy day and she was tooting every few minutes to help mariners locate the piers. The original wooden pier head lighthouse was a red square pyramidical lighthouse, with a ten-sided lantern room, and a small sixth order Fresnel lens. This lighthouse was ineffective and replaced by the large lighthouse at Point Beach State Forest. The old pier lighthouse now stands at the historic Rogers Street Fishing Village on the East Twin River, where you can climb her and see the restored Fresnel lens. Also, at the Village are artifacts from nearby shipwrecks including the deadly Vernon where 35-50 lives were lost, and the renowned Rouse Simmons, the Christmas Tree shipwreck.

If you enter the Two river harbor, on the north side is the US Coast Guard Station. It is an active lifesaving station continuing the daring adventures and rescues the original station did when commissioned in 1877. Across from the US Coast Guard Station is Seagull Marina and campground with a public boat launch.

A half-mile up the north side of the West Twin River is Veterans Park with a public boat launch. Shipwreck Adventures is located in downtown Two Rivers and they rent kayaks and canoes at Paddlers Park on the East Twin River. And oh hey, Two Rivers boasts of being the birthplace of the ice cream sundae, so while downtown stop into the historic Washington House on Jefferson Street, for a classic ice cream parlor where they serve sweet Wisconsin ice cream sundaes.

Time to head to the Nashotah Park beach, wow, you just can't miss it! It is a third of a mile long and 300 feet deep of beautiful cream-colored groomed sand. Swish your feet deep into the sand, lay out on the beach blanket, soak up some sun rays. Good times, and today is the Kites Over Lake Michigan Festival—hundreds of kites in the air, giant kites and colorful ground kites. Join in and learn how to fly a kite, free kite making for kids, and fly your own nighttime sky lantern. This is BIG, one of the largest kite festivals in the Midwest,

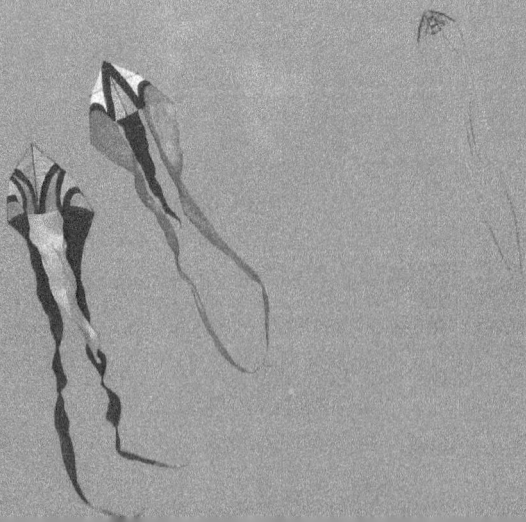

and you can enjoy it all and play on the beach! Marvel at the skill of the precision stunt teams with their dancing kites twining together and then magically releasing, doing the jig or romancing to music. You gotta catch it! Nashotah Park extends on shore with grass and shade trees, perfect for a picnic break. Across the street is Picnic Hill Park where the Rawleys Point bike trail begins and rides the sand dunes the same 6 miles that we are following north. The packed limestone trail takes bikers through the forests, over the dunes to Grandma's house we go, err, Point Beach State Park we go, and offers scenic views of the lake, so wave once in a while!

For a short half-mile, we are paddling past private homes and then the Point Beach State Forest begins as it goes past tiny Silver Creek (maybe the creek should have been named "Sliver" Creek).

We are entering an area, with a plethora of surf zone shipwrecks. All of which struggled in storms as they neared Rawleys Point. Most are newly discovered as they have been covered by soft sand. So, it's time to start looking down! Two miles north of Nashotah Beach lies the Tubal Cain shipwreck. She was a baroque, a small schooner, with three masts and square sails. Just a young 'un, she was less than two years old when she met her untimely end. In 1867 she headed out of Milwaukee, and ran into heavy rain and fog. Ahh, how grateful that we only have the fog! The Tubal Cain was pushed into shore and quickly her deck was below the lake surface. She lies about seven to ten feet deep about 400 feet off shore.

Now you can say you paddled the Ice Age National Scenic Trail, well—close anyway, as the trail walks the beach for two miles in Point Beach State Forest Park. The Ice Age National Scenic Trail is Wisconsin's only designated scenic trail. It starts at the border of

Minnesota and winds down into southern Wisconsin, climbs back up to Northeast Wisconsin by this lakeshore and heads across the Door County Peninsula and ends at Potawatomi State Park for a total of over 1200 miles. It follows the last continental glacier in Wisconsin and highlights unique glacial features.

Time to search for our next shipwreck. Less than a quarter mile before Molash Creek, and about 230 feet off shore lies the newly discovered Major Anderson shipwreck. She was found in 2013 by an ultralight pilot looking down and she only lies in three to ten feet deep water. You could actually stop and swim around to find her. The Major Anderson was a barquentine schooner with three masts but the front mast had a square sail which allowed good wind performance and required a smaller crew. She sank in 1871 in thick fog, umm. . .a lot like today.

Molash Creek opens its mouth to Lake Michigan. Today she is misty and eerie, in spring she is more awake and offers fishing opportunities. Native Americans lived in this area and on the south side of the creek, arrowhead making remnants have been found. We take a break to investigate the area with an opportunity for a swim.

While you are swimming, swim north just 1000 feet of the mouth of Molash Creek. Look for the Grace Patterson shipwreck which lays in 5 feet of water. She was a steam screw ship, with a steam engine and a propeller. Newly built only two years earlier, she sprung a leak (well at least it wasn't fog again. . .) and ground ashore in 1882. The Life Saving Crew found the crew hanging topside in the rigging and rescued all five crewmen.

If you are really lucky, the LaSalle shipwreck lies .53 miles north of Molash Creek, 600 feet off shore. She was a three-masted schooner with unique angle iron deck knees to be able to carry a heavier load. She left Chicago with a load of wheat and sailed into a gale. She tried to anchor, but struck bottom by Rawleys Point and filled with water. The crew needed to climb up into the rigging overnight, and were rescued the next day. She lies 12 feet deep.

Don't stop looking! Just a little more than a half mile north of Molash Creek, is another shipwreck to find. The Alaska, constructed in Sheboygan for the lumber industry, was pushed ashore and finally abandoned in 1879. She was a scow schooner, with a flat bottom and square sides, to have a shallow draft. She is only 100 feet off shore in about 5 feet of water. Another opportunity to swim and search for her!

And we aren't done yet! The Lookout, a clipper schooner with two masts is .74 miles north of Molash Creek and 300 feet off shore, about 12 feet underwater. She had two masts, square, rigging and an eagle figurehead! Wouldn't that be awesome to see! After 45 years of sailing the Great Lakes, in 1897, she was sailing empty north from Chicago and stranded in a northeast gale. All the crew were able to get ashore in their yawl, to the safety of the Life Savers on shore. Her bow and lower hull are mostly intact. All these ships lie in soft sand that covers and uncovers parts of the ships each year.

The beach and sand dune continue for another two miles. It's a rarity to see folks on the shore, even on an 80-degree day. Listen to the gentle waves lapping on the shore, time to relax and rejuvenate the spirit and soul. Take pleasure in this pristine view of the Point Beach sand dunes topped with forest greenery. Point Beach Ridge is truly an unusual piece of paradise with eleven alternating sand ridges and low swales between. Each ridge was formed through the slow lowering of glacial Lake Nippissing, Lake Michigan's great-grandma. The first ridge closest to us is a coastal sand dune with endangered dune thistle, goldenrod and sand dune willow. The next ridge has junipers and bearberry, successive ridges have maples and white birch, the ninth ridge is mostly white cedar, white pine and hemlock. By the eleventh ridge the trees are ash and tamarack.

As we propel past this irreplaceable landscape on the shore, our calm seas are alive, occasionally we see great schools of white fish beneath our boats, which suddenly dart away, chased by a large trout or salmon. Twice our white fish dance for us, jumping out of the waters, a hundred in a chorus standing on their tails on top of the water, waving and dancing on the calm lake surrounding our boats, and abruptly disappearing back under water! Just out a bit, the gulls and cormorants also sing and dance for us. The cormorants dragging their feet across the water as they boogie a short distance away, making the water glisten and sparkle and the air tingle with their tapping feet and flapping wings while the gulls croon.

Just as you begin to see the Rawleys Point Lighthouse in the distance approximately a little more than half-mile away, there is a little path heading up the dune, part of the Ice Age Trail, and if you get close you will see a small sign on a blue post. This is a wonderful addition to Point Beach State Forest—the landing for the two kayak (or hikers) wilderness campsites. They are just over the sand dunes and you may only rent them for a single night's stay.

We arrive at the Rawleys Point Lighthouse. After the original one built 1853 deteriorated, they erected this steel tower lantern room

which is 113 feet tall, the largest and brightest beacon on the Great Lakes, with a light that can be seen for about 20 miles—almost half way across Lake Michigan. Prior to this lighthouse, 26 ships floundered or were stranded on this point. The Vernon shipwreck lies out off this area 205 feet deep. Her story is a tear jerker. She was a large steamer ship that sank in heavy seas filled with at least 36 passengers and crewmembers. Only one survivor was found, in a lifeboat with a dead companion. Other ships were in the vicinity, but mysteriously none offered aid, breaking the maritime steadfast rule. Since the Rawleys Point Lighthouse was built she has successfully done her job and no new ship has joined the lost ones.

In a blink of the eye, okay, 700 feet, we are at the Rawleys Point lighthouse beach. Pull up on shore, and dive back into the water for another sandy beach swim. It has been a delightful day, why rush it now? As we slowly pack up, other kayakers arrive back at shore, they have been out fishing and caught a salmon with their kayak—thrilling! They were filling the back hatch with ice to keep the salmon fresh. Love to hear that fish story…

Logistics:

Rawleys Point Lighthouse beach launch, Two Rivers:
44.2121, -87.5068. 9400 County Road O, Point Beach State Park. State Park fee, pit toilets. Short carry to the shoreline.

Point Beach State Park Kayak Campsite, Two Rivers:
44.2012, -87.5103. About .7 miles south of the Rawley Point Lighthouse, where the Ice Age Trail comes to the shore. Look for a sign on a blue post.

Park Road, Two Rivers, Ice Age Trail beach access, Two Rivers:
44.1574, -87.5426. 150 Park Road. End of the road beach access trail. 900-foot carry to the beach. Parking on street, no restrooms.

Nashotah Park, Two Rivers:
44.1524, -87.5550. Zlatnik Drive. park in any of 5 parking areas by the beach! No fee, nice restrooms, short carry to the water's edge.

Parkway Boulevard Lake access, Two Rivers:
44.1364, -87.5864. Highway 42/Memorial Drive at Parkway Boulevard south of downtown Two Rivers. No fee, no restrooms, short carry down a few steps and over sand dune to shoreline.

Shipwreck locations:

Tubal Cain: 44.1729, -87.5223. Lies in 7-10 feet of water .9 miles south of Molash Creek in Point Beach State Forest.

Major Anderson: 44.1821, -87.5163. Lies in just 3-10 feet of water south of Molash Creek in Point Beach State Forest.

Grace Patterson: 44.1877, -87.5144. Lies in just 5 feet of water 1000 feet north of Molash Creek in Point Beach State Forest.

LaSalle: 44.1921, -87.5099. Lies deeper in 10 to 15 feet of water .56 miles north of Molash Creek in Point Beach State Forest.

Alaska: 44.1935, -87, 5113. Lies in 5 feet of water .62 miles north of Molash Creek in Point Beach State Forest.

Lookout: 44.1951, -87.5099. Lies deeper in 10-15 feet of water .74 miles north of Molash Creek in Point Beach State Forest.

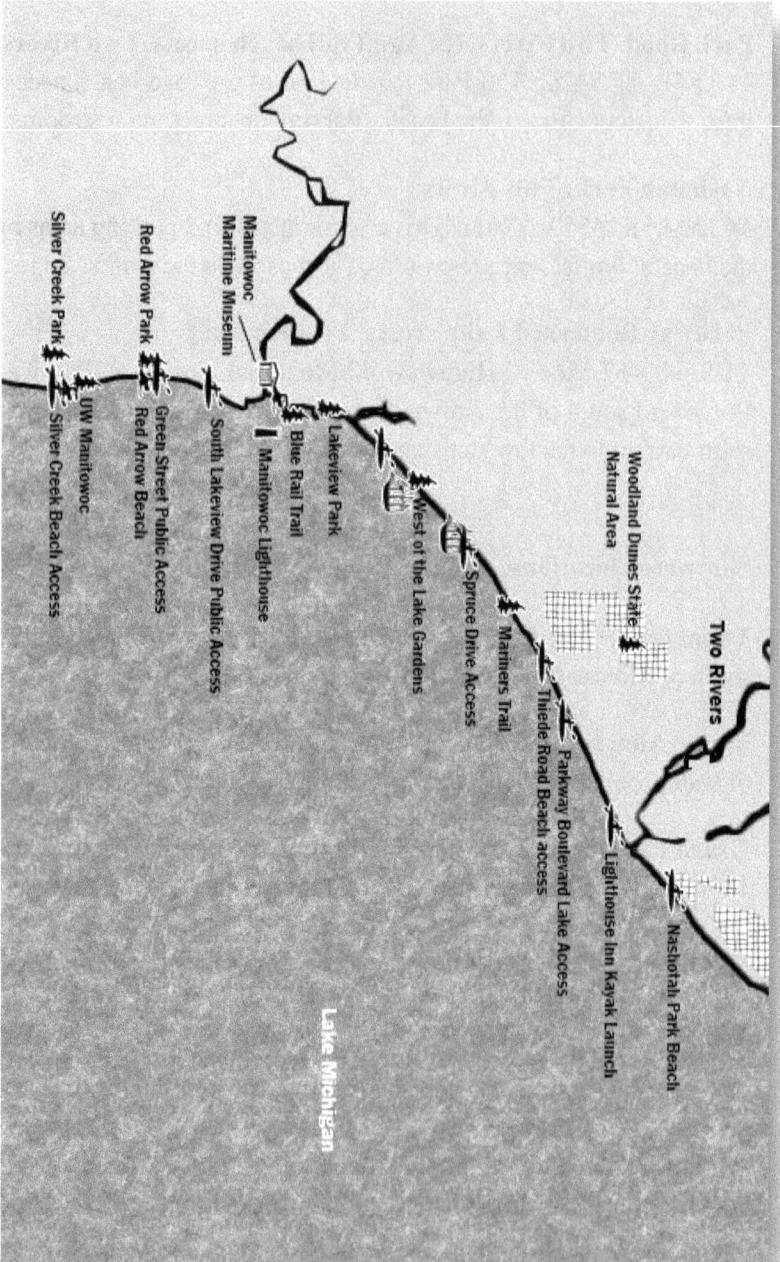

Silver Creek Park

Silver Creek Beach Access

UW Manitowoc

Red Arrow Park

Red Arrow Beach

Green Street Public Access

South Lakeview Drive Public Access

Manitowoc Maritime Museum

Manitowoc Lighthouse

Blue Rail Trail

Lakeview Park

West of the Lake Gardens

Spruce Drive Access

Mariners Trail

Woodland Dunes State Natural Area

Thiede Road Beach access

Parkway Boulevard Lake Access

Two Rivers

Lighthouse Inn Kayak Launch

Nashotah Park Beach

Lake Michigan

Leg 7

Submarine and Shipwrecks

Two Rivers to Manitowoc

With USS Cobia submarine, and 2 shipwrecks

9 miles

Up periscope, fire the torpedoes! Exciting opportunity to be up close and personal to Manitowoc's WWII submarine, then experience the massive SS Badger steamship car ferry as she docks. The rest of this paddle is a nonchalant relaxing paddle along beaches and streams with most of its public natural scenery as we race the bikers on the Mariners Trail from Manitowoc to Two Rivers. Stop to look down for the Francis Hinton, and Arctic shipwrecks, and "our" newly found shipwreck, read on for more of that story...

Divide this day into two paddles if you desire. Play around Manitowoc from Silver Creek to Lakeview Park Beach for a 3-mile paddle. Then paddle from that beach to Two Rivers for a 6-mile journey along the Mariner Trail.

We put in at the southern edge of Manitowoc at Silver Creek Park and paddled north with our extremely gentle wisp of a wind, veered up into Manitowoc River for the ferry and submarine, and then back out to Lake Michigan north to Parkway Boulevard beach access off the Mariner Trail before the twin rivers of Two Rivers for our 9 mile paddle.

Unusually gorgeous warm and sunny Memorial Day paddle with that whisper of a wind making the turquoise lake sparkle and dance. We discover that the best launch at Silver Creek Park is by the south side of the creek itself with a nice sandy trail down to the beach. Stop and explore the almost half mile of beach and the silver hue off the surface of the stream. Silver Creek starts four miles west in Silver Lake (gee, what a surprise) and meanders for over eight miles through meadows and woodland before becoming the highlight of this park. The park has a concession stand, fieldhouse, and one of the top-rated disc golf courses in the state with 27 holes. Its signature hole has the basket sitting atop a six-foot lighthouse surrounded by Lake Michigan—might want to wear your swimsuit for disc in!

Gently push off into Lake Michigan and immediately the calmness surrounds us as we ease into the day with the beauty of the lake and forested shoreline. Just north of the park is University of Wisconsin Manitowoc which gives even more beach and offers a switchback ramp down to the shoreline that may work for a launch site. All along Lakeside Boulevard is loads of natural conservancy super sweet beaches and then onto Red Arrow Beach Park with a wide open thousand-foot sandy groomed beach with a shower house and restrooms. At the north end of Red Arrow Beach Park is Green Street which is the designated kayak/canoe launch site. Manitowoc Lincoln High School Beach is next door as we paddle north, followed by Warm Water Beach with its little inlet. South Lakeview Drive offers a parking area with carry in access next to the inlet. Have you noticed that all this natural shoreline has added up to almost 2 miles of beach and public access? Marvelous Manitowoc!

Urbaness now begins, the Manitowoc Water treatment plant is protected by the built-up rocky shoreline with the old Budweiser plant behind. Now it is a malt house, but the Budweiser sign is still a historic landmark. Barley is brought in by train, and yes, it is still producing malt for making. . .what else but beer, yes, of course, this is Wisconsin. The company is the original site of the Manitowoc Rahr Eagle brewery that closed at the start of prohibition. Malt production continued for cereal and the company has been selling malt since 1891 with the original horse stable still there.

We head out past the harbor wall racing the SS Badger into port. It won—what a shocker. Probably a good thing as the harbor entrance is not that wide and the SS Badger car ferry is massive at almost 60 feet wide, 400 feet long and over 100 feet high. . .that equals 7 stories! She travels at 18mph, pretty sure we can't paddle that fast. The SS Badger is a national historic treasure as the largest lake crossing passenger service on the Great Lakes and has provided a real steamship experience for over 60 years. She is also the only coal fired steamship in operation in the US, with her coal ash off loaded and used to make cement. At least once, you gotta' treat yourself and take the SS Badger the 60 miles, four-hour cruise, across Lake Michigan to Ludington Michigan. We've enjoyed touring the Michigan side sand dunes, renting jeeps, and running down the mountain of sand into the lake. See Big Sable Lighthouse, sister to Wisconsin's Rawleys Point Lighthouse. Take an evening sail back on the SS Badger and enjoy a star lit night show, might want to bring a chart of all the constellations to revel in the show.

The SS Badger arrives in Manitowoc at 11:30 am and stays until 1:30 pm—your best opportunity to check out this legend of the lake. From the harbor entrance it is a third of a mile to her dock on the south side. Watch for boats coming into the harbor, making this portion of the day an intermediate paddle.

Just a thousand more feet along the north side of the river wall is the Maritime Museum, a great place to learn about Wisconsin's Schooner Coast and commemorate the marine heritage of Manitowoc and Two Rivers. First up, the Native Americans were here, scooping out their canoes. Then the first Europeans settled in the Manitowoc area in 1820, and by 1847 the first schooner was built leading the Manitowoc shipbuilding industry. By World War II, Manitowoc switched to constructing military vessels to assist the Navy's war effort. Visit the museum and let the kids play in the Children's Waterways room, tour Wisconsin built boats, step back in time to be part of Wisconsin ship building, and even start an actual Great Lake 1911 steam engine and make it pump and move.

For this Memorial Day, we have chosen to honor those who serve, and float quietly past the Maritime Museum's star the USS Cobia, a World War II submarine. 7000 local men and women built 28 submarines like the Cobia during World War II, working around the clock every day of the year. The Manitowoc submarines together sank 132 enemy ships. Four of the Manitowoc ships were lost at sea and are now on "eternal patrol". The USS Cobia herself sank 13 enemy vessels and was part of the attack of the Japanese convoy where she sank two vessels and was critical to the success of capturing Iwo Jima, remember the famous flag raising photo? One sailor from the USS Cobia died during a running gun battle with two enemy ships where the Cobia ultimately sank both of the vessels. She herself was almost sunk when attacked by a Japanese minesweeper that blasted her into the sea floor—she escaped heavily damaged. Paddle past the USS Cobia slowly, touch her with kindness, and salute all our veterans and especially those who gave all. Hooyah!

Now we head back out to the mouth of the river. The SS Badger car ferry dock on the south side of the harbor is considered to be a small craft launch site, but recommend using it when the SS Badger is not in port and use the beach by the parking area. On the north side of the harbor is an extension of the Mariners Trail that curves into the harbor with a public beach by the YMCA. Next to the break water is a beach access that could work as a gentle launch site. Inside the marina is the Manitowoc Marina which is a designated boat launch with six lanes and fish cleaning stations. Here is where you may rent a Hobie kayak for river pedaling, or the Hobie Mirage which is both a standup paddle board with the addition of pedaling instead of using a paddle—got that?

Head out of the harbor following the south wall, cross the marina entrance with heightened focus, and follow the Blue Rail Trail (duh Babs, it has a blue painted railing...) out to the Manitowoc Lighthouse on the tip of the pier. The first Manitowoc lighthouse was built in 1839. Then the parallel piers were built and the first pier head lighthouse was completed, with a fog bell added later. The angled breakwater that forms the north end of the Manitowoc marina was constructed to protect the harbor. The inside land between the pier and break water offers a dog play park and a little pond. The old pier head lighthouse was moved several times and needed replacing. The current steel lighthouse was built atop a concrete boathouse in 1919. The first story is the power room, and the second story housed the light keeper's office. The round diaphone fog signal room is the third floor, and the very top is the lantern room which had a fifth order Fresnel lens. This cool wedding cake looking lighthouse now has an electronic fog horn and an automated light. The original priceless Fresnel lens was removed for safe keeping and it is at the Maritime Museum just up river.

As we head back out and around the lighthouse and turn north, we follow the breakwater back to Lakeview Park which runs for over a half mile along the coast. Nice sandy beach tucked in the corner right by a parking area, perfect for an easy launch and enjoyable for a picnic lunch. Two classic Adirondack chairs are provided for lounging on the beach, along with picnic tables and an open shelter for lunch. Here is where the Blue Rail Trail begins its half mile walk on the break water and pier out to the Lighthouse—superb sunset screening! The Native Americans called this bay Manidoowaak "dwelling of the spirit" due to the natural beauty of the area, perfectly verified at Lakeview Park.

Paddle past the Little Manitowoc River, it spreads out inward with marsh and meadow and hardwood forest. Smelt and sometimes Rainbow trout spawn here. The north shore in Lakeview Park has three crib beds for old docks extending out into the lake (with a fourth submerged), fun to stop and climb around…"no, no, no… don't push me in Rick!"

A southern wayside, Waldo Boulevard, has a small beach path leading up the shore. Entertaining artistic sculptures line the Mariners Trail as it follows the shoreline. We wave to the bikers, hikers, and roller bladders as they traverse the paved path enjoying the vistas of Lake Michigan as we enjoy the shoreline. The trail starts in Manitowoc at the Maritime Museum and is the longest continuous scenic view of Lake Michigan with six miles as it coasts up to Two Rivers over craggy coves and sand dunes. It doesn't truly end there, as you can continue through Two Rivers and join the Rawleys Point recreation trail biking through Point Beach State Forest with the sweet smell of pine and hemlock woods for another six miles. Along our portion of the trail, are gardens loving tended by local folks, along with occasional telescopes, so smile sweetly!

As the bike trail curves away from the shoreline, the West of the Lake Gardens grow for six acres of unbiased glory. John West was President of Manitowoc Shipbuilding Company, and his wife developed an obsession with gardening. Now the gardens are free for all of us to enjoy, so when you walk or bike past, do not miss the blooming display. Unfortunately, there is no beach access as the shoreline is rocky along this portion of the paddle.

However, there are sights to be seen under the lake. The Francis Hinton shipwreck is located about 1200 feet off shore right before the West of the Lake Gardens. There is a mooring buoy floating on the Lake marking her location. She lies in approximately 15 feet of water, which is generally too deep to be seen from the surface as we paddle over her, but her boiler rises to within five feet of the surface, so there is a chance to glimpse her. . . And several portions of the ship are much closer to shore, only about 200-300 feet off shore, so head in close and search for those pieces. The Francis Hinton was a steam screw ship, a steam boat with propellers to move her, known as "screws". As she was heading to Chicago in 1909, a fierce gale blew up squelching her steam fire, and she was unable to make it to Manitowoc's harbor. The crew needed to abandon ship, climbed into their life boat, and rowed to safety through the pounding surf as the ship broke up in the storm.

And right after the Francis Hinton, is the Arctic shipwreck. Only 140 feet north of the Francis Hinton, but she is only 900 feet off shore. The Arctic served the Manitowoc area for over 49 years as an ice breaking tug boat. Then she was dismantled, beached, and abandoned. Her stem post and upper hull is 800 feet further north of her rudder, bilge and boiler.

After several houses, businesses, and the Chamber of Commerce, the Mariner Trail again rolls next to the shoreline by the Spruce Drive middle wayside, which used to have a beach access and possible launch site, but as the lake has risen, it is now not recommended to launch or take out here. But here is where we choose to stop on the beach for lunch and swim—well not quite, we only made it up to our knees, 50 degrees is burning cold, not reasonably ready for swimming, unless we put our wetsuits back on. Nah, lay out our beach blanket, and soak up some sun rays.

Then a boat moors right off our lunch spot, really? How dare! Look, miles of beach south, miles of beach north, not another boat in sight, why spoil our lake view? Then they put up a dive flag and for the entire time we cook and cut up our veggies, they are diving down in the deep blue about 250 feet off the beach. Pretty sure they aren't looking at sand and rocks. "What are they looking at?" We plan to ask them as we set off after lunch. Shoot, they pack up right when we are. . . and off they go. Fine, we'll check it out for ourselves…

I see wood! It has to be a shipwreck…but there isn't supposed to be one here. . .interesting. . . In the Manitowoc area, eleven ships have been lost, a few scuttled, but most have floundered in gales attempting to reach safe harbor in Manitowoc. Not quite making it, they capsized or beached and broke apart. None of these shipwrecks have "confirmed locations" so you could be the next explorer that discovers a lost treasure! However, the Magellan's unconfirmed location is just north of where we are picnicking. When a ship goes down in the surf zone, wind and ice can move the wreck a bit. We hope that our found shipwreck could be the Magellan. She was lost in 1877 in a storm and the shattered ship and mutilated bodies washed ashore. It was suggested that she had been run down by another ship. However, that same day, the Joseph L. Hurd reported "running through a vessel's rigging". It is now assumed that the Hurd ran over the remains of the wreck of the Magellan mutilating the bodies with its propellers. By noon of the next day, the hull of the Magellan was bottom up and beached between Manitowoc and Two Rivers. Gives us chills to "find" this wreck!

But no, it is not to be. I checked with the Wisconsin Historical Society which keeps track of Wisconsin's Great Lakes Shipwrecks. Caitlin, was one of the divers we saw! And no, this new wreck is not a schooner, meaning it could not be the Magellan, more likely one of the scuttled ships. Still cool that a new shipwreck has been discovered!

Ah, onward we paddle north with no further excitement—just serene splendid scenery. Rocky shore interspersed with small beach areas depending on the level of the lake. Less than a quarter mile inland is the Woodland Dunes State Natural Area where the Ice Age Trail has ditched the Mariner Trail to ramble through the preserve. The sand ridges are narrow parallel sand bars that were former beach shores of Lake Michigan during the post glacial times. Aspen, beech, hemlock and white pines dominate the ridges. Between the ridges are swales, wet low areas where ash, elm, willow and white cedar flourish. There are several other shorter trails through the Dunes with one giving you an overlook of the West Twin River in Two Rivers.

Soon we are in Two Rivers but the appealing coast line continues with bikers waving hello from the shoreline trail. Woodland Drive and a half mile north, the Davis Street bump out arrive, both wayside

areas, but without beach access. Another pretty picturesque half mile north, Thiede Road rest area appears with stairs on both ends leading through the boulders down to the beach for a possible take out spot. We have chosen to paddle yet another half mile north to the Parkway Boulevard wayside and its twin beach access steps and path to a quiet beach. After unloading, Rick took the scooter back to Silver Creek to pick up the car and trailer, while Chris and I had the difficult job of wading, relaxing and beach lounging. Cheers to a charming ending to a remarkable paddle day with ship, submarine, shipwrecks and sunbathing.

Logistics:

Silver Creek Park beach access, Manitowoc:
44.0613, -87.6535. 3001 S. 10th Street. Turn into the park entrance, then at the T intersection turn right/south and then immediately turn left and follow the park road to the small turn around/parking area by the creek and bridge. You may drive down the gravel road 200 feet to the beach path to unload and then move to park your vehicle. Short carry of about 200 feet to water's edge. There are rest rooms in the park, but not at this area. No fees.

Red Arrow Park, Manitowoc:
44.0760, -87.6567. 1931 S. 9th Street. Large parking lot with several paths to the beach. Short carry over sandy beach. Restrooms and showers available. No fees!

Green Street public access, Manitowoc:
44.0777, -87.6557. 809 Green Street. Parking available. No restroom (although there are restrooms and showers in walking distance at Red Arrow Park). No fees.

South Lakeview Drive public access, Manitowoc:
44.0842, -87.6540. S. Lakeview Drive. Parking area and beach path that curves next to the inlet to the beach. No restrooms, but no fees either!

Manitowoc Marina boat ramp, Manitowoc:
44.0955, -87.6502. 425 Maritime Drive. Boat launch fee, Hobie kayak rentals. May go to the right to the YMCA parking lot and beach (small sailboats on beach). May be possible to launch at the beach for free. Restroom in the Marina.

Lakeview Park (Blue Rail Marina Beach), Manitowoc:
44.1002, -87.6485. 600 Maritime Drive. Picnic tables, open shelter, nice beach, no restrooms, but no fee either! Blue Rail Trail to walk the half mile path to the Manitowoc Pier head Lighthouse.

Memorial Drive (Wayside South) at Waldo Blvd, Manitowoc:
44.1090, -87.6412. Memorial Drive just as Hwy JJ/Waldo Blvd turns onto Memorial Drive. Beach trail on north side of parking area. This is not listed as a kayak launch, but is considered a beach access. No fee, no restrooms.

Spruce Drive Wayside (Wayside Middle), Manitowoc:
44.1204, -87.6235. 1630 Memorial Drive. The wayside is just north of the Chamber of Manitowoc County building. This is an alternative launch site because the lake level has risen, and there is now a steep drop off to the water. Check before you unload your water craft or decide to use this as your take out spot. No fee, no restroom.

The next two Waysides on Memorial Drive have no beach access:
Woodland Drive (just south of Aurora Hospital)
Davis Street

Thiede Road Wayside beach access, Two Rivers:
44.1326, -87.5978. 3120 Memorial Drive, Two Rivers. First Wayside by Lake Michigan (has a fish sculpture by the trail). Steps to the beach, no fees, no restrooms.

Parkway Blvd Wayside beach access (Wayside North):
44.1369, -87.5870. 2848 Memorial Drive, Two Rivers. Blue signs indicate the beach accesses, curved patio at the north end with blue benches). No fees, no restrooms.

Shipwreck locations:

Francis Hinton: Main shipwreck: 44.1112, -87.6313, mooring buoy by her. Although she lies 15 feet or more below the surface, her boiler is about 5 feet under the water, so you may be able to see that.
Pieces of the wreck may be closer to shore, check out 44.1129, -87.6319, however these pieces may move with wave and ice action. The Francis Hinton lies about .25 miles off shore from the West of the Lake Gardens. There is a sign marker on the Mariner Trail indicating the wreck site.

Arctic: 44.1120, -87.6319. 1.5 miles north of the Manitowoc Lighthouse, 900 feet off shore, however her hull and stem post are 800 feet lays 800 feet more north. She is in 10-15 feet of water.

"Our shipwreck": 44.11923, -87.62405. This is the shipwreck that the divers were investigating when we were having lunch on the beach by the Spruce Drive Wayside. She is unconfirmed since she lies in the surf zone, she could be washed to variable locations.

Kayak Wisconsin, Lake Michigan Water Trail

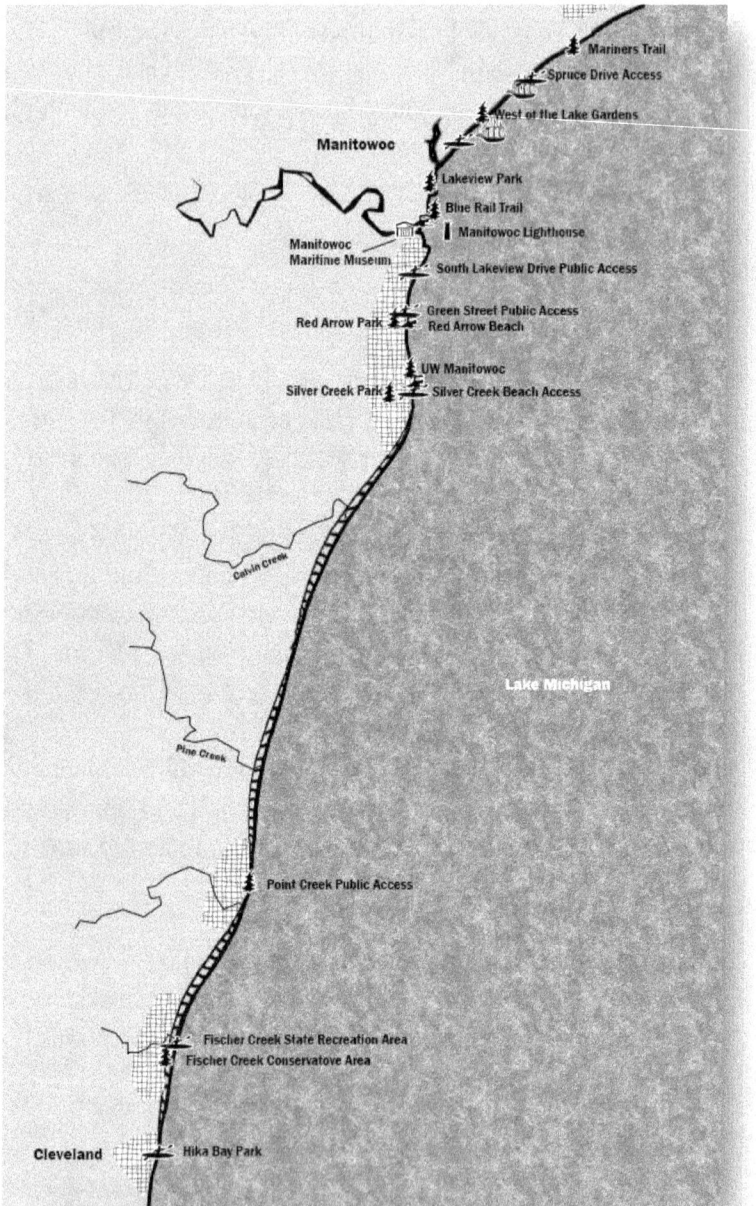

Leg 8

Bluff, Creek, Repeat

Manitowoc to Cleveland Wisconsin

With massive bluffs, and Silver, Point,
Fischer, and Centerville Creeks

11 miles

Summer Solstice Streaming. Now you don't need all 15 hours and 29 minutes of the longest day of the year to complete this paddle, but this scenic adventure is perfect for a summer fun day with its numerus sandy beaches and towering bluffs. Put in on the bank of the Silver Creek in the south side of the city of Manitowoc, paddle to the point—Point Creek for lunch, field Fischer Creek Recreation Area, and land at Hika Bay Park with its Centerville Creek. Then check off your choice for voting on your favorite stream: Silver Creek, Point Creek, Fischer Creek, or Centerville Creek.

Now, I don't want to say it would be impossible to shorten this paddle. . . but, Point Creek access is at the 7-mile mark, with a long boat carry to the bluff overlook, yes that is correct, the 30-foot bluff overlook. Fischer Creek Recreation Area is at the 9-mile mark, and it has a long trail leading to the beach, but paddling the 2 miles more to Hika Bay Park with its drive-up boat ramp seems like the best option. So, just accept that this is the day to dilly dally and check out the creeks and stay enthused for the full 11 miles.

We put in at Silver Creek Park at the southern end of the city of Manitowoc. Blue sky day after a week of storms. Consider being lazy and putting in at the main parking lot right into the swollen fast and furious creek and riding the current, and splashing out into the lake. After rethinking that plan, we park next to the creek in the middle of the park and lug our boats and gear for the gentle push off into Lake Michigan by the southern bank of Silver Creek. Perfect sunny day with 76-degree temps, but Rick persuades us to don our wet suits. His logic is that 60 degrees water temperature is 36 degrees cooler than our bodies prefer. He is almost becoming the safety patrol, but since he is correct and the water was breath removing icy cold, we dutifully gear up with wet suits and our PFD's personal floatation devices.

Head north to south today, because the weather report is breezy with northwest winds. We agree, the wind was brisk from the west, but Mother Nature isn't too sure about whether to blow from the north or the south. Today, Denise, Chris's stepmom joins us. She has paddled a lot of the river paddles with us, but today she considers herself a beginner on the "big lake" Lake Michigan. I'm sure she is nervous to set out in our mighty 3-inch waves, yup we are in the lee and our waves are just inches high with gentle soothing swells. A kayaker in a recreation boat waves to us as he passes by. Perfect morning to paddle close to shore in a recreation kayak.

On the water, we head south, with views of Silver Creek Park and the superb sandy beach. Just ahead is a metal clad peninsula jutting out with a little lighthouse. The lighthouse is one of the baskets for the first class 36-hole frisbee disc golf course that covers much of Silver Creek Park. On top of the little lighthouse is the disc basket. Throw too far and your disc is floating on the lake. It takes a lot of

tries, at least for me, to finally land the frisbee in the basket. Then climb the steps to retrieve it. The rest of the park is sandy shore with woodlands.

Looking at a map, you would swear that the coastline is straight for our entire paddle. But we pass a little point and enter a gentle bay. Head for the next point which is 6.5 miles away. Keeping your bow pointed at the point, does put you at least a half mile off shore, otherwise, hug closer to land. There are no public areas in the belly of the bay, but there are two small creeks you can explore. The first one is Calvin Creek which is a mile and a half into the bay. This little stream's origin is Hartlaub Lake three miles inland. The creek twists and turns and finally flows into Lake Michigan.

Sandy bluffs with green tufts rise up to fifty feet high. Topped with a lime green plateau and stately homes. Some of the homes add a hundred step staircases down to their beach. The shoreline is sand and cobblestone flanked by those bold and beautiful bluffs. Our lake is a stunning steely sage color today due to the recent rains. As the usually gentle babbling brooks, now running high and reckless, gush out into the lake they turn the water a dusty color today. The azure blue sky meets the new green bluffs completing this photo finish of a day. Wispy clouds float above us just off the shoreline as the cooler lake air meets the warmer land mass. A spreading jet trail slices the sky above us. We are joined by lines of squadrons of pelicans streaking close to us, checking us out as we enjoy these thank you God moments.

Pine Creek is three and a half miles after Calvin Creek. It is located where the bluffs begin to sag and the evergreen forest meets the sandy beach. The low-lying woods is the riparian ribbon of green alongside the stream. This creek begins at Carstens Lake four miles inland, but with all its curvy cues the creek length is probably double that. Lakeshore Drive follows us as we paddle, and two miles inland, Interstate 43 shadows the shoreline too. Right after little Pine Creek, the emerald and sand cliffs grow once more.

After the last home before the point, Point Creek Park begins. This is a newer Manitowoc County Park. There are 39 acres of forest and meadows above the coastal bluff with a half mile of beautiful sandy beach sprinkled with tiny yellow flowers on trailing vines clinging to the sand. The steep cliff is dotted with daisy wild flowers, and the bluff is topped with woodlands. Literally at the tip of the point is the properly named Point Creek. This is the southern end of the park, although the forest continues for another thousand feet. The

natural park extends inland a quarter mile following the north side of Point Creek. The stream itself wigwags westward until it finally trails out near Interstate 43.

Stop at Point Creek Park under the headland for our own personal beach. Pure quiet. Just for us alone. . .this is why we kayak, no sharing the beach with anyone. Lovely American Pelicans bobbing past. Sharing cooperatively our area of the lake. Swimming on the surface and dipping their extended bright orange bill into the water to scoop up fish in their pouch. Slapping their feet across the water as they as they flap their nine-foot wingspan to gain the height for soaring above us. Their tips of the wings black against their pure white body. They fold their neck back on their body, with the flattened horn on the tip of their upper mandible evident. Appreciate them making Wisconsin their home.

Attempt to swim with our wet suits on, manage to make it waist high. Nope, can't do it, settle for some ice-cold drinking water instead. Explore our beach as we munch on our sub sandwiches and trail mix snack, smooshing our toes into the sand. Pack up the cooler, and shove off shore, ready for our afternoon paddle.

Rounding the point, brings us to the beginning of shallow Hika Bay, which extends to Sheboygan. Back to green sand cliffs interspersed with brown sand patches sloping down to the sandy cobblestone and sometimes rocky shoreline. Spring greens darkening to shamrock green dot the bluffs and deeper hunter green trees frost the top of the bluffs. Fluffy clouds floating on the bright blue sunny sky with turquoise blue water below us. The wind and waves have increased with the waves making it all the way to 12 inches high with occasional little sparkly whitecaps. Several small duck looking grebes swim close then skim over the lake away from us.

Only one and a half miles leads us to the start of Fischer Creek State Recreation Area. Volunteers saved this land for us from condo development. Now instead, we have a picturesque half mile of shoreline before the creek and another half mile of park coast after the creek. That is a full nice mile of public access for us to stop and

explore, as several couples and families are doing. There are two parking areas off Lakeshore Drive both before and after the creek, with a restroom located at the southern parking lot. Picnic areas overlook the lake both north and south of the creek. An old sturdy steel bridge crosses the stream. This historical bridge dates back to an old military road that connected Green Bay to Milwaukee. Trails lead down the slope to the beach where thousands of migrating waterfowl travel through. Fischer Creek trout spawn here in Spring. The stream itself meanders west for over three miles before gently petering out.

As we paddle past Fischer Creek State Area, we are almost to the end zone. The cliffs decrease in size and dwindling trails wiggle their way from homes down the slopes to the beach. Only a mile of paddling left to arrive at Hika Bay Park. First, we see sandy beaches leading up the ridge to a forested top, with sandy swales and meadows behind the trees. There is 600 feet of beach before Centerville Creek, so named because it is half way from Manitowoc to Sheboygan. After the creek, there is 300 more feet of beach, before the can't miss it dock with the bright yellow sign indicating you have arrived at Hika Bay Park. A gentle sloped boat ramp, makes the landing a breeze. Paddle lift to celebrate Denise's first Lake Michigan adventure!

I decide I will swim, even if it necessitates doing it in the wet suit. Rick dares me, I need to have wet hair and feet off the bottom to count it as swimming. Little by little, I am able to tolerate the cold, cheating and splashing water over my hair, but I do achieve actually floating for at least a whole half a minute, and duck my head under water. "Pay up Rick!" He bows to my accomplishment— swimming in the 60-degree lake. I feel refreshed!

Hika Bay Park is a delight. Striking green grass picnic area with a wonderful bench to enjoy the Lake Michigan views as Rick heads out on the scooter to retrieve the trailer left in Manitowoc. Nice covered pavilion with picnic tables. Chance to freshen up in the restroom with true flushing toilets. Hang out the gear to dry and relax before the drive home. Stroll down the beach to check out the creek. Applaud the scenic beauty this paddle shared with us.

Logistics:

Silver Creek Park beach access, Manitowoc:
44.0613, -87.6535. 3001 S. 10th Street. Turn into the park entrance, then at the T intersection turn right/south and then immediately turn left and follow the park road to the small turn around/parking area by the creek and bridge. You may drive down the gravel road 200 feet to the beach path to unload and then move to park your vehicle.

Short carry of about 200 feet to water's edge. There are rest rooms in the park, but not at this area. No fees.

Directions to Point Creek public access, Manitowoc:
43.9682, -87.6990. 11000 Lakeshore Drive. Emergency access. Beautiful picnic area on the beach front, but steep bluff limits access from the road. No fees, but no restroom.

Fischer Creek State Recreation Area, Manitowoc:
43.9373, -87.7191. 13350 Lakeshore Drive. This is a carry-in access, which means from the north parking lot you have a 600-foot carry and a slope to access the lake. Whereas from the south parking lot you have a 1000-foot carry but a gentle slope to a larger beach area. State park fee required. Restroom is located at the south parking area.

Hika Bay Park, Cleveland Wisconsin:
43.9156, -87.7237. 1116 Lakeshore Drive. Easy launch on the two-lane boat ramp. Launch fee, but A+ restrooms.

Kayak Wisconsin, Lake Michigan Water Trail

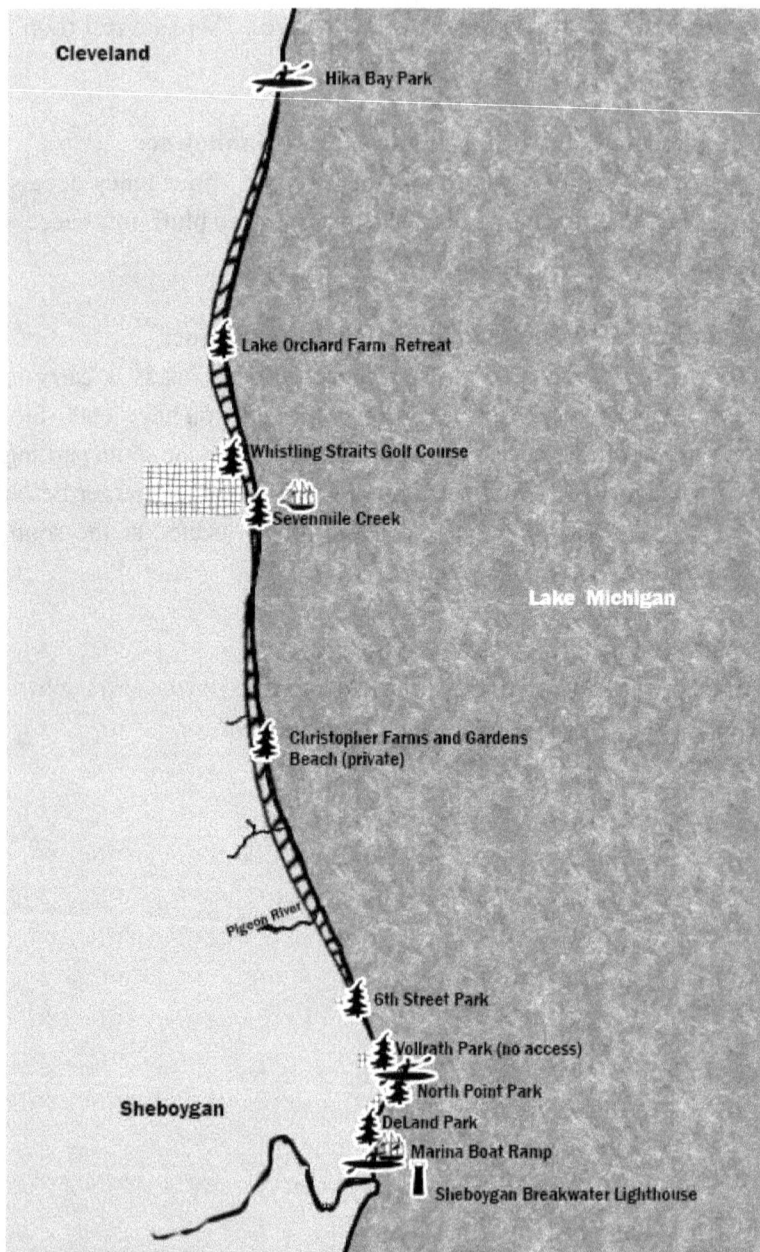

Cleveland

Hika Bay Park

Lake Orchard Farm Retreat

Whistling Straits Golf Course

Sevenmile Creek

Lake Michigan

Christopher Farms and Gardens
Beach (private)

Pigeon River

6th Street Park

Vollrath Park (no access)

North Point Park

Sheboygan

DeLand Park

Marina Boat Ramp

Sheboygan Breakwater Lighthouse

Leg 9

Whistle While You Paddle

Cleveland to Sheboygan

With prominent Bluffs and Whistling Straits Golf Course

11 miles

Heron Heaven.   We've been transported into heron heaven. Honestly, we lost count, over two dozen sighted, but since they played tag with us, there might have been a few of the same.   Add a couple eagles and this paddle was an aviary rapture. The birds were hiding against the greenery at the bottom of the massive sand bluffs. Topping the cliffs are lime grass frosting dripping down the sides of the headlands.   Homes, meadows, and forests sprout from the summit.   About half way, the bluffs become sculpted toward shore and the smooth bright green fairways of Whistling Straits Golf Course become discernible.   Whistle while you watch the golfers wind through the course.

Sorry, no way to shorten this paddle . Remember that famous golf course in the middle? I'm pretty sure, we would be run out trying to cart our boat to the shoreline. Maybe we could hire a caddie to carry our kayaks? But, don't panic, in the middle of Whistling Strait is Sevenmile Creek, and if we stay under the highwater mark, we are allowed to rest and have a nice lunch break.

We drop the chase car, Rick's scooter, off at Hika Bay Park with its nice boat ramp.   Then we drive south to launch our boats on the north side of North Point, just north of Deland Park beach in Sheboygan. A nice little drive way leads gently to the sand and smooth rock ledge shore. A man and his very wet and friendly dog are playing catch with an also very wet soft orange buoy dog toy. Ruff wants us to join in the game, but isn't so quick to give up his prized toy. North Point offers an open shelter and, for safety, has an emergency life ring and phone. There is a walking path all along going south towards the sand beach of Deland Park in the bay before the harbor and lighthouse.

We choose to paddle north today with a light, gentle breeze coming from the south. The sun sparkles causing the lake to effervesce like a mermaid's green fin. The water is so clean and clear, perhaps she is lurking just under the surface. To help this Disneyish movie theme, are the cotton ball fluffs of clouds lounging in the sunny blue sky. A float plane with his large tubular pontoons instead of landing wheels ascends above us.

'Search for more mermaids as we paddle north past the water utility building on the shore. Check out the old pier forms jutting out off shore. Just after the building, three more archaic concrete dock forms protrude out into the lake from the now appealing fern green shore line. This is Vollrath Park. This pretty park, with its large rock boulders lining the shore, is home to Wisconsin's oldest disc golf course. And like its big cousin, Whistling Straits Golf Course, this too is a killer difficult course with many shots over the ravine and one along Lake Michigan.

As we settle into a relaxed paddle mode, just a half mile north is the 6th Street Park with a little path kindly descending the hill to the rocky shore. This could be an alternative launch site, albeit with a long carry of the boats. The park itself is a small neighborhood park just a block in length with no shelter or restrooms, but has the wonderful distinction of access to Lake Michigan.

A mile of a mix of clover and avocado green cliffs, topped with distinguished homes with a few ladder stairs steeped down to the beach. At times, the homes are replaced with stately pines reaching up to the light blue sky with a few wisps and the occasional mark of Zorro clouds. A helicopter whirls above heading south. After a timeworn stone wall, the bluffs dip and the Pigeon River meets the lake. Although not labeled public, the Pigeon River valley has a thousand feet of undisturbed coast. Nope, no statues, but lots of driftwood trees for the pigeons to land on. Although technically, we only see herons, not one single pigeon. One and a half mile up river, the Pigeon River opens up into the Quarry Park lake where a beach Adventure Park is located. Kiddo's (and those that can't seem to grow up, but we won't name names. . .) can have fun on the inflatable obstacle course with bouncers, slides and lily pads. The Pigeon River is considered navigable in high water times.

We, remain stoic adults, as we paddle on north. Cresting the tops of the bluffs are meadows and woodsy greens. At our four-mile mark, a small point lags out into the lake. On top of the cliff is the Christopher Farms and Gardens. If you request permission, you may stop below the bluff for a rest break. If you are successful at climbing the mound, you may schedule a tour of their gardens. The petals and paths of their gardens include an Asian water garden, astilbe flowers, lilies, hostas, and a brook and evergreen experience.

The huge lake carved hillsides continue with green drapery flowing over the edges. Corn stalks top the bluffs with quiet trees swaying in the breeze. Intermittently, a heron or two, take flight out of the trees, circle near us and then fly away to a more inland perch.

When the bluffs are sculpted and step down toward the lake, we spy tailored green fairways and putting greens with little white flags. We have reached the famous Whistling Straits Golf Course with 18 holes of views of Lake Michigan mixed with two thousand massive sand traps. One of the top greatest American golf courses, Whistling Straits has hosted the PGA and Senior Open Championships with its dynamically rugged and windswept fairways. As we paddle past, we watch and scrutinize the golfer's techniques—as if we could do better. We giggle as a golfer hits his ball on top of a rock lining the shore near the lapping of the gentle lake waves. . .I guess this is called a water hazard. Originally, this land was a farm, and free roaming sheep now call Whistling Straits their home—moving hazards? In the 1950's this area belonged to the US Army as an antiaircraft training facility. When the new owner, Mr. Kohler (of bath fixture fame), was strolling the bluffs, the name of the course occurred to him. He could hear the wind whistle over the cliff as a

north-to-south gale badgered the shore and white caps were breaking along the rocky beach of the straits of Lake Michigan.

The little green point in the middle of the course is our goal. The first 9 holes of the course are on the southern mile long shore before Seven Mile Creek. Whistling Straits allows us to land by the creek, hidden by the woods lining the stream (as long as we stay below the highwater mark). We wave away a heron standing guard to the creek. This is pretty close to a half way mark starting from North Point in Sheboygan. Seven Mile Creek zig zags through Whistling Straits golf course, then meanders through the grasses and dunes of The Irish, the second golf course at the American Club of Kohler.

Time for a light lunch as we relax on the sandy shore. Meet a new friend, Mr. One Claw Crayfish. Wish he could tell the story of how he survived losing this claw, perhaps in a deadly fight with another crayfish, or even an eagle or heron? Today, we will swim. Mid July, the lake is refreshingly chilly. But we quickly adapt and enjoy the clean clear cyan blue water with the sandy bottom rippling under our toes. Swimming toward the horizon, the lake color deepens to aquamarine where it meets the dark navy-blue sky at the horizon and then the sky lightens up to a bright baby blue sky.

Reinvigorated and satiated, we climb back into our boats, stretch quick, and paddle off shore. Head straight out from the creek, less than a half mile out lays the remains of the three masted Montgomery shipwreck in 12 feet of water. She survived several collisions with other ships, was stranded once, and even sunk once, but always saved. But, not this time, in 1890, during a storm, she was washed ashore onto rocks. There were attempts to rescue her, but to no avail, and she was abandoned.

There is another mile of the Whistling Straits golf course to relish. The hole names are fun explanations of the course: On the Rocks, Sand Box, Cliff Hanger, Shipwreck, and Grand Strand. One is even called O'Man, the way many of the golfer's probably feel as they tee off!

As we wave goodbye to the golf course, the bluffs rise again, with deep green trees cascading down the cliff to the water's edge. This is heron heaven. As we get close and catch a glimpse of them, they fly north and land where they can see us on a log or branch. They watch as we approach, and then swoop up and out of the bushes to fly forward again. On and on, several herons frolic with us. The herons stand statue like on long thin legs and a narrow neck, poised up to five feet tall, with a long dagger like bill searching for prey. The heron's blue grey plumage blends in well with the hillside, making it a game of I Spy as we search the shoreline. Just as we notice one, off it flies, curling its neck into an S shape with its long legs trailing behind. The wing span spreads out to five or six feet as he slowly flaps his wings with deep wing beats.

The heron sport of tag continues as we approach the Old Orchard Farm Retreat. An old six generation farm with rolling fields atop the bluff. The farm house and cottage is a bed and breakfast, and the long standing elegantly refurbished event barn is a local wedding favorite. Although it is a historical farm, they have developed a state-of-the-art aqua phonic farm for fish and vegetables. Below the bluff, is a small sand and cobblestone beach that can be a rest break.

As we follow Lakeshore Road high above the bluffs, Rick spots an old white fallen shed that intrigues him. Could it be an ice shanty? Nope, it is a long-forgotten outhouse, tipped on its side. Gives new meaning, to a term potty break. . .think we'll pass.

The last couple of miles continue with the massive cliffs, tree lined, with some trees that have slid down the cliff or tipped over into the lake. This is an area the herons love, as we still are relishing our heron encounters. Then an eagle decides to join the game. He stands sentry above on a tall tree, eagle eyeing us, then soaring along the shoreline to be a lookout again. Eagles are big, up to three feet tall, with females larger than males—way to be dominant! With a yellow hooked beak, and their head and tail a snowy white, helps to identify them on the shore. Eagles prefer tall trees with, near large bodies of water, pretty sure Lake Michigan suffices. They love to eat fish, can fly thirty miles per hour, and then swoop down and snatch their prey in their talons. Glad they have such good eyesight, so they know a kayak from a tasty fish.

The breeze has increased in intensity and now we have rolling swells of one to two feet of height, but far enough apart to not be breaking and white capping, except at shore. We have chosen the correct direction to paddle, as the swells help push us north. Sometimes, we can surf the tops of the swell and be propelled up to ten feet forward. Helping us reach our destination!

Soon, we spot the bright yellow sign at the end of the dock of Hika Park boat ramp. Rick speeds ahead, lands, jumps out of his kayak, and then motions us to come in one at a time. He catches us and steadies our kayaks against the breaking waves.

Chris is enticed to join Rick on the scooter for the pleasure of a motorcycle ride back to pick up the car. Denise and I empty out the boats, hang the skirts and PFD's to dry and then lounge on the shoreline appreciating the lake view. We are blessed with another great beautiful day of paddling, and start gearing up for frying some great perch with our Great Lake view!

Logistics:

Hika Bay Park, Cleveland Wisconsin:
43.9156, -87.7237. 1116 Lakeshore Drive.
Launch fee, but A+ restrooms!

Sevenmile Creek at Whistling Straits Golf Course:
43.8512, -87.7285. No launch access, but a nice break along the shoreline. Whistling Straits allows us to land only by the creek, hidden by the trees as long as we stay under the high-water mark.

Pigeon River, undeveloped area:
43.7905, -87.7153. Not public, but does offer 1000 feet of undeveloped shoreline. Please stay under the high-water mark on shore. The Pigeon River is two miles from North Point, Sheboygan.

6th Street Park, Sheboygan:
43.7762, -87.7069. 2828 N. 6th Street. 700-foot carry down a hill to the rocky shoreline, a little shorter carry if you park on Evergreen Parkway. No restrooms. No fee.

Vollrath Park, Sheboygan:
43.7682, -87.7015. Vollrath Blvd. 200-foot carry, but down a steep hill and across the path of the disc golf course to a boulder lined shoreline. I'd use North Point instead. No fee, restrooms available.

North Point, Sheboygan:
43.7650, -87.6969. Broughton Drive, Sheboygan. Parking lot 600 feet south. No restrooms. No fees. Does have an emergency phone.

Other possible rest stops on the shoreline, call for permission:

Christopher Farms and Gardens, Sheboygan:
43.8152, -87.7265. W580 Garton Road. 920-565-2291.
No launch site, but a possible rest break on the shoreline.

Lake Orchard Farm Retreat, Sheboygan:
43.8753, -87.7359. W839 Lake Orchard Court. 920-693-8336.
No launch site, but a possible rest break on the shoreline.

Shipwreck location:

Montgomery: 43.8520, -87.7196. By Sevenmile Creek at Whistling Straits golf course .44 miles off shore in 12 feet of water.

Kayak Wisconsin, Lake Michigan Water Trail

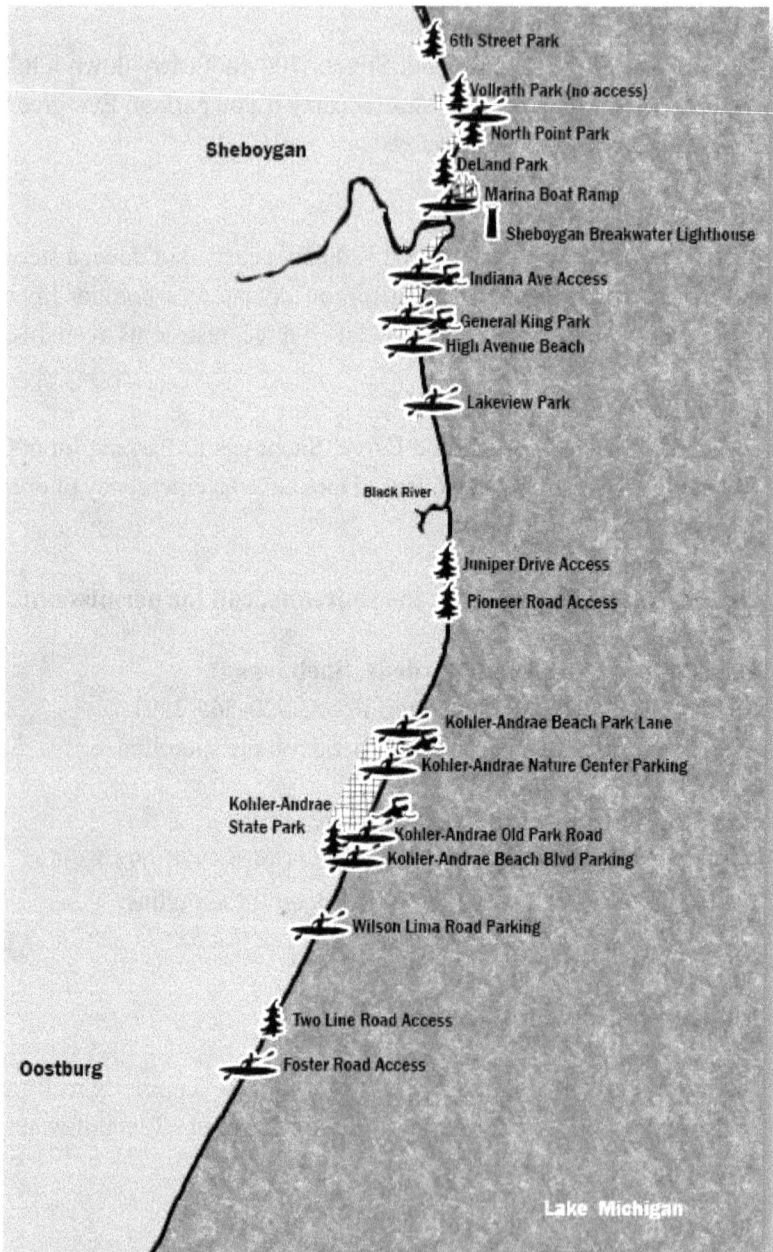

6th Street Park

Vollrath Park (no access)

North Point Park

Sheboygan

DeLand Park

Marina Boat Ramp

Sheboygan Breakwater Lighthouse

Indiana Ave Access

General King Park

High Avenue Beach

Lakeview Park

Black River

Juniper Drive Access

Pioneer Road Access

Kohler-Andrae Beach Park Lane

Kohler-Andrae Nature Center Parking

Kohler-Andrae State Park

Kohler-Andrae Old Park Road

Kohler-Andrae Beach Blvd Parking

Wilson Lima Road Parking

Two Line Road Access

Oostburg

Foster Road Access

Lake Michigan

Leg 10

A Swell Time

Sheboygan to Oostburg

With Kohler-Andrae State Park

11 miles

Windy has wings to fly. . .Who's reachin' out to capture a moment, everyone knows it's Windy (Ruthann Friedman, recorded by the Association). Yup, windy Sheboygan, "the Malibu of the Midwest", is a favorite spot for surfers, and kayakers seeking to ride the waves. We decide to capture the moment, and paddle from the city of Sheboygan south, enjoying the pure sandy beaches and the beautiful Kohler-Andrae State Park, with its superb sand dunes and forever beaches. Ready for our swell time!

Our planned take out spot is Foster Road access, although there are several other possible take outs. The midway point on our paddle is Pioneer Road access in Black River. Or to shorten the paddle, choose to launch at some of the nice Sheboygan park accesses south of the harbor, or plan to exit at one of four take out sites at Kohler-Andrae State Park. Launching at High Avenue beach in Sheboygan and paddling south to Kohler-Andrae State Park would be a 5-mile paddle.

We face the waves at North Point in Sheboygan, paddle past the lighthouse and harbor, follow the nice city parks and beaches in Sheboygan. As the city sputters out, the beaches begin. Black River flows out to the lake and shortly after the combined state parks of Kohler and Andrae begin with over one mile and a half of beaches, not counting the extra miles of undisturbed nature areas.

As I steel myself to face the daunting breakers at North Point, Denise, our never have done a white cap—ever, is excited for the challenge. The wind is about 10 miles per hour and there are one to two-foot curls hitting the shore. Rick steadies our kayaks, as we skirt up. With a big push to help us on our way, we paddle hard confronting the breakers straight on. Up and over the waves as they splash directly into our faces! We wait and group up in the swells off shore, and dry off our sunglasses. Rick has predicted correctly, breakers on shore, but just large swells with five seconds between, once we are on this big pond of Lake Michigan. The swells are kind of fun, and we are all able to manage and enjoy them.

Stunning blue sky with thin white clouds are striping over the horizon. The translucent turquoise waves sparkle on their pinnacles with strings of little white beads of water. We steer clear of North Point, which has a rocky tip that surges out into the lake. After which there is a dip into a bay before the north pier head harbor wall. The Lakefront trail tours all the way from North Point into the bay, passing by four timeworn north side jetties to Deland Park Beach. This is an exceptional beach with perfect sand box sand four hundred feet deep. Grass picnic area and park benches line the trail out to the north pier and Sheboygan's lighthouse.

Deland Park is the final resting place of the Lottie Cooper shipwreck. This one you can't miss—literally. She is on shore and you can actually walk right through her and discern her sad tale. It was an early spring gale in April of 1894, with a northwest wind that

doomed the Lottie Cooper. She dropped anchor by the river harbor, signal flagged for rescue, but unfortunately capsized before the rescue team could help. The life boats were able to save five of the six crewmen. The sixth sailor, used the cargo wood to makeshift a life raft, but drowned trying to ride the surf to the coastline. The schooner with three masts was washed ashore on the beach. The lake reclaimed her, but she was rediscovered when the new marina was being constructed. She was raised and is now on display on shore in Deland Park, the only opportunity to walk through a real shipwreck without getting wet in all of the Great Lakes.

As surf boarders paddle out at Deland Park, we bee line it toward the red lighthouse on the north pier. Sheboygan's first light house was erected at North Point in 1839, then the harbor walls were built and a lighthouse was placed on the north pier. Unfortunately, that one burned down, a constant concern when using oil for the lantern lights. The classic vivid red pier head lighthouse of today was built in the early 1900's of cast iron. She originally had an octagonal lantern room, that has since been removed. The lighthouse now uses a modern plastic lens giving her the look of a stolen roof. She shines nine miles out to sea and has an electronic fog signal. The lighthouse has been successful at preventing further catastrophes as the Sheboygan area has had sixty-two known shipwrecks.

The Sheboygan River is larger than Chicago's River and has the protection of solid land mass on her shores, making it one of the busiest ports on Lake Michigan. With the Riverfront boardwalks on both sides of the river, lined with quaint restaurants and fishing boats, the harbor and marina are very popular destinations. Crossing the 500 feet of harbor entrance is exciting, and wide swells bounce us around and limit our view. We cross together, keeping alert and staying clear of the cement pier heads.

Sheboygan, is named for a Chippewa word meaning "great noise" such as the mouth of the river. We agree, that Lake Michigan is making a great noise as we cross the needle of the harbor with the waves crashing on the piers. Besides the Chippewa, the Menomonie, and Ho-Chunk/Winnebago's lived in this area. Jean Nicolet, Jolliet, and Marquette were the first European to explore Sheboygan. Mr. Farnsworth established a fur trading post in 1818. In 1845, Sheboygan began its great shipbuilding legacy when the Pilot schooner was built. At its heyday, seven shipbuilding companies were located in Sheboygan. Today, Sheboygan continues the spirit of the lake, with an abundance of charter fishing boats and several commercial fishing companies.

For over half a century, Sheboygan has been the surfing capital— the Malibu of the Midwest, due the whopping waves and surf that is generated when north or southeast winds blow. We ride the swells past the south pier and with the wind blowin' from the northeast, we get a tiny relief from the surf as we paddle past the gorgeous Blue Harbor Resort. With her brilliant red roof and rows of white balconies, the resort is reminiscent of bygone eras and grand resorts. Folks are splashing in the breakers, playing beach volleyball, and lounging on beach chairs on the shore.

Indiana Avenue ends south of the Blue Harbor Resort at the terminal point of the south side river boardwalk, and is a lake access with a little carry over the dune and swale. Following shortly after, is General King Park. This park has a beautiful long sand beach with grass areas for picnics. It has a nice pavilion and outdoor shower to rinse off the sand. The roof has a squawking gull weather vane to keep sea gulls away. Such a nice park, we return here for our evening cookout and enjoy the dimming sky. The perfect Sheboygan barbecue: Johnsonville brats on Sheboygan hard rolls! I do it correctly with two brats, a double, on my roll. Classic topping Sheboygan style: brown mustard, ketchup, and raw onions. 'Not from Wisconsin? The word brat rhymes with pot, but don't you dare make a brat in a pot. . .it just is not done. A brat is a German heritage sausage, a bratwurst, which is chopped pork in natural casing. Now in Wisconsin, we often parboil our brats, in beer, of course, and then grill them. . .got that—always grilled, even if we call it a brat fry!

After supper, we learn the Swedish game Kubb, from some fellow park goers. It is kind of a cross between horseshoes or bowling on sand. Music from fellow picnickers, traces of Liberace? Rumor has it that the Wisconsin celebrity used to play at a local hotel just across the street from here. Children are still out dancing on the beach, chasing sea gulls, and swimming as we say good night.

The King Park beach continues with us as we kayak past, now nearing one mile, to High Avenue Beach with a nice parking area right next to a great access to the lake. Well used, as three vehicles in the parking area have kayak racks on them!

From here, the bluffs began to grow, all shades of emeralds, with houses peek-a-booing on the top. As we follow Lakeshore Drive, there are rows of dilapidated cement docks, more than a baker's dozen. All the way to Sheboygan's next collection of lake parks—Lakeview Park. Perched above the timeworn jetties, is the dog friendly park with an open pavilion and outside eating spaces. Parking is available and a feasible carry down the hill to launch kayaks. The beaches between the berths are the same fine white sand and the hill is wildflower covered with blue fringe flowers and dainty Queen Ann's Lace. While we roll through the swells, a standup paddle boarder, a SUP'er, impresses us by paddling through the rough surf and balances successfully!

Next door to the Lakeview Park, is Sheboygan's Waste Resource Recovery Facility. Here they restore ten million gallons a day and return the clean water back to Lake Michigan. The solids are treated to make a biogas that is converted to electricity and heat. The heat is used to dry the biosolids for fertilizer, making the plant almost 100% self-sufficient.

They share the lakeshore with the gigantic Sheboygan Power Plant with its two tall smokestacks. Alliant Energy Edgewater Plant is a coal to electricity power plant. Way up on top of the smokestack is a peregrine falcon project nesting box. Since 1992 over seventy-eight young peregrine falcons have been hatched here. . .and we don't notice a one. There are two large permanent towers off shore.

As we try to decide whether to explore close to shore or the tower buoys in the water, we meet up with two kayakers heading towards Sheboygan and enjoying Sheboygan's celebrated large surf.

Following the tree high piles of black coal, is the Black River. The Black River starts in Oostburg, flows northwest through Kohler-Andrae State Park then to Sheboygan. There is no public access to the mouth of the river, but just inland is the Jerving Conservancy, an estuary of Lake Michigan and migratory birding site. The Black River has spawning runs of smelt, trout, and salmon. Just a little more than a half mile south is Juniper Drive turn-a-bout access. Unfortunately, there is no parking, but a nice public walk in area. It's possible to land here and stroll up the narrow country road to one of Sheboygan's best restaurants, the Black River Grill. Nestled in the evergreens, their fresh lake perch is well-known, and one of the few restaurants located near the shoreline.

We dance through our waves past Pioneer Road, another dead-end road with walk in access to the lake. We sway and see-saw our way over the swells. The rolling waves have increased to three feet high, obvious as we keep losing sight of each other when we are in a low of a swell. Chris closes her eyes to feel the sway, but quickly decides this is not an advantageous idea prior to lunch.

The little Black River Point is ahead of us, then followed by a mile of undeveloped shoreline. Dunes dotted with evergreens with a nice sandy shore. This is the magic of this paddle. Soon the start of Kohler-Andrae State Park beacons and our lunch break arrives. Rick scans the shore, chooses a sandy beach with breakers to the north and white caps to the south. He beckons us to the quiet water between the surfs. Fantastic job landing safe, he calls Chris in who

duplicates his maneuvers. Now, it is Denise's turn. The newbie faces her biggest Lake Michigan challenge and wins the award landing smoothly on the beach. And here I sit, eyeing the shore, the breakers now encase the entire shoreline. I should wait to see if the white caps calm, but no, I have floated too close to shore to change plans. I've hesitated too long and now must face the curling surf. I've done this many times before. . .right? As Chris explains to Denise on shore, "watch how Babs will brace into the breaking surf—umm. . .maybe not". I flip over and roll with the seas, looking like a yellow submarine. Underwater, I have a second to see if my kayak skirt will magically come off and I will be out of my kayak. Nope, I need to grab the orange handle in front of my skirt and self-rescue myself. I grab my paddle as Rick runs to me to save the kayak. I wash—walk ashore embarrassed, my dignity skewed along with my hat and sunglasses.

Rick reviews my mistake to help me learn, but I don't actually remember my kayak stern being swirled and me being sideways to the surf, I just recall being upside down under the water. As I dry out under the nice warm sun, I continue to dredge up my humiliation. Chris encourages me to "let it go", and when I am a little slow with that, she finds the song "Let It Go" from the Disney musical Frozen, and makes me sing, the group joining in. "The wind is howling like this swirling storm inside. . .let it go, let it GO!!"

Kohler-Andrae State Park's incredible beach, lake shore helps me let it go. We relax and enjoy a wonderful hot meal by camp Chef Rick, as the surf howls before us. The park is actually two state parks now managed as one. John Kohler, the founder of the Kohler bath company, and Terry Andrae, a past president of a Milwaukee Electric Company, both donated lands to create this exceptional dune wildlife park. Over 1.5-miles of pristine sandy beach and dune cord-walk and creeping juniper trails is backed by the Black River and marsh trails. If you kayak in and wish to camp, the rangers assure us they will find a place for you. There are lots of parking areas and small craft launch sites available at the park. All just need a short carry over the soft sand of the dunes to the beach.

Over fifty ships have floundered and sank. . .just like me, near the Kohler-Andrae shoreline. Most of the shipwrecks have broken up and not been located. A piece of the keel of the Challenge, a schooner, washed ashore here. She was built in Manitowoc, a Great Lake clipper schooner with square sails. The Challenge was attempting to reach the Sheboygan harbor when she sank. Her washed up keel is on display at the Kohler-Andrae Nature Center.

Speaking of sinking, it is time to sneak off the shore, without the crashing waves noticing. Just to add some pressure, Chris and Denise both traverse the waves and rock and roll off shore in the swells, ready to watch my performance. Unknown to me, Chris films my launch off shore, not sure if she is hoping to capture a repeat performance, or if she has faith in my true abilities and wishes to capture my success on camera. Either way, off I go, thumping through the never-ending breakers that hit me squarely in the face, again and again, and then large mountain swells, some must be four feet in height! Finally, success! I've redeemed myself; I do know how to tackle the breakers—and I've got great video to prove it!

Rick swamps several times attempting to skirt up before the next crashing waves. He empties his boat and tries again. We wait off shore, hoping he can do this independently. Of course, he can—why worry? He smashes through the wave curls safely and joins us bobbing in the big lake. Together, where-ever we go, off once more on this swell adventure.

For more than three-quarters of a mile, we shadow the unspoiled sandy shoreline. Dunes speckled with evergreens and blowing shrubbery. The Wilson Lima Road ends at the lakeshore on the sand dune, another gorgeous and easy access to the lake. We paddle past a small stream before the next access at Town Line Road. A dead end with no parking, but with a clearing in the trees to the lake shore.

Just a half mile more to our planned take out spot at Foster Road. The road opening is hard to spot from the water, Rick needs his GPS to help. A little sandy beach surrounded by large rocks. Did I notice those boulders when we dropped off the scooter this morning? Hmm, those could hurt. . .also not much calming of the seas. Waves are still breaking on shore, perhaps we can just keep paddling until the lake composes herself? No, Rick has landed and is calling me in. I head in, not hesitating this time. A neighbor is out with his boogie board ready to rescue if needed—that builds confidence, right? No problem, I know what I am doing, I am an experienced paddler. I handle the white caps, no problems! Sure, I never had a question or concern. I jump out, drag my boat up and help lead Denise in. She stops paddling as she sees the rocks looming, "keep paddling", "don't let the waves turn your boat", "I'll catch you!" Denise lands safely and Rick steadies her kayak in the surf as I give her a hand to stretch out of the cockpit and a high-five hand slap for her facing the challenge. She loves it!

All safely ashore, and a thank you to our would-be rescuer who acknowledges that we are obviously experienced kayakers, yup, yup, we are! Now, it is play time, these waves are perfect for body surfing and diving into the breakers. Paddle lift!

Logistics:

North Point, Sheboygan:
43.7650, -87.6969. Broughton Drive, Sheboygan. Parking lot 600 feet south. No restrooms. No fees.

Deland Park, Sheboygan:
43.7556, -87.7028. 801 Broughton Drive. Go north in park lot to be close to the beach. Restrooms and outdoor shower for sand removal.

Sheboygan Marina public boat ramps:
43.7515, -87.030. Corner of Broughton Drive and New York Avenue. Fee to launch, restrooms and fish cleaning station available.

Indiana Avenue public access, Sheboygan:
43.7427, -87.7074. 600 Indiana Avenue. Parking spaces at the end of street. No fee, but no restrooms either. Need to carry the boats 350 feet through the swale to water's edge.

General King Park, Sheboygan:
43.7367, -87.7095. 1540 S. 7th Avenue. Street parking only. Restrooms and an outdoor shower at Park pavilion. No fee to launch, but about 400-foot carry to water's edge.

High Avenue beach parking, Sheboygan:
43.7346, -87.7097. 700 High Avenue. Parking at the bottom of the hill. Short carry to water's edge, no fee, but no restrooms either.

Lakeview Park, Sheboygan:
43.7209, -87.7074. 3200 Lakeshore Drive. Parking on side of street. 200-foot carry of boats. No fee, restrooms in the park.

Juniper Drive public access, Sheboygan:
43.6962, -87.7039. 216 Juniper Drive. No parking, walk in access.

Pioneer Road public access, Sheboygan:
43.6921, -87.7033. 299 Pioneer Road.
No restrooms or fee, and no parking signs galore, walk in access.

Kohler-Andrae State Park and kayak launch sites:
1020 Beach Park Lane, Sheboygan. State park fee:

North Beach, Beach Park Lane 43.6724, -87.7119.
Parking area. No restrooms available at this access.

Sanderling Nature Center. 43.6671, -87.7156.
Restrooms available in the Nature Center.

Old Park Road beach parking. 43.6570, -87.7222.
Restrooms available in the pavilion. This is the location of their kayak campsite location by the parking lots.

Beach Boulevard parking area. 43.6549, -87.7236. Carry boats over the dune to water, no restrooms.

Beach Boulevard playground parking area. 43.6535, -87.7244.
Pit toilets available.

Wilson Lima Road public access, Oostburg:
43.6435, -87.7309. 1800 Wilson Lima Road. Beautiful sand dune access, parking on side of road, easy carry to water. No fee, no restroom.

Town Line Road public access, Oostburg:
43.6295, -87.7420. W971 Town Line Road. Very limited parking and brushy carry in on a small trail. No fee, no restroom.

Foster Road public access, Oostburg:
43.6222, -87.7475. 2315 Foster Road. Limited parking, small carry in trail to water's edge. No fee, no restrooms.

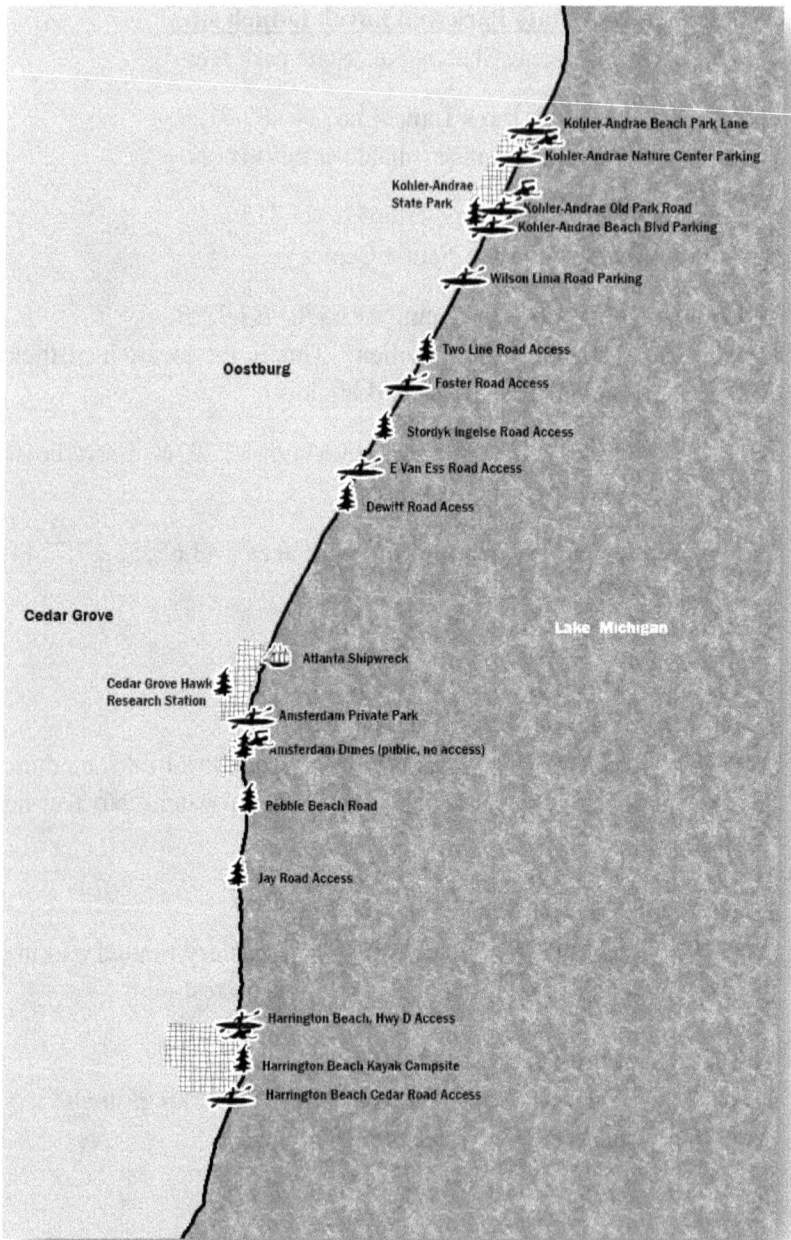

Kohler-Andrae Beach Park Lane

Kohler-Andrae Nature Center Parking

Kohler-Andrae
State Park

Kohler-Andrae Old Park Road

Kohler-Andrae Beach Blvd Parking

Wilson Lima Road Parking

Two Line Road Access

Foster Road Access

Oostburg

Stordyk Ingelse Road Access

E Van Ess Road Access

Dewitt Road Acess

Cedar Grove

Lake Michigan

Atlanta Shipwreck

Cedar Grove Hawk
Research Station

Amsterdam Private Park

Amsterdam Dunes (public, no access)

Pebble Beach Road

Jay Road Access

Harrington Beach, Hwy D Access

Harrington Beach Kayak Campsite

Harrington Beach Cedar Road Access

Leg 11

Beach Party!

Oostburg to Harrington Beach State Park

With Amsterdam Dunes beach

10 miles

Beach, baby, beach, out there in the sun! Having fun on the beach at the lake in Wisconsin is what this paddle is all about. A true "up north" typical cottage weekend experience. Non-stop fun on a long hot day, and we can join the beach party at Harrington Beach State Park and at Amsterdam Dunes beach. Grab your juke box song, and sing along for this paddle!

Amsterdam Park is the midpoint on this paddle. It is 5 miles if you paddle from Foster Road to Amsterdam Park or from Amsterdam Park to Harrington Beach State Park. Both provide ample beach opportunities. If you wish to paddle from Kohler-Andrae State Park beach to Amsterdam Park, it is a 7 ½ mile paddle. Kayaking from Kohler-Andrae State Park to Harrington Beach State Park is a minimum of an 11-mile paddle. Whichever paddle you choose, just make sure you bring your swimsuit and your beach blanket.

We launch our kayaks at the south end of Harrington Beach State Park at the Cedar Road access. Lunch at Amsterdam Dunes Preservation Area beach and then north to Foster Road. Our day, was a fairly calm day, a perfect Wisconsin beach day. A slight northly wind, making our paddle easier starting from the south.

Cedar Road access has limited parking, but parking at Harrington Beach State Park is very limited, especially on warm summer days. The parking lot at the Welcome Center, closest access to the lake, is so often full during the summer, that the rangers offer a wagon ride shuttle from the Puckett Pond parking lot, with no room for kayaks on the shuttle. The north end of Harrington Beach State Park, offers an ideal launch site with great parking at the Highway D access.

Immediately, we have our toes in the sand as we load up our kayaks at Cedar Road. A trickle of water sculpts the sand as it flows from the tree lined shore, searching for Mother Nature's mother-load of water—Lake Michigan. Sand granules smoosh between our toes, as the flip flops are already discarded into the kayak cockpits. Rick, our all-American male, tosses the sun screen to his sis. Chris ties her hair into a ponytail, flowing out the back hole of her cap—helps to keep the cap from flying off as she races across the water. Denise, joins us again today, dons her Tilley hat, ready for an easy paddle. We all are beach equipped. . .swimsuits and sunglasses on!

Harrington Beach State Park offers over a mile of beach front. From the south, the shoreline is sand beach backed with a carpet of forest. Yes, there are White Cedars at Cedar Road access, mixed with birch, oaks, and maples, creating a kaleidoscope of greens. A miniature brook exits the woods and stumbles into the lake, passing by white wildflowers dotting the shore.

An open picnic area appears to the north with the picnic shelter poking up over the soft dunes. This is the kayak campsite, marked by a small blue sign posted on the metal stairway. It has a grassy area with a stone fire ring and a picnic table and wooden benches for surveying the expanse of Lake Michigan.

The shoreline before the petite point is a beach area shared with pets. A black dog and his white bellied human are playing at the lakeshore as we paddle past. The trivial trifling point is actually an old pier that was used in the early 1900's for ships carrying limestone from the Harrington Beach old quarry. Watch for artifacts of the pier as you paddle over the forgotten wharf.

On shore, by the point is the anchor from the ill-fated Niagara wooden steamship with sidewheel paddles. On her last voyage in 1856, she carried about 300 passengers. As she passed this area, she caught fire (remember that wooden steamship part) with the passengers and crew jumping ship. Some of the lucky ones were rescued by nearby schooners, but over 60 folks lost their lives. She lies less than a mile off shore just south of the mini point in about 70 feet of water. Her portside paddle wheel is partially preserved and has portions of the water buckets still attached to the wheel.

The north beach in the park, past the point offers the most sand beach lounging area. Already, beach goers are staking out their corner of the sugar sand, laying down polychromatic colored beach blankets. They drag their coolers across the deep sand along with lounge chairs, some set up at water's edge to allow tootsies to be cooled in the lake. A few tent canopies to provide a bit of shade. Some beautiful beach bikini bodes mixed in with Mom's and Dad's and grandparents with the kiddos on the beach. Colorful plastic sand toys are clutched in children's hands as they stagger across the soft sand to the shoreline. They plop down into the sand with shovels and forks to transform the beach into small towns of sand castles. The Mom and Dad's join in on hands and knees, to help create trench rivers, or be allowed to be buried in sand by their laughing young ones.

We meet up with a Sheboygan kayaker, who has Fido in the basket on the front of the kayak. The puff of fur turns and smiles at us and licks his lips as he directs his buddy toward the beach. It's all about teamwork, one can't paddle without the other! The Sheboygan paddler has his shirt off working on his tan, with a baseball cap to shade his blonde hair, which closely matches the bright yellow of his boat. He's heading south as we go north, so with a wave and smile we pass each other by.

After at least a third of a mile of expansive beach, the shoreline develops a few small rocky bluffs, just a few feet high, while the lake bed continues to be sandy ripples below our boats. Harrington Beach State Park has a full mile of beachy lake shore, but that is only one of its attractions. The park itself is a 700 acre preserve with restored wetlands and ponds and a limestone quarry lake. The old quarry lake is a deep placid loch lined by limestone ledges and bordered by white cedars. The lake is encircled by a quiet trail which has a diminutive arched bridge over a small stream. You can fish off the bluffs of Quarry Lake or at Puckett's Pond for trout, crappies, bluegills and other panfish. Didn't bring your fishing pole? No problem, you can borrow fishing gear free at the park office. The Lakeshore hiking trail follows the north and south beach fronts. Besides camping, there is an accessible cabin, and several picnic shelters. This is one of the few state parks that offers an Astronomy Observatory with a twenty-inch telescope which is open to the public for monthly viewings!

As we approach the north end of the park, we realize that we've only seen a glimpse of what Harrington Beach State park offers. County Road D, at the north boundary of the park, is an ideal launch spot, wide open access with parking for cars and trailers.

Past the park, we enter a true Wisconsin up north cottage experience. Take a deep breath and enjoy the "up north" smell, the aroma of cedars and evergreens, which always takes me back to my childhood at Grandma and Grandpa's cottage. True to my memory, there are birdhouses perched on shore, flagpoles with marine flags, and windsocks. We paddle past a modest log cabin, probably with cedar paneling inside matching Grandma and Grandpa's home, with white Adirondack slat chairs tucked under a tree.

Next is a flat roofed golden oak home with a full panel of lake view windows with a front portico covered by a wooden slat trellis to provide a bit of shade. Matching oak benches under the porch. A kayak is nestled under a tree, as Mom and Dad lead the charge of children to splash into the lake as squeals of glee erupt.

Light wicker chairs sit under two bright sunshine yellow canopies at the water's edge with a tri hull trimaran sailboat, just waiting for her captain. Then there is a quiet section of tree lined beach which is the Felician Sisters Sacred Heart of the Lake Chalet, a private retreat. A small limestone rock path with layered stone steps is huddled in the trees.

And then, more folks come out to play. Bright yellow, blue and red Adirondack chairs loop around a bonfire pit. A picnic table next door with a party going on. A Bahama mama with her daughters lounging on teal blue and yellow floaties, while Dad gears up the ski-doo to make some waves.

We paddle past the Jay Road access, a tiny path to the beach with dainty blue wildflowers and white dotted Queen Ann Lace that joins Sauk Beach Road as it follows our path north. The everlasting sandy beach continues. A young 'un in a canary yellow child kayak paddling away—making very little headway, as Mom supervises from the top of a stand-up paddle board with her son in front, teaching big brother the tricks of the trade.

It is questionable how Pebble Beach Road and its lake access got its name, as there is only powder sand beach to be seen. . .maybe the road was a pebble road at one time? It is another sandy path tracing through the yellow and white wildflowers and through tall rushes to the shoreline.

North of Clear Vue Shores is our midway point, Amsterdam Dunes Preservation Area. Amsterdam Dunes is a series of ridges and swale formations with wet meadows and hardwood forests, below the bluff line. Barr Creek and several other intermittent streams divide the shoreline. Amsterdam Dunes is an important migrating rest stop for songbirds, hawks, owls, and other birds of prey. There is 1900 feet of our own private beach shoreline—or so it seems. If we don't tell anyone about this new park. . .opps, I already gave it away, didn't I.

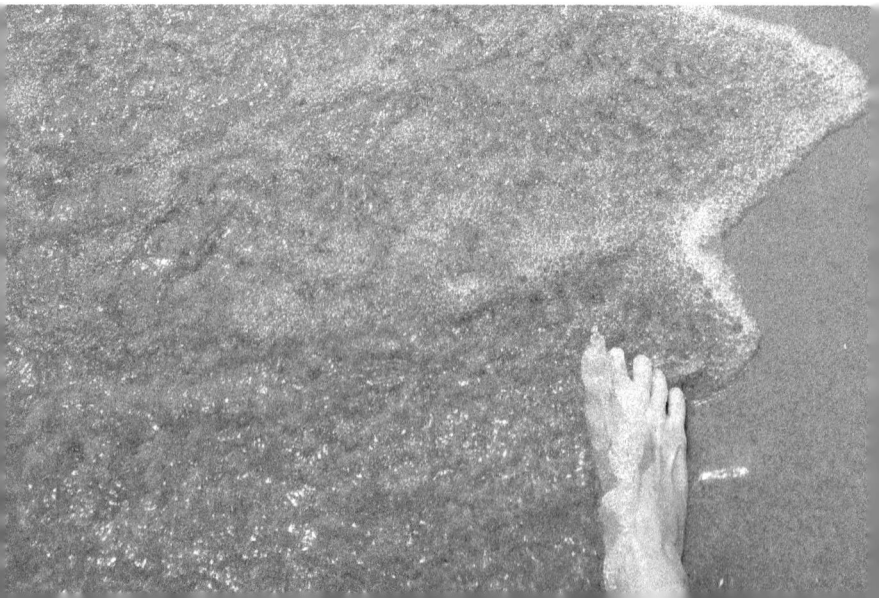

We pull up on the sand beach next to Barr Creek, with its little wooden bridge and a sun-dried beach log. Perfect for our picnic lunch and for strolling the beach. The women ditch Rick to cook us lunch as we explore the beach and play on the sand. But later, Rick and Chris sneak off hand in hand for a romantic ramble.

Rick is our camp chef, and we eat well. My fav is his white chicken bruschetta pizza individually personalized with garlic, spinach, and tomatoes. Yummy! After lunch and much needed clear water hydration, we run, splash, and dive into the lake. . .our turn to enjoy this perfect Wisconsin beach party!

Slowly, we repack the kayaks and do a beach check for litter. We would truly hate to spoil this paradise by leaving anything behind. Reapply sunscreen and adjust our hats, back to our paddle day.

Just after a few beach homes is Amsterdam Park. A beautiful shoreline park, with a playground for children, picnic tables and benches, and grills, all in a grove of shade trees. The boat launch is a metal grate, along with the dock. . .ouchy, ouchy, ouchy if you aren't wearing your flip flops—although the teens seem to be doing just fine as they jump off the end of the dock! A group has set up a large Wisconsin Badger red canopy on the shore with its large W. A rainbow collection of coolers and lounge chairs on the beach. A threesome of jet ski's weaving lazily on the water.

Behind Amsterdam Park is the Cedar Grove Hawk Ornithological Research Station and State Natural Area. This station has the distinction of having the longest sustained record of measuring, banding and releasing raptors and the perching passerines. The station has exceeded banding over 38,000 birds of prey for research!

I have no difficulty looking up for eagles, falcons, and hawks, although I do not think I can tell apart Harris, Cooper, or sharp-shinned hawks. The Cedar Grove ornithological station has even banded the gry falcon—the largest of the predator falcons.

A mile north of Amsterdam Park lies the Atlanta shipwreck. She was a passenger and freight steamer with boilers and propeller. On her fatal day, she was carrying 65 passengers and cargo from Sheboygan to Milwaukee, when a fire broke out in her hold. The crew could not stop the blaze and all 65 passengers were transferred to the life boats, but a crewman tried to jump to the lifeboat off the Atlanta, missed and fell to his death. She lays 17 feet deep, which would make seeing her difficult, and is 765 feet off shore.

It seems that all Wisconsinites are out enjoying this gorgeous sunshine day. Mom in blue jean mini shorts with black puppies playing on the beach and trying out the water. Her faded green lounge chair with a bright towel draped over it rests on shore. We

race a rainbow striped sailboat of yellow to orange to red stripes. Want to guess which of us won?

Next to traditional cottages that blend into their surroundings is a modern flat roof home with a khaki green tower, flanked by red deck chairs. There are two tents, a blue and green one, next to a cottage with a red umbrella and matching red chairs. Nearby is a tiki hut in front of a classic chalet by the beach with white chairs. There's a party going on, dance. . .err paddle in rhythm to the music!

The summer gear is getting more outrageous! Kayak past a huge floatie that sits eight easily with a step-up launch pad, a bright gold and teal checkerboard back rest on the inflatable chairs with inner circle with a mesh that allows splashing toes in the water. Wow, a party right on the water!

In front of a small hut with arched door, is a rowboat, kayak, sailboat, and a pedal boat. Along with all those water crafts is a green alligator floatie, very reminiscent of my son's blow up shark that he rode for years up at Grandma and Grandpa's cottage. Pin the blue-ribbon award for the most possible water toys on this home!

Not to be out done, a nearby lodge has a wave runner blue inflatable ball, seemingly as big as the redwood cottage. Players walk inside the ball on the surface of the water. Shhh. . .no one is looking, shall we check it out? Try it? That has got to be a blast!

Rick has our own toys hidden in his cockpit. Water guns! One for each of us, what a sweet brother. Before I can figure out how to fill mine up, I am soaked from a waterfall blast from that sweet brother—hmm. We have an entire lake to fill and squirt at each

other. Pirate battle on the water. Paddle and fire, paddle and fire, turn and attack, fire the water cannon! Dangerous to lean too far over trying to be fastest at filling up your gun in retaliation for a brotherly attack. Hide behind Chris, my sweet sister in law, Rick won't squirt his lovely wife. . .right?! No—I'm attacked by both!

Past a manor flanked by two patio umbrellas above the two deck chairs, marine flag, and bathing beauties lazily tanning by the blue leaning beach umbrella. . .laughing at how soaked I am.

After miles of fun in the sun and sharing this incredible freshwater ocean with vacationers escaping to Wisconsin, we pass a series of lake shore accesses. Dewitt Road access is a marshy path to the shoreline. But less than a half mile later is the nice E. Van Ess Road access with is slight sandy path leading to a lovely sandy beach, where you have 49.5 feet of public access and shoreline to lay down your beach blankets and join the merriment on Lake Michigan.

Double paddle boards strapped on top of a jeep, waiting to be unloaded, while the beach party under the red and orange large umbrella is a happening. A happy dog begging a teen to throw a toy and little brother playing in the larger than life Flamingo floatie with his multicolored wings matching the little boy's life vest.

We pass the Stokdyk Ingelse Road access with its 50-feet of public sandy beach. There is a small sand path next to a hedge leading to the beach access. After this, we know we are nearing the small village of Oostburg, which was settled by Dutch immigrants. It is known for tulips and windmills. We wander past a white cottage with a large Dutch windmill. It has a round porch surrounding the tower of the windmill and the owners are lounging in its shadow. The sails of the windmill are not moving, due to little breeze today.

Half a mile later, we arrive at Foster Road access, our planned take out site. Foster Road is a dead-end road with a tiny trail through the wooden rails with the trees curving above to form a grotto. Sandy beach with large boulders for chairs at water's edge. Today we can float gently on the lake's surface with a relaxed rhythm of the placid swells of the lake. Perhaps we should blow up our paddle floats for pillows as we relish the end of a fantastic day playing at the beach. If you choose to paddle park to park (Harrington Beach State Park to Kohler-Andrae State Park), you have two and a half more miles of paddling to land on the beaches of Kohler-Andrae State Park.

Logistics:

Kohler-Andrae State Park Beach Boulevard, Sheboygan.:
43.6435—87.7309. 1020 Beach Park Lane. Pit toilets available. State park fees apply.

Wilson Lima Road public access, Oostburg:
43.6435, -87.7309. 1800 Wilson Lima Road. Beautiful sand dune access, parking on road, easy carry to water. No fee, no restroom.

Town Line Road public access, Oostburg:
43.6295, -87.7420. W971 Town Line Road. Very limited parking and brushy carry in on a small trail. No fee, no restroom.

Foster Road public access, Oostburg:
43.6222, -87.7475. 2315 Foster Road. Limited parking, small carry in trail to water's edge. No fee, no restrooms.

Stokdyk Ingelse Road public access, Oostburg:
43.6155, -87.7532. W1167 Stokdyk Ingelse Road. Limited parking, small carry in trail. No fee, no restrooms.

E. Van Ess Road public access, Oostburg:
43.6068, -87.7602. 1300 E. Van Ess Road. Some off-road parking, small carry in trail to nice beach on the lake. No fee, no restrooms.

Dewitt Road public access, Oostburg:
43.6012, -87.7644. 1450 Dewitt Road. Limited parking, marshy trail to water's edge. No fee, no restrooms.

Amsterdam Park and boat launch, Cedar Grove:
43.5576, -87.7920. Amsterdam Road.
Parking, shelter, and restrooms available. No fee.

Amsterdam Dunes Preservation Area, Cedar Grove:
43.5534, -87.7925. No road access. Only accessible by water. Public beach between Clear Vue Shores Road and Westshore Road. Beautiful beach area. No fee, No restrooms.

Pebble Beach Road public access, Cedar Grove:
43.5430, -87.7916. W1934 Pebble Beach Road.
Grassy trail and high reeds to water's edge. No fee, No restrooms.

Jay Road public access, Cedar Grove:
43.5284, -87.7942. 180 Jay Road. Limited parking, grassy/marshy path to water's edge. No fee, No restrooms.

Harrington Beach State Park Highway D north of park access:
43.4994, -87.7937. 180 County Highway D, Belgium, WI.
Nice parking, easy access. No restrooms.

Harrington Beach State Park Kayak campsite, Belgium WI:
43.4913, -87.7925. Harrington Beach State Park, 531 County Road D. Access by the lake: look for the metal stairs with the small blue kayak sign south of the small point. You may reserve the site.

Harrington Beach State Park Cedar Beach Road public access:
43.4848, -87.7955. 205 Cedar Beach Road, Belgium, WI. Limited parking on side of road, no fee, no restrooms.

Shipwreck Location:

Atlanta: 43.5709, -87.7827. Lies 1 mile north of Amsterdam Park south of Oostburg. 17 feet deep and 765 feet off shore.

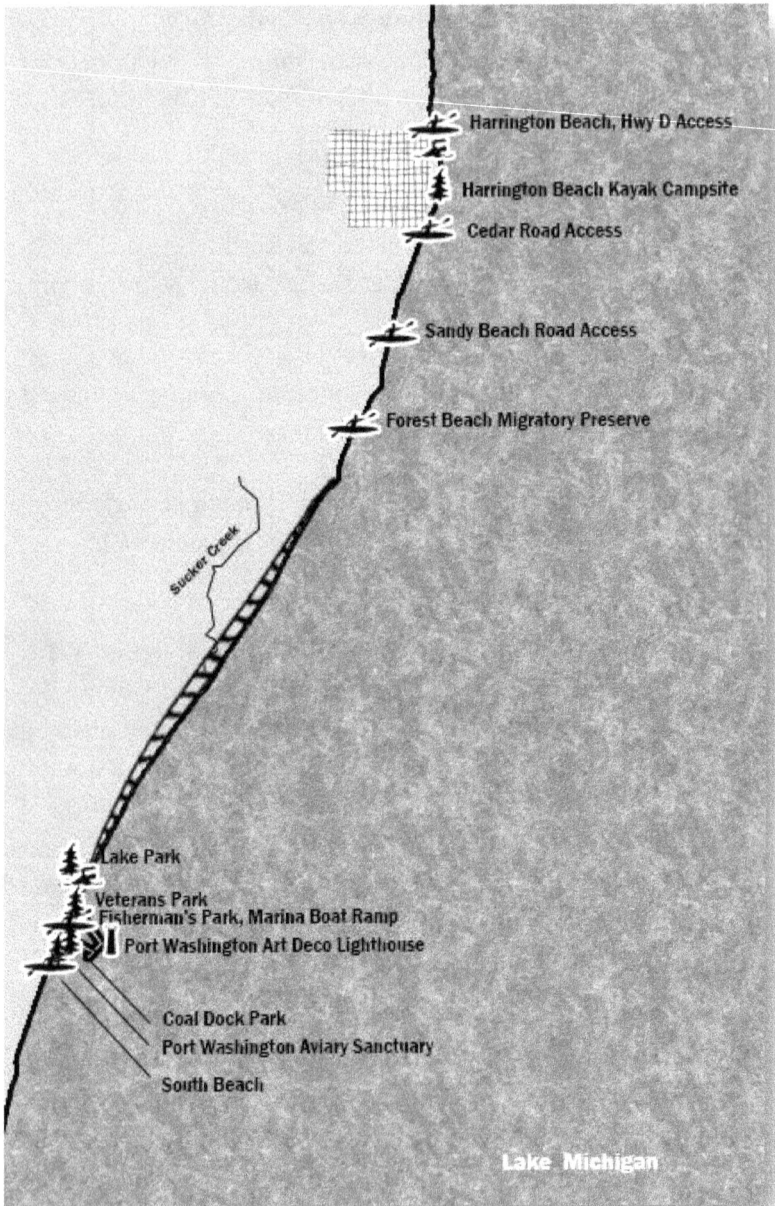

Harrington Beach, Hwy D Access

Harrington Beach Kayak Campsite

Cedar Road Access

Sandy Beach Road Access

Forest Beach Migratory Preserve

Sucker Creek

Lake Park

Veterans Park

Fisherman's Park, Marina Boat Ramp

Port Washington Art Deco Lighthouse

Coal Dock Park

Port Washington Aviary Sanctuary

South Beach

Lake Michigan

Leg 12

Bountiful Splendor

Harrington Beach State Park to Port Washington

With forested beaches and bluffs

9 miles

Golden Fall Day. Charming colors adorn the shore and bluffs as you paddle past a migratory bird preserve, golden beaches, and steep vibrant forested precipices. Awesome Autumn paddle, but the golden sand beaches contrast stunningly against the deep green wooded cliffs in the Spring and Summer also.

We start at the southern end of Harrington Beach State Park, but you could add another mile to the day by beginning on the northern end of the park at the Highway D access and enjoy the beach park also. Could shorten the paddle slightly by starting off your day at Sandy Beach Lane access a mile south of Harrington Beach State Park. However, once the bluffs start, it is impossible to shorten the paddle, unless you'd like to carry your kayak up the 83 steps at Veterans Park at the North Beach of Port Washington!

Even the drive to Harrington Beach State Park announces that Autumn has arrived. The corn stalks have turned flaxen, the leaves are changing colors, and there is an early morning chill. Approaching the Cedar Beach Road access, Rick slows the car down and backs up for us to relish a small herd of deer munching the russet grasses along the lane.

The early morning light glistens off the soft fawny sand beach with honey yellowed ash trees gently quivering in a placid breeze. A light mist harbors off the lake. Wade into the quiet lake and—squeal like a baby! Lake Michigan has cooled to its Fall temperature of 55 degrees. Yup, we don our wet suits even as the afternoon is expected to warm up to 70 degrees. If the lake water takes our breathe away at shore, we can imagine the impact if we tip and have full immersion during the day.

Gliding gently off the shore, we settle into our boats. A tranquil morning. Looking off shore, it isn't always so. On an Autumn day in 1856, the Niagara, a side wheeled steam palace paddle boat, caught fire, with passengers jumping off ship into life rafts, or into the cold of the lake. 60 passengers perished. Today, the Niagara sits on the bottom of the lake a mile out from Harrington Beach under 65-feet of water. Yup—I am glad I am wearing my wet suit.

The first mile of shoreline is sandy beachfront property. We marvel at the mansions with small cottages tucked just next door. The morning sunlight reflects off the wide paned glass windows of the large homes, and the little lodges often have screened front porches.

Sandy Beach Road access peeks out between some homes with a sandy trail leading to the water's edge. The lake is a clear celeste blue, allowing us to see the sand ripple patterns ten to twenty feet beneath our boats. The bungalows and manors are nestled between the shadows of the trees, the leaves have generally turned golden butterscotch and lemon with a few pops of radish reds and oranges. The sky is powdered blue dotted with a light white vapor as the morning dew slowly evaporates. The faint edge of the three-quartered moon still hangs over the shore.

As the next mile passes, and we round a gentle point, a small trace of a path wanders up the shore into a shallow ravine. This is the Forest Beach Migratory Preserve with its sliver of land that dawdles to the shoreline of Lake Michigan. This is a public human rest stop on the shoreline, with most of the preserve behind the cottage homes. It previously was a Country Club, but has been transformed into a "five-star bird hotel". Great opportunity to look up into the blue sky for raptors including hawks, eagles, and osprey. Stop on shore to search for small migratory shorebirds such as plovers with orange legs, sandpipers with bobbing tails, or the woodcock with its cinnamon coloring. The Preserve has acres of hardwood forests, prairies, and ponds. We note a flying hawk, ducks on the water, and geese in flight. The Forest Beach Migratory Preserve is a "treasure of Oz"—Ozaukee County that is.

The bluffs have already begun with a two-tiered timber land, with crimson maples and medallion oaks against deep green cedars. We aim for the forest beach point with its rock outcropping draped by the white bark of ash and birches with their fluttering butter leaves. Here is uninterrupted natural autumn splendor all to ourselves. A Monarch butterfly flitters by, landing on the calm lake surface to dance with me as I paddle. His vivid orange and black contrasts exquisitely against the cerulean waters and the azure blue sky. He shares his rest break with me on his way south.

Inland, above the flamboyant high point headlands, Sucker Creek is making its way zig zagging and turning, slowly coming to meet us. The shoreline is sand and cobblestone with the multicolored forest behind. This seems to be our paradise; we head into shore for a rest break and snack. Rick heads in, silhouetted by the sandy bluff with bursts of hues, such as a child gone wild in finger painting. An eagle, sitting in an evergreen, flies up to survey and consider our landing. Satisfied, he returns to his perch to master over his domain.

We peel off our wet suits to cool off and wiggle our toes into the chilled lake (but no ice cubes, yet). We wander the sandy beach enjoying this superior Fall day. The mouth of Sucker Creek angles into Lake Michigan flanked by the bluff and trees as they maintain their root hold in the sides of the steep bank. In addition to the hardwoods and cedars, beeches and hemlocks join the choir. The brook supports chub, stickleback, minnows, and darters. Game fish of bass, pike, bluegill and young rainbow trout can be found, and trout and salmon are stocked annually.

We relish the view south to Port Washington. We can already see the profile of the four smokestacks and the pierhead lighthouse. Hopping back into our kayaks we push off shore for act two of our day. We still have over a mile of pristine bluffs polka-dotted with trees turning currant red, apricot orange, and the mustard yellows against the oat sand tan bluffs and deep avocado green of the evergreens. Our blue sky has galvanized into a solid cobalt blue sky without a hint of mist to dull the vibrant colors of the trees.

Slowly, Port Washington homes dot the top of the bluff overlooking our lake. The closer to town we get, the homes cluster on the ridge trail above us. Then, a lull in homes indicates we have arrived at North Beach nestled under the Upper Lake Park. The beach is a third of a mile long, splashing all the way to the outcropping of the Port Washington Water department. In the summer, this beach is a popular beach with soft sand for beach blankets and sand castle building. It offers refreshing swimming in the warm summer months. Today, the beach is quiet with only a lone romantic couple holding hands and leisurely strolling the beach.

At the south end of the beach is the only access, the staircase with over 80 steps. Above the sand and Autumn tie-dyed bluff lies Upper Lake Park, still green, grass park land with an expansive view of Lake Michigan. The huge Possibility Playground is a popular feature. It offers a poured soft ground surface with the usual swings and slides, but also has a Pirate Ship with waves, rain wheel, climbing net, and motion surf board. Lake Park flows directly into Veterans Park with its concert band shell.

We turn and head out to the Art Deco Pierhead Lighthouse on the end of the north pier. It's intriguing. It's iconic. Who has ever seen an art deco lighthouse? It is like no other lighthouse we've seen. Built in 1934 at the heart of the art deco era, it stands on a large concrete base, with arched concrete footings to increase its elevation. It starts as a square steel riveted panels and swoops up symmetrically into a smaller square tower with its corners angled to almost be geometrically octagonal. The lighthouse has traditional art deco round maritime windows. The Art Deco lighthouse initially was topped by a black lantern room with a fourth order Fresnel prism lens. In the 1970's, the lantern room was removed.

This lighthouse was never intended to be the dwelling for the lightkeepers. The older Port Washington lighthouse is located in town. When the north pier was completed in 1934, the lantern room and Fresnel lens from the old lighthouse was moved to the Art Deco pierhead lighthouse. The entire former lighthouse continued to be the residence for the lighthouse keeper. The city lighthouse has been completely restored and the lantern room rebuilt. The lighthouse is open for tours and has an authentic recreation of the original fourth order Fresnel prism lens.

A lighthouse is required at the harbor as the Toledo shipwreck is testimony to. The Toledo was a large double decker passenger steamer with a propeller. In 1856, the Toledo docked in harbor in Port Washington on its way to Milwaukee. A sudden summer storm blew in, the Captain and the Toledo started struggling and piled onto the beach and broke up quickly. Only two passengers were able to be saved, with estimates of thirty to eighty souls dying that day. Wreckage is strewn off of North Beach from two to twenty feet

deep. With such clear water, look down, you may spot artifacts trapped around underwater rock piles.

We cross the serene harbor entrance, waving to the only boat bold enough to head out on this Autumn day, and share a moment with fellow kayaker with his bright yellow kayak heading into port. Inside the harbor is Rotary Park with a pavilion and rest rooms. It is the site of the annual Pirate Fest and Maritime Heritage Fest. Paddling down the south side of the south pier is the new Coal Dock Park. Originally this was the location of the coal pile used by the power plant next door. Now that the power plant has switched to natural gas, the city has made this land into a park with a two-story red roofed gazebo, paved walking paths, picnic areas and benches to enjoy the views of Lake Michigan, the bluffs, lighthouse and city.

The squared off rock lined area next to the south pier is the WE Energies Migratory Bird Preserve. The hiking path from the Coal Dock Park crosses over to this floral plant community with marsh and meadow. Over one hundred bird species have been documented here. The power plant dominates the shoreline behind the bird preserve, south of the city's harbor. The tall structure is cleanly painted with four tall smokestacks uniformly fronting the building.

We land at South Beach next door to the power plant. There is a sand path to the beach with a large boulder to prevent cars from interfering with the beach. Two life rings on posts are on each side of the access path. Even today, there are several families enjoying the beach and view. Jumping out of our vessels, we stretch and peel off the wet suits. I wade into the lake, accomplishing all the way up to my knees, hurray!

We use Chris's fleece blanket changing "booth" to convert into street clothes. Our plan is to eat out at one of the historic restaurants in downtown Port Washington with a vista of the lake. Port Washington is located in a natural U-shaped ravine carved from the Sauk Creek. The lakeshore bluffs make a three-quarter mile retreat to form the natural recess. The first people to benefit from this geologic haven, were the Sauk tribe. French missionaries traveled to the area in 1835, and as the city grew, the Smith Bros had a thriving commercial fishing business. A fire in 1899 destroyed half of the budding hamlet, but the city rebuilt and to date has the largest collection of pre-Civil War buildings in Wisconsin. Port Washington is also noted to be the half way point on the original trail from Sheboygan to Milwaukee and was a great rest point, including Abraham Lincoln, who once hiked from Sheboygan to Milwaukee and stayed over-night in Port Washington.

Downtown Port Washington is a historic charming tree lined community "Main Street" with boutiques and markets. Choices for our lunch include, Italian, Mexican, Barbecue, Chinese, Ice cream, or coffee shops. Newport Shores, chosen as one of America's best seafood dives by Coastal Living magazine, is located right at the north end of the marina, and it would be possible to paddle the inside marina north beach to land the kayaks and stroll to the restaurant, or there is curtesy docking at the marina for up to three hours for lunch. We choose one of the deli's fronting the Port Washington Marina. This allowed us to have front row entertainment of the marina, and the opportunity to watch several fishermen catch salmon right from the marina docks.

Logistics:

Highway D access, north of Harrington Beach State Park:
43.4994, -87.7937. 180 County Highway D, Belgium Wisconsin.
Parking lot, no fee, but no restrooms.

Cedar Road Access, south of Harrington Beach State Park:
43.4848, -87.7955. 210 Cedar Beach Road, Belgium Wisconsin.
Parking on side of road, no fee, but no restrooms.

Sandy Beach Road lake access, Belgium:
43.4705, -87.8023. 310 Sandy Beach Road. Very limited parking
on side of road, no fee, but no restrooms either.

Forest Beach Migratory Preserve, Port Washington:
43.4578, -87.8090. 5000 Lower Forest Beach Road. Unload
kayaks, and drive back to the Preserve parking lot (.45-mile walk).

Sucker Creek (no vehicle access):
43.4232, -87.8375. Natural area, beach shoreline and high bluff.

North Beach, Upper Lake Park, Port Washington:
43.3943, -87.8637. 500 N. Lake Street. 83 steps of the staircase
down to North beach. Restrooms in the park.

Veterans Park, Port Washington:
43.3916, -87.8654. 440 N. Lake Street Port. Would be a hard put
in, recommend one of the other access points.

South Beach and kayak launch site, Port Washington:
43.3826, -87.8701. South Beach Road.
Parking lot. No fee, no restrooms, there is a picnic area.

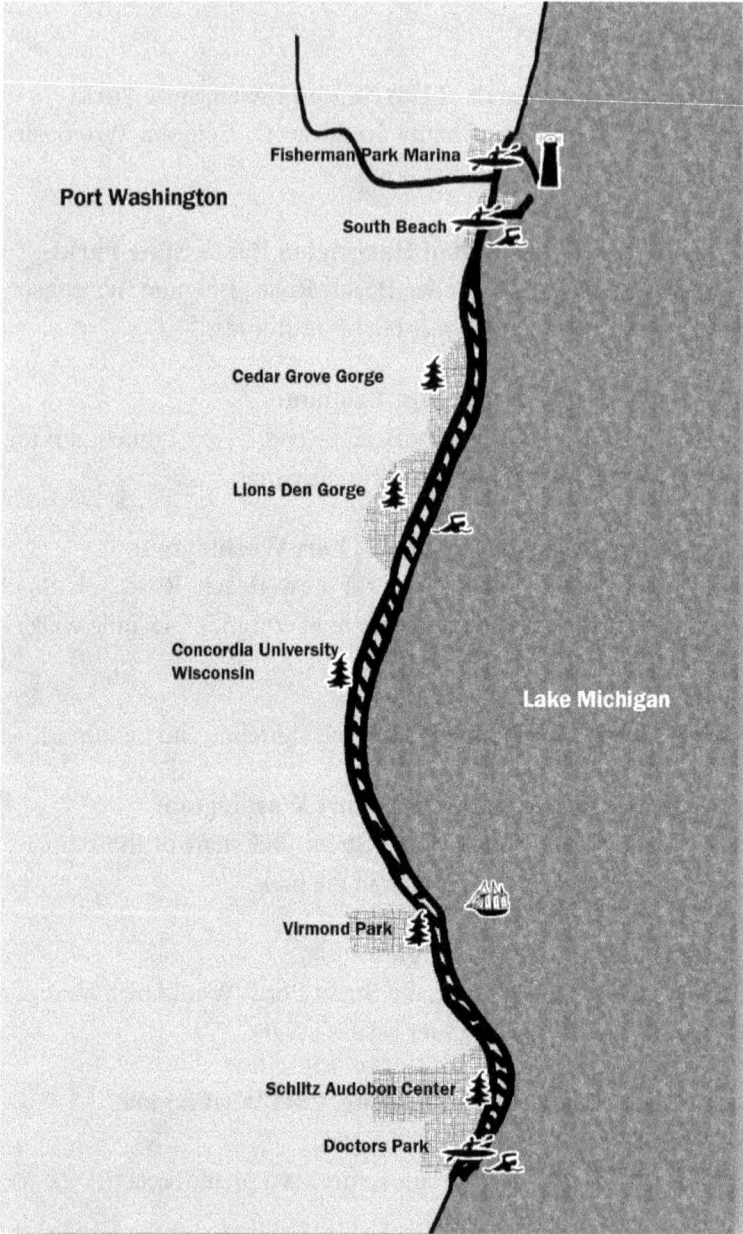

Leg 13

Gorge-ous Bluffs

Port Washington to Fox Point

With bold bluffs and deep gorges

16 miles

Man, vs Mother Nature. Stay tuned to who won. Highlights include the high sand bluffs (like the pun?), sliced with yawning cedar woodland gorges. The gorges *are* gorgeous. Stunning deep green dew dropped, quiet ravines. The green chasms that slice the tall headlands temper the splashing blue waves at the bottom of the bluffs. The catch is the bluffs go on forever, miles at least, and the gorges have long staircases or steep paths to the lake shore.

Mother Nature guaranteed us a long day's paddle with her non-stop bluffs. Score 1 for Mother Nature. Need to get an early start as we have hours of paddling ahead of us. There is no way to shorten the paddle due to those dazzling bluffs that seem to reach up to the sun — or at least the sun got in my eyes every time I look to the top of the cliffs. But that doesn't mean that there aren't pretty and public rest areas along the way. . .as long as Mother Nature concurs.

However, there is a possibility of a stunning shorter paddle. If you paddle from South Beach, Port Washington south to Cedar Gorge it is only 2 miles. A nice paddle, and at this time, the only way you can see Cedar Gorge, as there is no road access to this new public nature area. Add on only a half mile more to the largest sand beach area of Lions Den Gorge, which is just north of the creek and staircase down to the shore line. Delve into the gorges at these two VIP's (very special parks) for swimming and exploring. Kayak back to South Beach for a 5-mile round trip paddle.

It could also be possible to paddle north from Doctors Park in Fox Point and explore Virmond Park beach, 3 miles north. Or you could continue paddling north another .4 miles to search for the J.M. Allmendinger shipwreck, or add another 3 more miles to Concordia University, and enjoy their hospitality on the shoreline. A round-a-bout paddle back to Doctors Park would be a 12-mile excursion.

Rick, our weather man, checked the forecast, and broadcasted that a slight south to north wind is predicted for the entire day, making it a perfect day to roll our kayaks down the hill at Doctors Park in Fox Point and paddle north, with a wee bit of help from the waves and wind to make our long paddle seem like a breeze. Excellent! We arrive at Doctors Park, lug our kayaks onto our wheeled carts and load them up in prep to pull them down the hillside path to the beach. We do not want to climb up the hill multiple times.

Then Mother Nature pulls rank. Rick did seem to mention something about a slight chance of a thunderstorm. . .nothing to worry about. Nope, Mother Nature wants us to know who is in charge. That slim thunderstorm risk plops herself directly over our heads and with a roaring thunder clap, and slice of lightening, the cloud opens up into a raining deluge. We quickly cover the kayaks and gear and jump into the car.

Thunder and lighting, buckets of water falling from the sky. We wait it out. Hmm, hmm, hmm. Precious time is ticking away on our longest scheduled paddle day. How long can this freak storm possibly last? I start encouraging the idea of an early lunch in the park. Rick prefers to wait for a lovely picnic site on the beach during our paddle route. Hmm, hmm, hmm. Still storming. OK, guess it is an early lunch. Lift the hatch back on the car for a canopy and start the camp stove. Fry up the gyro meat, and cut up the onions and tomatoes in the back of the car. Gyros are great no matter the weather or location, even as we huddle at the back of the car.

Magically, Mother Nature decides we have bowed to her power long enough. The rain and lightning ends, and the skies slowly clear. Game on! Paddle is on! Off we go pulling the kayaks down the hill . . .or should I say, the kayaks on the wheeled carts push us down the hill. The gorge at Doctors Park is a gorgeous tree canopied valley. All fresh after the summer storm. Still dripping with raindrops off the leaves and berries.

Should we be surprised that we have the beach to ourselves? Looking south, there are three concrete beach protective jetties. The beach is still expansive, even with Lake Michigan at record high water. Driftwood adorns the sand and cobblestone beach which spreads almost a half mile.

Doctors Park is a picturesque park with a fun tot lot, and has two frisbee golf baskets. It even hosts a traveling beer garden with Feasts on the Beach several times a summer. The park was donated by Dr. Schneider, an eye doctor from Milwaukee. His old school doctoring ways included no appointments, everyone just waited their turn. All cash payments were tossed into a basket to be counted after all patients were seen for the day. This land was the doctor's summer home.

Our lake today, is fairly calm, considering we just had that passing storm. Dark storm clouds still line the horizon, but white puffy clouds are over the shoreline, with sunshine streaming through with a pink glow. The white caps are less than one foot at the shore, and it is an easy glide into the lake. We head north with a slight push from the gentle airstream.

The serene beach continues under the woodside bluff. The shoreline is public for another half mile. We glide past the Schlitz Audubon Nature Center which has a 60-foot observation tower peeking above the cliff. The center offers 6 miles of hiking trails with a terrace trail with a viewing deck overlooking Lake Michigan. The Audubon Center is a Lake Michigan migratory flyway and over 260 species of birds have been identified. The Schlitz Center also has a raptor program and have birds for viewing, all of which cannot be rehabilitated back to the wild. Glory and Valkyrie are bald eagles, the only eagle unique to North America. Cutright, a Peregrine Falcon, the fastest animal on the whole planet, can dive at a speed over 200 mph! Red faced Tallulah, is a turkey vulture who can smell her food over a mile away. Loki, is a black crow, one of the most intelligent animals—he can paint and do puzzles. Rounding out the raptors are six various types of owls, and 3 varieties of hawks.

Stay close to shore and you'll never even see the homes perched on top of the bluffs. The cliff heights are dramatic, over 130 feet high! Just north of the end of Lake Drive is a small unnamed stream cutting through the escarpment.

After three miles of pleasant paddling is our first planned break, Virmond Park. High up on the mesa is a pretty park. They have breathtaking views overlooking Lake Michigan. A few folks, have managed to thread their way down to the shore. I'm thinking down is easier than getting back up. . . The park does offer restrooms way up on top, over a hundred plus foot climb up the cliff which slumps and slides down into the lake. Since there is a quarter of a mile of beach underneath the park, we find our own quiet neck of the beach.

Back in our boats, onward we paddle. Most of what we see is a green hillside or sandy tan cliff with slipping forest greenery on the top. Occasionally, a home owner has managed to create a stair way or a deck part way down their bluff. A delightful quiet paddle.

Just a half mile north of Virmond Park is the resting spot of the J.M. Allmendinger shipwreck. Fun ship name with a salty reputation. She ran aground four times prior, always lucky enough to be pulled off. Once on the Menomonee River, a bridge swung open, hitting her and causing significant damage. Five times you're out? In 1895 in a November blizzard, the J.M. Allmendinger ran aground, loaded with lumber and bound for Milwaukee. But this time, she was not so lucky, and could not be saved. A lifesaving team was able to rescue all the crew. The wooden single masted steam barge was abandoned as a total loss. Today she lies about 1000 feet off shore, just south of Mequon Road in about 15 feet of water. In our hurry, we saw no sign of her and there was no buoy marker for her.

Rick wonders if we want to skip dipping into the bay to land at Concordia University due to getting a late start—what with Mother Nature delaying us and all. Yup, no problem there are several rest stops after the bay, and perhaps we can shave off a little time and muscle energy. This means we paddle straight across the shallow bay, about a mile off shore. Chris mentions how great it is that we have the kind and tender push from Mother Nature with the light wind from the south. I swear that temperamental lady hears Chris and whips her magic wand, and the wind literally swivels to a stronger breeze from the north. What the heck? If you don't believe in Mother Nature's revenge, then this is a perfect lesson of how Lake Michigan makes its own weather.

Now the lake responds and becomes choppy. We need to tighten our hats and lean into the wind, digging deeper with our blades. This is becoming work. Score 2 for Mother Nature. How far is our next rest break? Paddle, we can do this, paddle, we can do this.

We can see Concordia University on the shore. The bright white rock shoreline stabilization and the eleven switchbacks of its pedestrian path to the beach is striking against the green flora plain. Concordia is a liberal arts college, with a lovely Greek styled open-air theatre and a sloping pedestrian path swerving around the hillside to the shore. This is a great rest area, but only considered an alternate launch access, and would be a long haul to the beach. Concordia University has a half mile of shoreline and in the rough and tumble of the open water it seems to take forever to make headway past the college.

Slowly, we get closer to shore as we near the end of the bay and are adjacent to the shore. Since the change in the wind, the bluff does not provide us any quiet lee, as the waves are crashing on the shoreline. The gusty wind is in our face and we fight for forward motion. The shoreline continues stunning with the craggy bluff half covered in forests. The homes up above are mostly hidden, crested on top of the flat land.

After seven miles of paddling, we arrive at our next planned rest break, Woodland Shores. The beach below the vista is a recognized access on the Lake Michigan Water Trail. There is no access from the bluff to the lake and the natural beach. We head into shore, and search for a beach area large enough to land on. The surf is brown and churning. "Don't make me land here, don't make me land here", I say with a worried frown on my face. Finally, Rick agrees, "it's not safe to land here". Whew. . .but my butt is sore and I need a stretch. Our final decision—raft up and each take turns to lift up and lean back and stretch out our backs as the other two steady the boat. Works in a pinch. Score 3 for Mother Nature.

Onward towards the main feature on the day's paddle: Lions Den Gorge. Only two miles, we can do it, we can do it. Slowly, the wind quiets and actually settles back to a gentle breeze—mostly from the south again. Thank you, Mother Nature. We bow before you. The evergreens on the bluff bow down too, and nice homesteads sit back on the upper meadow. The sandy cliffs become sheer, straight down at almost a ninety-degree angle with no trees to adorn them.

We are arriving at Lions Den Gorge. Established in 2002 as a Land Trust property, it is considered an ecological jewel. The sharp precipitous, one hundred feet high, vertical bluffs capped with meadow and woodlands. The bluff trail leads to the gorge, a verdant green ravine with bridges and stairs down to a salmon spawning stream. From here is a short path to the mile-long shallow shoreline beach. Did you catch the part about a shallow, narrow beach? Yup, after Mother Nature whipped up the north wind, the waves are literally crashing into the bluffs. Even though the breeze has settled, and the lake is calming, the one-foot white caps are quick, sharp and continuous. There is no way to land or even stop, we'll smash into the bluff wall. Mother Nature, how could you?

Our next hope is almost next door—Cedar Gorge, the newest public nature area. At this time, there is no parking lot, restrooms, or trail to the water's edge. It offers a mile-long beach stop for small water crafts. But no such luck today. . .it too has the steep brown bluffs with a shallow beach. No kayak landing again for us today. No choice, we must grin and bear it, and paddle on. My arms are now aching, my back is mad at me. We shall persevere, we shall, we shall, as we dig the paddle in and work our arms. I'm pretty sure, I'll be paddling in my sleep tonight. . .

Only a mile and a half more to Port Washington's South Beach. We can see the four white smokestacks as we round the next point. Almost there, almost there. Enjoy the beautiful bluff with the V shaped green ravines. Quite a striking shoreline.

Soon, we can make out the rare Port Washington Art Deco lighthouse on the end of the north breakwater wall. Built in 1935 at the height of the Art Deco period, it is typical of this type of architecture with its square cement block base with a large arch underneath all four sides. The modern looking white tower is squarish with small round classic Art Deco windows. Originally, the light station had a fourth order Fresnel lens, but the lantern room has been replaced with its current red light.

The southern pier wall beckons us and our eyes follow it to South Beach shore to the superb soft sandy shoreline. I glide in and hunch forward, allowing my arms to rest. Do I still know how to stand on my own two feet? With a tender tug, Rick pulls me up and out of my boat.

Mother Nature challenged us today, but we were up for the challenge. We paddled for a non-stop twelve miles, seven which were against the switcheroo north wind that Mother Nature whipped up for us. Mother Nature scored many points and was winning after every quarter. Yet we persisted, and believe that at the last buzzer, we won, and we cheer our accomplishment. Paddle lift!

Logistics:

Fisherman Park Marina boat ramps, Port Washington:
43.3879, -87.8667. 106 N. Lake Street.
Free courtesy docking for 3 hours, public restrooms, picnic areas.

South Beach and kayak Launch site, Port Washington:
43.3826, -87.8701. South Beach Road.
No fee, no restrooms, there is a picnic area.

Cedar Grove Ravine Nature Area, Port Washington:
43.3601, -87.8795. Rest stop only on a shallow beach. No vehicular access at all. 1.6 miles south of South Beach, Port Washington.

Lions Den Gorge Nature Preserve, Grafton:
43.3468, -87.8824. 511 High Bluff Drive. Rest stop only on a shallow beach, can enjoy the Gorge Steps. Restrooms on top.

Concordia University/Kapco Park Alternate Access, Mequon:
43.2532, -87.9112. 12800 N. Lake Shore Drive. This is considered an alternative access due to long hill or switchback trail.

Virmond Park Emergency Access, Mequon:
43.2110, -87.8958. 10606 N. Lake Shore Drive. Nice rest area, no launching due to high steep bluff. Parking lot.

Schlitz Audubon Society Nature Center shoreline rest stop:
43.1756, -87.8826. 1111 E. Brown Deer Road, Bayside. Great aviary, no access to shoreline from Nature Center above.

Doctors Park, Fox Point:
43.1717, -87.8810. 1870 E. Fox Lane. Parking area off Fox Lane. Trail hill starts here to shoreline. Restrooms available.

Shipwreck location:

J.M. Allmendinger: 43.2181, -87.8942. Lies .4 miles north of Virmond Park in Mequon, 100 feet off shore in 5-15 feet of water, scattered wreckage.

Kayak Wisconsin, Lake Michigan Water Trail

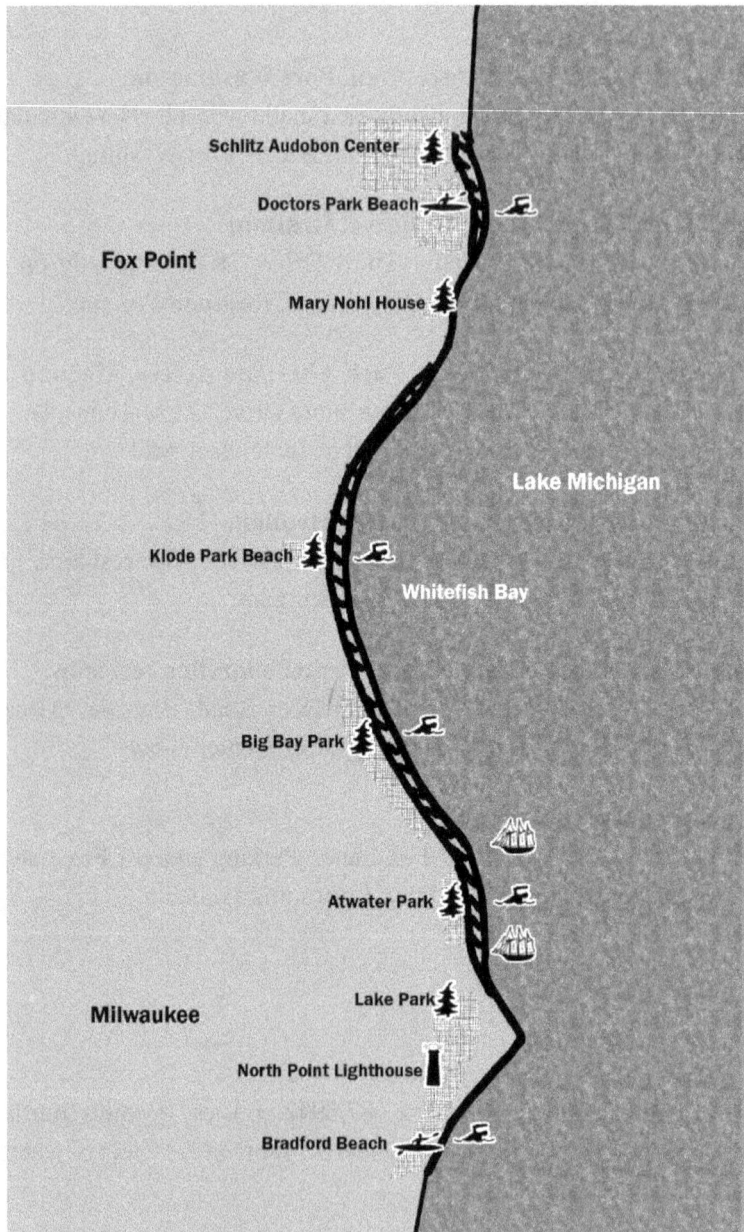

Leg 14

Beaches Below the Bluffs

Fox Point to Milwaukee's Bradford Beach

With Beaches, Sculptures, and Mansions

9 miles

"Oh, what a beautiful mornin', oh, what a beautiful day, I've got a wonderful feelin', every thing's goin' my way" (by James Taylor). The paddle has suburban sandy beaches scattered into the lovely bluff shoreline, with unique sculptures, and stately mansions perched on the bluffs.

Although there are numerous delightful beaches along this paddle, they all entail a long one hundred step staircase or long, steep curving paths down to the shoreline. All the beaches are listed as "resting sites" and not actual launch areas on Lake Michigan's Water Trail. But that being said, they are beaches—perfect places to stop and relax, swim, and sunbath. Therefore, don't rush your paddle trying to do your best race, take it slow and appreciate the summer day.

We pick a flawless summer day, 85 degrees, sunny—no hint of rain, and Lake Michigan is a balmy warm 70 degrees. Swimsuits on, an impeccable Wisconsin midsummer day for exploring the coast. A minor breeze coming from the north, perfect for paddling south from Doctors Park to Milwaukee. We drop the "chase" car, actually Rick's scooter, which fits perfectly on his homemade kayak trailer.

The trailer can strap on two kayaks on each side, a fifth kayak on the top, with room for the scooter in the middle. Then we head back up to Doctors Park, in Fox Point, to initiate our journey. Again, we use our kayak carts, they are becoming indispensable on the Lake Michigan's western bluff sides, with the extended curving paths to water's edge. Saves our backs a lot!

The small town of Fox Point was initially a Dutch settlement, named after the first hump on our paddle, Fox Point. Doctors Park, our launch beach, was the summer home of an eye doctor, Dr Schneider. He donated his land after his death, exclusively for a park for all to enjoy, hence the name, Doctors Park. A grassy plain on top of the bluff, with a protracted sloping paved trail through the gorge to the lakeshore. Two youngsters and their babysitter beat us to the beach. They play in the teepee created by long pieces of driftwood as we pack up the kayaks for the day. Cute with their little pails and scoops to carve into the sand beach—I'm sure they have the ability to permanently change the geology of the shore. . . With a wave, we push off from shore and head south along the sandy beach of Doctors Park. The park has almost a half mile of beach, protected by four old concrete jetties to save the sand from sifting away.

It's a mesmerizing day, Lake Michigan showing off to us in all her glory. Close to shore, the lake is a light cyan, darkening to turquoise, and a deeper teal on the horizon. Whereas, the sky is a light baby blue developing into a darker azure above the puffy white marshmallow clouds. Streaks of white jet lines cross the sky, and occasionally a roar of a plane rounding over us, curving to land in Milwaukee after the long crossing over the lake.

Round Fox Point, and after the park, the homes begin, sheltered up a gentle sloping hill. Stay close to shore, not necessarily to scrutinize the houses, but because the Mary Nohl House is coming up. Her unique cottage of folk art is now on the National Register of Historic Places. The house is just a mile and a quarter south from Doctors Park, right after when N. Beach Drive is closest to shore for the second time. Although Mary was known as the "Witch of Fox Point" in her life time, due to her seclusive nature, she actually trained as an artist at the Art Institute of Chicago. She donated her home to an Art Foundation, and her money for Art Fellowships. Her home is adorned with wooden reliefs of swimmers, waves, and boats, and her yard has an eclectic collection of statues created right from her environment—the sand and pebbles on the beach. Mary's art is now being celebrated for her colloquy with the land and lake. The home is in the process of being moved to Sheboygan as a Museum to Mary. As her concrete porch, decorated in beach stones says "BOO", Mary finally gets the last laugh!

Inland, secluded from shore or road is a Frank Lloyd Wright home. The Adelman House, built in 1948, is a typical Prairie School home. Characteristically, it is a one story, concrete block, L shaped home with some full wall glass windows mixed with above eye level clerestory windows. Part of the home is a flat roof, and the rest is cedar shakes with wide cantilevered overhangs distinctive of Frank Lloyd Wright's Usonian style.

As we round into the belly of Whitefish Bay, Cardinal Stritch University, is just a half mile inward from shore, in the city of Whitefish Bay. It is a Catholic liberal arts College founded in 1937. This Whitefish Bay, was first settled by Native Americans, and then grew up with fisherman. . .who incidentally netted whitefish—go figure. Whitefish Bay, was a northern resort for the city folk of Milwaukee for many years.

The home lined Whitefish Bay, is interrupted by Klode Park. It is a true neighborhood park with tennis courts, and a soccer field. To us, it is the first opportunity for a rest break and swim. The Klode Park beach is protected by the three white rock reefs defending the two curved sand and pebble beaches. Above the beaches, is your choice of a hooked path or endless stairs up the green bluff to the manicured emerald lawn above. There is a string of benches to enjoy the view from the top of the mesa.

Perched above the cliff are elegant "old money" homes, many Tudor style, built with brick or stone and capped in red tiled roofs. Silver Spring Park is a slit of a park with a scenic overlook o'er a rocky embankment mingled amongst the mansions.

Another half mile of stately manor homes and we arrive at Big Bay Park interlocked with Buckley Park. Time for lunch. Rick, our chef, makes us pizza on tortillas on his tiny propane tank kayak stove. Delicious! We sit on the stone shoreline protection wall. Relishing our pizza on the beach, with the delectable expansive view of our water playground—Lake Michigan. We explore the park, south is a large rock wall, haphazardly dumped as a groin to prevent erosion. We have landed our kayaks next to the only cement jetty at the park. North of us is a superb sandy beach sheltered by the jetty. Chris and I climb up the one hundred and ten (I counted) old stone stacked steps of the gorgeous ravine to the grass plateau above. Take a short breather, then survey the astonishing view of the turquoise lake all the way to the horizon. We skip down the wide U-shaped blacktop path lined with wild flowers including Queen Anne's Lace, and native Black-Eyed Susan's, with a few monarchs flittering on the petals. We meet back down on the beach with Rick doing the lunch clean up, generally my job. . .opps, derelict in my duties.

A few bikini clad young ladies are near us, wading into the lake preening. While pre-teen boys ignore them and scamper past us to find their own slice of Lake Michigan heaven. The lake summons us. I splash in, Rick trails me in, and Chris is enticed in with the promise of "it's warm"! The sandy bottom is comforting as we leisurely float and lightly swim, delighting in nature's huge swimming pool, Lake Michigan.

Then I notice the boys that had scurried past, are jumping off a rock wall just north of us. Big eyed, I turn to Rick "we gotta!" as I point to the kids. Assenting, Rick and I start hiking and swimming towards the boys and the wall, while Chris just shakes her head "some kids never grow up. . ." We arrive at the protruding wall, only to find out it is just a beach protection wall, 18 inches wide sticking out into the lake about 15 feet high. Reconsidering, I hesitate. "It doesn't look very deep" Rick voices about the water level. "You gotta' run" the boys agree, to get into a little deeper water. "You gotta' bring your knees up. . .like a cannon ball" the boys urge. Rick shrugs and looks at me and says, "you're shorter, you go first—you gotta' run!" With a scream, I run like an old fool hurdling into the lake. I survive without injury. So, of course, Rick dashes forward off the wall, safely joining me in the lake. "Awesome!", as we swim back towards Chris. She laughs at the fun photos of each of us careening off the wall that she has taken with my camera.

After two hours of lunch and playing in the sand and waves, we hop back into our kayaks and off we go paddling south towards Shorewood. The village of Shorewood was settled between Lake Michigan and the Milwaukee River about a mile and a half inland. Before the Europeans arrived, Shorewood was the territory of the Sioux and Algonquin Native Americans. The first explorer was Pere Jacque Marquette who canoed right along this shoreline.

Now we kayak past a mile of old traditional estates built in the early 1900's. Each home is unique with its own character, no cookie cutter houses sometimes seen today. These revival homes, take their cue from Europe, with steeply pitched multiple roof lines with gables and dormers. Often brown or cream-colored stone or brick on the main floor, with stucco and half-timbered framing on the upper floors. Arched multipaned windows, and highly embellished doors sometimes with classic columns. Most with massive chimneys capped with chimney pots. These million-dollar manors sit high up on the flat plain above the cliff, a joy to gape at.

Just 540 feet north of the northernmost jetty of Atwater Beach, and about 260 feet off shore, lies the remains of the Appomattox steamer. She was the largest wooden bulk steamer in the Great Lakes. Her builder used pioneering steel crossed bracing and plates and arches that exhibited the transition from wood to steel in shipbuilding. The Appomattox had a huge capacity of 3000 tons and generally towed a barge capable of holding another 5000 tons. The fact that she was connected to the barge was her undoing, as this made her ungainly. In November of 1905, both the Appomattox and her barge were loaded with coal heading to Milwaukee. They ran into a thick cloud of smoke, cloaking the shoreline and the range lights of Milwaukee. The Appomattox and her barge ran aground. The barge was quickly freed, but the Appomattox was too deeply stuck and had suffered irreparable bottom damage. On her 13th unlucky day, she was abandoned and lost to the sea. Today, she is marked by a mooring buoy, but lies about 18 feet deep, and we are unable to sight her wooden beams on the lake floor.

Three longstanding concrete breakwater quays with groomed sand beaches between, announce that we are at Atwater Beach. A very popular beach, especially on such a warm wonderful day. A soft sand raked sun warmed beach, backed by a boardwalk, lead to a not quite centered steep hundred step staircase up the long flowing grass and wildflower hill—thankfully with resting platforms along the way. For those with coolers and strollers, there is a switchback path curving down the hill as an alternative. There are restrooms, and two playgrounds, one on top and one at beach level. The crowning jewel of this beach is the Plensa sculpture, Spillover. Spillover is the form of a man crouched and hugging his knees as he gazes out over the Lake Michigan vista. Formed by letters of the alphabet, spilling out, the sculpture symbolizes a dialogue with the lake.

Pretty much right after Atwater Beach is the Shorewood Nature Preserve. Only accessible by land by a small path between Newton Avenue and Menlo Boulevard on North Lake Drive. The trail is a steep climb straight down to water's edge. However, by lake access, you have almost a third mile of coast line to discover under the stately homes above. Much of the shore is exposed rock strewn, pebbles and sand, so be careful if you land. You are rewarded by a quiet natural area that is much more peaceful than the public raked sand beaches.

We are arriving at North Point in Milwaukee. The metal wall lined square point with the massive light-colored building is the Linnwood Water Treatment Plant. This is one of two plants in Milwaukee that take the clear Lake Michigan water and purifies it for human drinking for Milwaukeeans. Don't worry, the intake pipe is over one mile off shore and over sixty feet deep, therefore there is no effect on boats plying the lake near the plant. However, water waves created by the many pleasure boats hit that solid metal wall, bounce off and creates confused clapotis waves.

Just as we pass the metal protruding water works wall, by Lake Park, it happens. Rick asks me to check my map on my phone. I finally upgraded to a smart phone with a curved tempered glass screen to decrease cracks and scratches, with an excellent camera, that is water resistant and repels splashes and dunks up to five feet underwater for thirty minutes. Perfect for a crazy kayak lady. I have it wrapped in its rubber backside case, with an attachable two-foot long floatable camera cord, carabineer-ed to my front kayak elastic deck lines. As I dutifully pull out my phone from under the lines on my kayak deck, the rubber case kick stand—that I never use—catches and the phone flips out of its case, flies in the air as I stumble to grab it, and sinks quickly into the lake. "My phone!" I yell. "What about it?" Rick says, as I shake the now empty case, "It's sunk!". Rick and Chris immediately turn around to start a search and rescue. "Phones don't float" I moan. . . "paddle on". So, for all my carefulness, and unless the phone has a black box with a bing beacon and red flashing light, my phone is gone, gone to its watery grave, along with all those great photos I took today. So much for my song this morning; "Oh, what a beautiful mornin'. . .every thing's goin' my way".

I stay poised and composed and paddle on, accepting the inevitable. We are passing Milwaukee's Lake Park with virtually a half mile of grassy plain on the lake right after the deep brown metal wall of the water works. The park is one of the original parks of Milwaukee, designed by the premier landscape architect, Frederick Law Olmstead. He encompassed the existing natural ravines and Lake Michigan into his design, with trails for passive sports with nature. One of the ravine paths has a waterfall. The large meadow areas have a golf course, bowling greens, tennis courts, and a children's playground for active sports. The Oak Leaf paved trail, which started miles inland, now curves to follow the lakeshore. In Lake Park, Olmstead also included romantic features such as the two Lion Bridges by the lighthouse ravines. Eight lions were sculpted out of sandstone in 1897. The Grand Staircase has two curving staircases circling a green natural area meeting together in a wide promenade coming down the hill, which is visible as we paddle past on the lake. There is an equestrian statue that honors Brigadier General Erastus B. Wolcott, Wisconsin's Surgeon General during the Civil War. Incredibly, the park also has one last, real, prehistoric Indian Mound, commemorating the original owners of this land. It is the sole survivor of a group of mounds that was once part of a stone age village at this site. Indian mounds were used for religious, ceremonial, or burial purposes of the Native Americans.

Interestingly hidden from view when close to shore is Lake Park's North Point Lighthouse. There has been a lighthouse at North Point since 1885. By 1886 this new lighthouse was built higher up the bluff when the shoreline fell near the original lighthouse. Then the lighthouse was still not tall enough as the trees grew taller, so they raised the lighthouse tower on top of a steel structure. Now it stands 154 feet above the lake level, and still it is hard to discern when we paddle close to shore! In 1893, Lake Park was developed around the lighthouse. The lighthouse tower is octagonal cast iron sections bolted together. The light first burnt mineral oil, then coal gas, and now electricity. The pretty white lighthouse keeper's quarters was built in a Queen Anne style.

Lake Park continues a mile long, behind the large Bradford Beach that we are arriving at. "Now this is a beach!" my son, Matthew, has proclaimed. He is correct, Bradford Beach was designated a Top Ten urban beach by USA Today in 2016. It is a massively long beach—a half mile, and three hundred feet deep of groomed soft sand. Three tiki hut bars, over forty sand volleyball courts. Rows of bright blue lounge chairs, umbrellas, and cabanas that you can rent. A large bathhouse with restrooms and concessions. Truly, a perfect people watching paradise. Beach blankets galore, and sandals strewn over the sand. Kids building sand castles, while mamas and papas relax, with an eye on the kiddies. But so large, that it is easy to find an open area for ourselves to land in our kayaks. Kick off our flip flops and sprint into the waves! The lake is clear, and the bottom is repetitively rippled sand designs. Feels delightful as we dive in again and again. Finally, exiting the lake, the Milwaukee skyline is a superb backdrop. Flop down on the beach blanket and chill out. OK, I'm back to singing "oh, what a beautiful day"!

Logistics:

Doctors Park, Fox Point:
43.1717, -87.8810. 1870 E. Fox Lane, Fox Point. parking area off Fox Lane. Trail hill starts here to shoreline. Restrooms available.

Mary Nohl House for folk art collection:
43.1503, -87.8915. 7328 N. Beach Drive, Fox Point. Follow the road to the shoreline and continue south, when it curves west again with a little paved area by the shoreline, this is the Mary Nohl House. The house and sculptures are in process of moving to downtown Sheboygan.

Klode Park Beach:
43.1246, -87.8998. 5900 N. Lake Drive, Whitefish Bay. Nice beach stop, not a launch site. Rest rooms up on top of the bluff.

Silver Spring Park, Whitefish Bay:
43.1187, -87.8968. E Silver Spring Drive, Whitefish Bay. Natural area, with rock and sand shoreline, possible rest break stop. Limited street parking, no rest room.

Big Bay Park and Buckley Park, Whitefish Bay:
43.1090, -87.8881. 5000 N. Lake Drive, Whitefish Bay. Only 1-hour parking on N. Palisades Drive. Nice natural beach by the jetty at Big Bay Park. Rock groin for all of Buckley Park. Nice curved paved path to shoreline, but the posted sign prohibits launching here.

Atwater Beach, Shorewood:
43.0895, -87.8724. 4000 N. Lake Drive. Emergency access only. But very nice life guarded and roped off beach! Spillover sculpture above.

Shorewood Nature Preserve:
43.0848, -87.8705. 3600 N. Lake Drive, Shorewood. Street parking only, no restrooms. Natural beach, look for sandier beach areas.

Lake Park, Milwaukee:
43.0682, -87.8666. 2975 N. Lake Park Road. Shoreline is rocky groin, so no access by the lake. Can stop at Bradford Beach and walk north .36 miles to the Grand Staircase up to the park.

Bradford Beach, Milwaukee:
43.0598, -87.8746. 2272 N. Lincoln Memorial Drive. Parking lot for Bradford Beach and Northpoint Custard stand.

McKinley Beach or McKinley Marina dock boat ramp:
McKinley Beach: 43.0513, -87.8818. McKinley Marina boat ramp: 43.87.8824. 1750 N. Lincoln Memorial Drive, Milwaukee. They share the same parking lot.

Shipwreck locations:

Appomattax: 43.0928, -87.8732. The largest wooden bulk steamer ever on the Great Lakes, lies north of Atwater Beach in Shorewood, 540 feet north of the northernmost jetty of the beach, and 260 feet off shore in 18-20 feet of water.

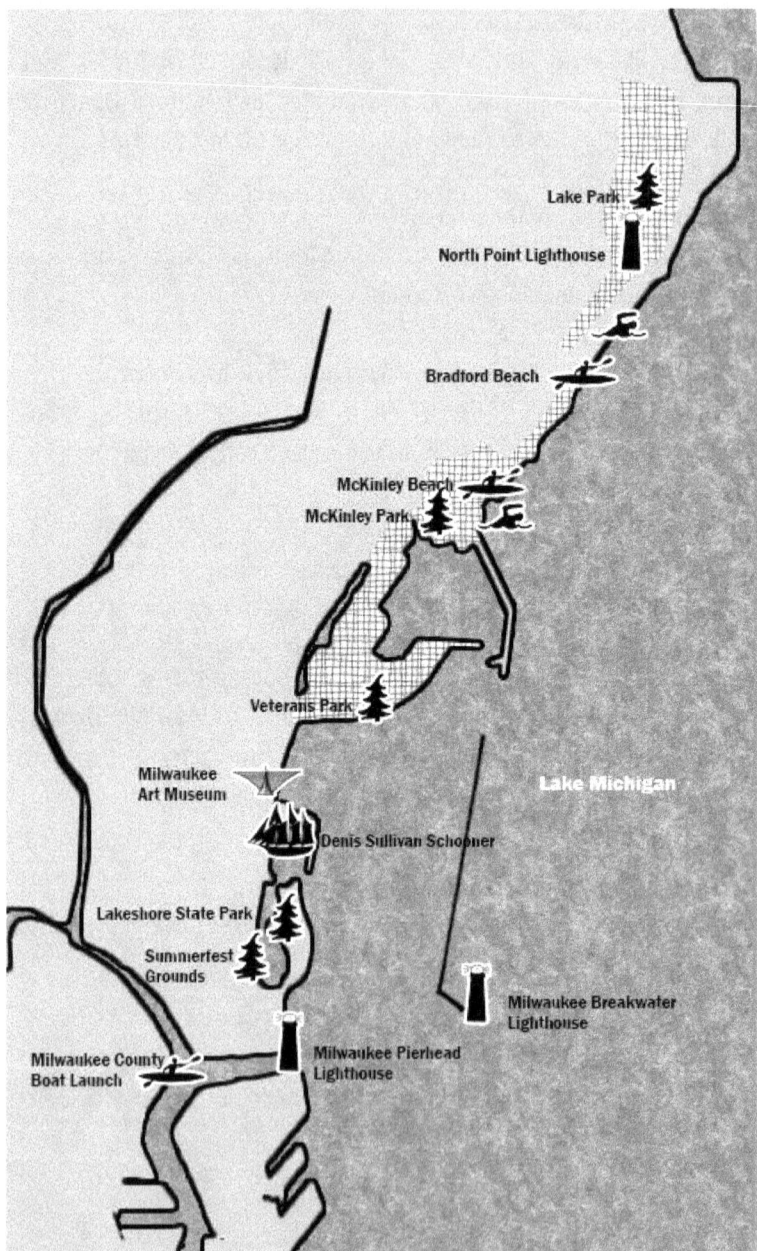

Leg 15

Milwaukee Skyline

Bradford Beach to the Milwaukee River

With beaches, lighthouses, a real schooner and the Milwaukee skyline

5 miles

Milwaukee might be known as the city beer built, but you need water to make beer, and Milwaukee has lots of water. Visit Milwaukee says: "The fresh coast is the best coast". Most of the Milwaukee shoreline is a parkway, and there is a four-mile long breakwater wall to tame Lake Michigan's wild ways. The best features of this urban paddle are two beaches, the Milwaukee Art Museum's flying wings architecture, Milwaukee's tall ship the Denis Sullivan schooner, three notable lighthouses, and of course, that awesome skyline.

Making the Milwaukee shoreline its own destination, gives you lots of time to relish all the sights. Start out at the north end of Bradford Beach, or shorten the paddle by a bit and start at McKinley Beach.

Bright blue sky, clear Lake Michigan water, sunny temperatures nearing 90 degrees, and we are starting at Bradford Beach, an award-winning urban beach. A half mile long, with an extensive sandy beach that is a popular summer hang out. No matter, there always is room for another beach blanket. Dig our toes into the sand and dive into the pure water with the natural sand lake bottom.

Hop into our kayaks and start the tour! As we paddle out into the water, we need to turn around and see if we can spot the North Point Lighthouse, up on the bluff in Lake Park. Lake Park is one of the oldest parks in Milwaukee and designed by the same landscape architect who designed Central Park in New York, and the U.S. Capitol grounds in Washington D.C. The park has some of the original old growth trees dating back 180 years. Hiking paths with ornate bridges with natural ravines covered in wildflowers. Lake Park has open meadow areas for baseball, golf, and lawn bowling.

The North Point lighthouse is located above the northern end of Bradford Beach. The original lighthouse was closer to shore, but became endangered when the bluff collapsed. This traditional lighthouse was built in 1888 between two of the park's ravines. The white cast iron octagon lighthouse tower had to be doubled in height when it started to be obscured by trees—can we double its height again? Formerly the light house had a fourth order Fresnel lens that has since been replaced. The light was initially powered by mineral oil, then coal gas, and now electricity. The lighthouse was decommissioned in 1994 and is now a Maritime Museum open to the public and displays the original fourth order Fresnel lens.

Paddling south, we kayak the full length of the bountiful Bradford Beach. Past the rows of blue beach loungers, umbrellas, and cabanas. Numerous nets for beach volleyball. There are three Tiki huts, the bathhouse, restrooms, and concessions. Behind the swimmers and tanners, are cyclists touring along the Oak Leaf trail.

As the beach sand fades away, we come to the southern tip of Bradford Beach when large rocks protect the shoreline. Can't miss Northpoint Custard with its black and white spotted cow design.

They have matching dotted picnic table and benches. Northpoint Custard sells true vanilla flavor custard, malts, and sundaes. If you are hungry, they have charbroiled burgers on Milwaukee rolls, Wisconsin brats, and deep-fried white cheddar cheese curds. About as Wisconsin-y a menu as you can get!

We paddle on toward the skyline of Milwaukee. Notice the incredible spire rising high up—the North Point Water Tower. Over a hundred and forty years old, the tan colored Wauwatosa limestone pillar stands on a bluff overlooking Lake Michigan. Its ornate features decry its original boring purpose of serving the pulsating water pumping engine house. The square Gothic base has buttresses at the four corners, with a castle looking tapering circular tower with a wooden observation deck near the top. Then it flushes out with pinnacles, gables and finials high above the urban landscape.

The green space with the rocky rip rap shoreline border is Back Bay Park which continues across Lincoln Memorial Drive. We are now in the belly of Milwaukee Bay. Tucked in the corner by the pier wall is the quieter McKinley Beach. McKinley Beach is a horseshoe curved sandy beach that is defined by the flag pole at the north end. The two jumbled rock buttresses, north and south, provide protection to the beach. Thus, making it a great kayak launch site.

We head out around Government Pier with its blue rail trail and cut into the North Gap of the four-mile long breakwater wall. It has a small white with a wide green stripe light tower. The breakwater was first built in 1882. The water calms down inside the protective barrier. But to the north is the entrance to the McKinley Marina. A busy, and popular boat launch and harbor, and we give a wide berth to the boats coming out of the marina.

Stay close to the north wall and follow Veterans Park. The park is popular for walkers, cyclists, and runners along the Oak Leaf Trail. Perfect also for lounging and picnicking. A large lagoon is a quiet water sport area with a vendor renting paddle boats, kayaks and stand up paddle boards, along with a variety of bikes. Veterans Park is dedicated to all Milwaukeeans who have served in the military and is home to the Southeastern Wisconsin Vietnam Veterans Memorial. Three Wausau red granite monoliths stand tall with sloped tops representing those who were killed, those who returned, and the third for those Missing in Action or were Prisoners of War. Veterans Park has a large grassy area that is popular with kite flyers and every Memorial weekend, the park hosts the Family Kite Festival. Great place to watch the intricate dancing of kites to music, as the experts make the kites kiss, hug, tangle and untangle magically to music. The kites do the salsa, tango and waltz, whatever their handlers choreograph for the colorful kites.

Next up is the highlight of this paddle: The Milwaukee Art Museum with its architectural landmark, the Burke Brise Soleil. The Quadracci Pavilion designed by Santiago Calatrava is a ninety-foot

high vaulted cathedral glass vestibule. That in of itself is mightily impressive, but its sunscreen wings folded over the outside of the glass ceiling is actually moveable art! The white seagull like wings open into a wingspan of 217 feet, then flap at noon, and close at museum's close, or whenever there is threatening weather. Absolutely extraordinary unique and astounding in its beauty.

Inside, the Milwaukee Art Museum is also remarkable. With over 25,000 works, it is one of the largest art museums in the United States. Many famous works of art can be viewed including by the masters Degas, Monet, and Picasso, and American artists Winslow Homer, Frank Lloyd Wright, and Andy Warhol. The museum also has one of the largest collections of paintings by Wisconsin native, Georgia O'Keeffe.

Behind the Milwaukee Art Museum is the stunning Milwaukee Skyline. Just to the south of the Art Museum is the 833 E. Michigan Street office tower. Behind the south peak of the Art Museum wing is the US Bank Center skyscraper, the tallest building in Wisconsin with its 42 stories, and it won the Distinguished Building Award. Behind the north peak of the Art Museum wing is the Northwestern Mutual Tower, the largest building in Wisconsin by square footage. The smaller building just north, is the Northwestern Mutual North Tower with its light blue pyramid at the top, that is lit at night. The white building is the Cudahy Tower, with shining white marble and glazed brick. Looming large is the University Club Tower, a snowy white colored condominium skyscraper, it was designed originally by Santiago Calatrava and has a unique curved south corner. Right next door is the Kilbourn Tower, another residential structure built in a modernist style. Across Kilbourn Avenue is the Regency House

Condos, with round porches on the corners facing the lake. The skyline is spectacular in daylight, and gorgeously golden at sunset.

After ogling the skyline, paddle east around the harbor wall past the Harbor House Restaurant with outside patio eating. Curve around the rip rap rocky fortress and pier path and then kayak inside the harbor of the Maritime Water Basin. The white building with the round edifice at the end is Discovery World, a science and technology museum. They have several exhibits that explore the Great Lakes including; "The City of Fresh Water" which explores how Milwaukee pulls water from Lake Michigan, purifies it for drinking, and cleans the used sewerage water before returning it back to Lake Michigan. The "Great Lakes Future" is an interactive model of the Great Lakes where you can interact with creatures around our region and you can create Lake Michigan weather— make it rain with a thunderstorm or create fog!

Discovery World also has two aquariums, one with saltwater with ocean and the Caribbean Sea creatures with a glass enclosed viewing tunnel. The second one is a freshwater Great Lakes aquarium with a petting tank to pet sturgeon! Lake sturgeon are the largest freshwater fish, and can grow to be six feet long, and weigh over 200 pounds. They are a prehistoric fish, dating back over 350 million years. Sturgeon look like they should be extinct like the dinosaurs, with rows of bony plates on their sleek sides, and two pairs of whiskers—barbels, tactile organs by their mouths. Sturgeon can live over fifty years. Seldom actually seen when kayaking, because they are bottom dwellers, they do however come by shore for spawning season in a fabulously exciting splashing display!

One of Discovery World exhibits is a replica of an 1800's Great Lake Schooner, where you can experience the living conditions on a sailing ship. Or, like us, you can paddle right next to the Denis Sullivan schooner, which docks at Discovery World. The Denis Sullivan has a 95-foot high mast, truly a tall ship. She is the world's only re-creation of a 19th century three masted wooden Great Lake schooner. She is gaff rigged, her sails are four cornered squares, and has a pole, a gaff, at the top of the sails. Like a typical great lake schooner, the Denis Sullivan has the unique raffee, a triangle rigged top sail. Her inspiration came from several real schooners: The Rouse Simmons; the Christmas Tree ship, and the Clipper City; a ship built in Manitowoc. The Denis Sullivan's rigging and decking is authentic to a Great Lake schooner, but below deck, she is modernized. Whereas the original Lake Michigan schooners would have had a flatter bottom with a centerboard to sail in shallow waters, the Denis Sullivan has a deeper hull and a weighted keel with bulkheads, to comply with modern sailing requirements. She is so much fun to paddle past and marvel at, or maybe, she'll be out on the horizon and you can see her with her sails up. Even more cool, is to take an afternoon or sunset cruise and experience firsthand sailing a Lake Michigan schooner. You can even help the crew hoist the sails! No matter how you marvel at the Denis Sullivan, she is a true Wisconsin treasure.

On the south dock of Discovery World, is Lakeshore Paddle boat rentals. On shore, The Oak Leaf Trail has now connected to the Hank Aaron State Trail, and we can go under its arched foot bridge into the Lakeshore State Park Inlet. Lakeshore State Park is a curved peninsula rooted at its southern end of the Summerfest grounds. Harbor Island, now the peninsula, is the main feature of Lakeshore State Park, Wisconsin's only urban state park. Besides the hiking trail, it is a nice area for fishing and has wheelchair accessible fishing areas. The park is part of the Lake Michigan flyover for birds, and grey and red foxes roam the prairies on the island. There is a watercraft sand beach inside the inlet and there are docks for boat camping.

As there is no outlet on the southern end of the Lakeshore Inlet, we curve around the third of a mile lagoon, and head back. The shoreline opposite of the peninsula prairie is the Milwaukee World Festival Grounds which is a permanent infrastructure event location under the Milwaukee Skyline. The largest amphitheater can sit 23,000 fans for the hottest stars. Then there are eight other midsize theaters, along with the Klements Sausage and Beer Garden—Wisconsin all the way! For family entertainment, the festival grounds have a Sports Zone Theater, and the Captivation Station. There is Children's Theater and Play zone, which is so large, it is easy to misplace your child. . .just when he climbs up and plans on that slide, he is distracted and goes a totally different direction. Each year the Festival Grounds features heritage festivals such as Polish Fest, Festa Italiana, German Fest, Black Arts Fest, Irish Fest, Indian Summer Festival, and Mexican Fiesta. Newer repeat events include Big Gig BBQ, Petfest, and Pridefest. But the Henry Maier Festival Park is, for sure, best known for Summerfest. Summerfest debuted in 1968 and has become the World's Largest Music Festival! And it is right here in Milwaukee. Party on!

Paddle back under the Hank Aaron Bridge and then turn to our starboard side to exit the manmade harbor. We are still in the protective waters inside the breakwater barrier, although it is a busy waterway and all the boat traffic does create wavy conditions.

We head out to explore Milwaukee's Breakwater Lighthouse sitting on the southern end of the northern breakwater of the center gap. Before the establishment of the breakwater, the Milwaukee Lightship—yup a ship, was stationed three miles off shore in 1912. The lightship had a red hull with lanterns at the top of its mast. This present white lighthouse was constructed in 1926 and is known as the gateway to Milwaukee. She stands in 34 feet of water on concrete pilings, the foundation pier, inclosing the basement, which stands twenty feet above water and holds the fog signal machinery. The lighthouse has interior steel columns with a steel framework and covered with white steel plating with a flat concrete roof. The first floor contains a boat room, kitchen, living room, and dining room, while the second floor has bedrooms and the bath. A square tower rises two more stories and is topped with a balcony and the cast iron lantern room painted black. Two lightkeepers stayed here two at a time, three days on/three days off, working twelve-hour shifts. This was a dangerous job. When storms thunder in off Lake Michigan, the waves can crash higher than the five-story lighthouse! The lighthouse was automated in 1966 and the Fresnel lens removed in 1994. The original Fresnel lens is on display at the Maritime Museum in Manitowoc.

We however, are not done with Milwaukee's lighthouses. Head the half mile back to the mouth of the Milwaukee River, towards the yellow arch of the Harbor Bridge. On the north pier head is the red iconic Pierhead Lighthouse. Over the years, there have been several antiquated lighthouses by the river and pier. As the pier has been reshaped and expanded, range lights were built on the pier in 1906. Originally there was a rear range light five hundred feet west of the front light, but when the Milwaukee Breakwater Lighthouse was completed, range lights were no longer needed and the rear light was dismantled. The lighthouse on the pier today is the original front range light that was a dull grey. The now bright red cylindrical Pierhead Lighthouse is forty-two feet in height with five porthole windows circling the tapered top. Topped with a round black gallery and a ten-sided lantern. It had the Milwaukee Breakwater Lighthouse's fourth order Fresnel lens, but it was given to the breakwater light when it opened in 1927 and replaced with a smaller fifth order Fresnel lens, now removed for safety.

As we paddle past the red Pierhead Lighthouse with the red railing on the continuation of the Hank Aaron trail, we are entering Milwaukee's Inner Harbor. This walled channel is not the historic natural harbor. The primary natural mouth of the rivers was originally south across from Greenfield Avenue, but was filled in and this channel cut in 1857. The name Milwaukee, is derived from an Ojibwe Native American word meaning "gathering of the waters". The confluence of the Milwaukee, Menominee and Kinnickinnic Rivers forms the inner harbor as we paddle under the yellow arch of the Daniel Hoen Harbor Bridge. Named after one of the longest serving mayors in Milwaukee, this beautiful arc of a bridge was at one time called the "Bridge to Nowhere". Although completed in 1972, and opened to traffic in 1977, the bridge connections were never finished until 1998, due to complaints about the future plans for Milwaukee's Interstate system. The Hoen Bridge is part of the Lake Freeway, Interstate 794, and is tied arch bridge. Her gentle curve has a grassroots effort underway to light her at night to showcase Milwaukee's gateway.

Heading straight west under the bridge, not veering to the left for the Kinnickinnic River, or to the right for the Milwaukee River, we head straight to the boat launch. The Riverfront Launch Site has two very

Popular boat ramps, with limited parking and a small amount of greenery. But we spend a fun hour after Rick left with his scooter to get the car and trailer. Chris and I dry out our boats, skirts, and PFD's and chat with the "sitter" guarding his canoe as his partners went to get their vehicle. His observations of the folks launching their boats was hysterically funny and right on. With one couple, his observation was that she owned the boat, as the gentleman appeared to have no idea what to do with the boat as he held the tow rope as she left him alone to park the car. Another group of kayakers arrived, and a teenager was slipping and sliding as he attempted to step out of his kayak as I grab his arm to keep him from landing on his a**—buttock.

Milwaukee with her vibrant lake front is fun to explore on land, and a delight to sightsee by water. Her panoramic skyline soars above the beaches, shoreline parks, unique architecture, and lighthouses. As we travel Lake Michigan's Schooner Coast it is thrilling to share it with a real live tall ship schooner.

Logistics:

Bradford Beach, Milwaukee:
43.0598, -87.8746. 2272 N. Lincoln Memorial Drive.
Parking lot for Bradford Beach and Northpoint Custard stand.

McKinley Beach and boat dock ramp, Milwaukee:
McKinley Beach: 43.0513, -87.8818. Shared parking lot.
McKinley Marina boat ramp: 43.87.8824. 1750 N. Lincoln Memorial Drive.

Milwaukee Art Museum:
43.0309, -87.8963. 700 N. Art Museum Drive. Parking garage accessible from Lincoln Memorial Drive. No access from the water.

Denis Sullivan Tall Ship at Discovery World, Milwaukee:
43.0369, -87.8945. 500 N. Harbor Drive. The Denis Sullivan sits at dock in the Discovery World Harbor.

Summerfest Grounds, Milwaukee:
43.0321, .87.8984. 639 E Summerfest Place. No landing area, just enjoy from the Lake Shore State Park Inlet or inside the Milwaukee breakwater wall. Parking in lots A, H, or P.

Lakeshore State Park Beach, Milwaukee:
43.0316, -87.8959. 500 N. Harbor Drive. Street parking or in the Summerfest parking lots. Use the Hank Aaron Trail to carry your boats .64 miles to Lakeshore State Park Beach.

Milwaukee County Boat Launch, Milwaukee:
43.0249, -87.9040. 600 S. Water Street. Fee, port-a-potty. Very busy boat ramp with limited parking.

Kayak Wisconsin, Lake Michigan Water Trail

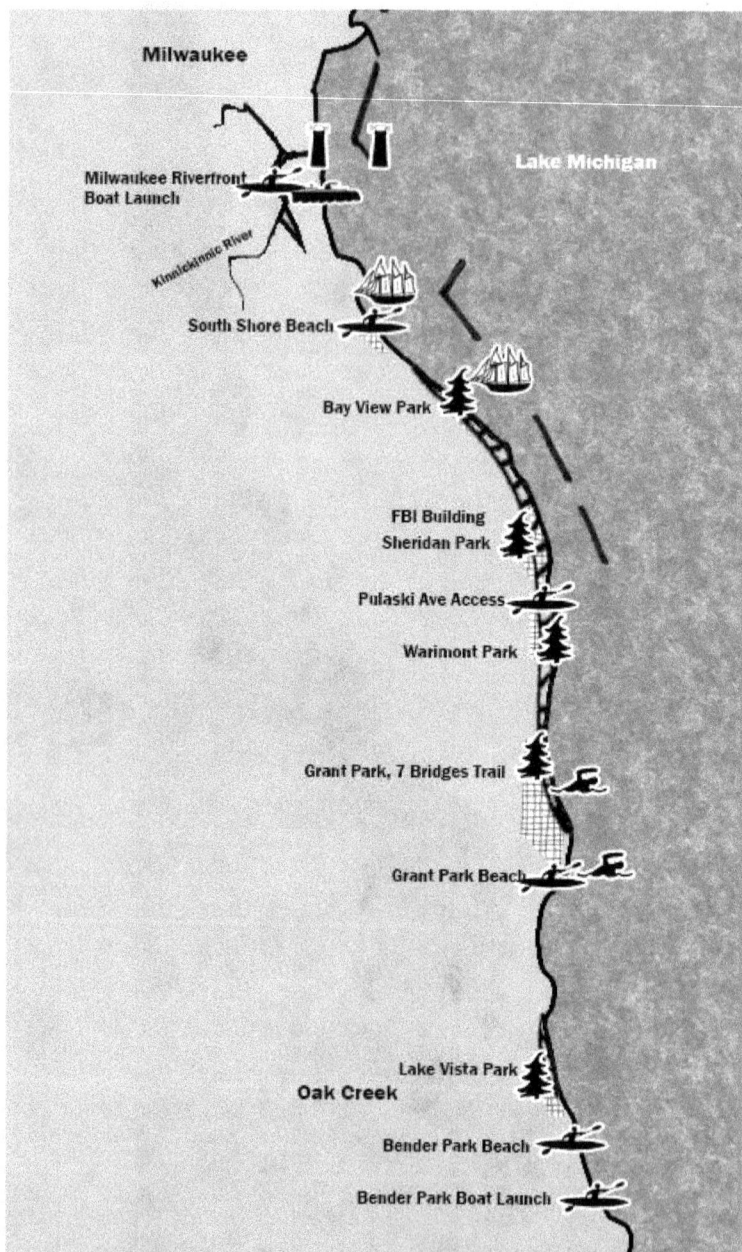

Milwaukee

Lake Michigan

Milwaukee Riverfront
Boat Launch

Kinnickinnic River

South Shore Beach

Bay View Park

FBI Building
Sheridan Park

Pulaski Ave Access

Warimont Park

Grant Park, 7 Bridges Trail

Grant Park Beach

Lake Vista Park

Oak Creek

Bender Park Beach

Bender Park Boat Launch

Leg 16

Beach Parkway

Downtown Milwaukee to Bender Park Beach Oak Creek

With a plethora of Parks and Beaches and Shipwrecks

12 miles

Day dream believer. This was a dreamy, delightful day. Warm summer day, mild textured water. And oodles of beaches and parks to explore. Bender Park beach is a beautiful start, and then Grant Park with its beach, shoreline and the "must see" Seven Bridges Trail. Continue on past more parks up on the bluffs with shipwrecks below, past the FBI building, to the South Shore Beach in the harbor with an unusual shipwreck—the Lightship 57. You may sail on past Milwaukee's Breakwater lighthouse, and the red pier lighthouse, under the golden arch bridge into the Milwaukee River. Lots of enlivening adventures await to make it a truly dreamy day.

The middle of this paddle is beautiful bountiful bluffs—making a midway launch unlikely. Technically, Pulaski Avenue with its stunning round building on shore is a nice midway point. But it is a long steep carry down to the shore with a cement wall and large boulders on shore. You could shorten the paddle on the north side by skipping the Milwaukee River and using South Shore Beach to eliminate about 3 miles. On the southern end, you could save 3 miles and stop or start at Grant Park beach. Shortening the two ends would make a 7-mile-long paddle along the bluffs and parks.

With the typical southern summer wind, we choose to launch at Bender Park's protected beach and paddle north with a gentle push from the breeze. Large parking lot and easy beach carry. Rick lost his wallet, so while he makes stressful phone calls, Chris consoles him. I however, wade, swim and lounge on the beach, while I "watch" the kayaks and gear. Really rough job… The beach is partially protected from the breakwater rock pile. Nice walkway on the breakwater to a lightly flapping flag. The flagpole path is the divider—north is the sandy beach, south the protected boat launch. Mounds of purple lavender planters by the beach house. Natural soothing scent for starting our day. . .just a gentle hint Rick.

Paddle, relax, repeat. Rick uses the mantra from paddling.com. Literally only takes about ten minutes to slowly start to unwind and be able to revel in the stunning views and the day. . . I notice a tiny smile begin to form at the corner of his lips. Sweet!

How can you not ease the tension and start to beam? The water is Lake Michigan turquoise, sparkling in the sunshine. The vivid white limestone rocky protective shoreline, with brilliant green grass growing up the hillside, and the bluff topped with deep evergreen trees against the intense blue sky, crowned with fluffy puffs of white clouds way up high. This is Lake Vista Park. From the top of the mesa, there is a colorful modern playground, and a glass walled picnic pavilion which offers panoramic views of Lake Michigan. Hiking trails are carved into the hillside with open air bluff overlook shelters nestled into the hills for your own private vistas.

Soon the Oak Creek Water Treatment Plant peninsula sticks out from shore. From water, the most notable structures are the two large balls on stilts. The water treatment plant serves over 70,000 folks in Milwaukee County and cleans 34 million gallons of water a day. On the north end of the water treatment plant is the South Metro Pier and sandy beach access. Locals come here to fish salmon, steelhead, and brown trout, or to enjoy the quiet beach. After the beach, is a wooded hillside, cleverly hiding the South Milwaukee Wastewater Treatment facility. Besides the typical open pond drying beds, there is a huge dome for sludge filtering. The smokestack next door belongs to the Everbrite Company, an electric sign company, or as they say "visual identity managers".

The harbor for the South Milwaukee Yacht Club is obvious by the sun-bleached protective breakwater and the white hulls of the boats with multiple masts sticking up. A green arch bridge marks the connecting walking path over Oak Creek to Grant Park beach.

We have arrived at the magical park, Grant Park. This is a huge park, with over 1.75 miles of shoreline. The groomed beach is just the beginning of this marvelous park. The beach is a popular spot, and offers one of four playgrounds in Grant Park. Beach goers are swimming, frolicking, and lounging by their coolers. The park has white beach chairs with umbrellas. Ferch's Beachside Grill offers Wisconsin dairy treats: cones, malts, and root beer floats. The menu also includes Angus burgers, fish and chips, and Wisconsin brats, with blue umbrellas over the patio or on the wrap around porch.

Behind the beach is a wooded hillside, and up on the plateau is the Grant Park golf course. This was Milwaukee County's first golf course. They still use an 1892 historic farmhouse as the clubhouse. The golf course has breathtaking views of Lake Michigan from the bluffs. The clubhouse parking area is the southern access for the Oak Leaf bike shoreline trail. The Oak Leaf trail now follows us along the rest of our day paddle north to Cupertino Park. Over eight miles of delightful pedaling through parks with stunning scenic overlooks and down to the shoreline to swim and explore.

Just after Grant Park's only concrete jetty is the beach access for the Seven Bridges Trail. This is the gorge hiking path that makes this park so magical. Picturesque dew drop greenery that winds up and over the gorge stream at least seven times. "May the peace of this leafy solitude rest upon and abide with thee"—as the covered bridge trail head states so eloquently. It is worthwhile to take a little detour from the Seven Bridges Trail a little south to an ancient pavilion. While the restrooms are a welcome relief, the true enchantment of this pavilion are the carved heads at each end of the rafter logs. Every one is a unique and fun character, some grumpy, some laughing—each delightful and amusing!

After the Seven Bridges Trail, we still have a half mile of shoreline of Grant Park to explore! This is a gem of a park, whether kayaking, hiking, biking, swimming, golfing, or just to sightsee and discover your own special spot.

Looming north, just after Grant Park is the high-rise Lake Tower Apartments. Being a slim building up on the bluff, provides renters a sunny observatory of the shimmering blue Lake Michigan. This tower is the divider between two parks.

If you stop on shore just after the Lake Tower Apartments, you are at Warnimont Bluff Fens State of Wisconsin Natural Area. This is a one of a kind wet-land. What makes it special is the calcium rich springs atop the hundred-foot high banks. Numerous rivulets run down the bluffs and carve mini gorges into the hillside. The damp seeping cliffs, are dappled with unique botanical fen wildflowers including Grass of Parnassus with five small white star petals, and Kalm's Lobella with irregular blue bell-shaped flowers. Because of the moistness, the hillsides are ever changing, and . . .unstable.

Warnimont Park continues after the Fen Natural area. Tall sandy clay banks continue with a mix of emerald and juniper greens on the uplands. Warnimont Park hosts an 18-hole golf course, an archery range, and a large fenced in dog park with trails through the woods. The Oak Leaf paved trail runs the one and a half miles through the park, which means we have a long sandy beach area to delve into for ourselves!

The park continues all the way to Pulaski Avenue, in Cudahy. A mix of suburban neighborhoods, Cudahy is blended with parkland. The only glimpse we have of Cudahy by the lake is Pulaski Avenue. You cannot miss this street. A round building with arches surrounds the red brick structure. The roof slants inland. Outstanding. This is considered an alternative Lake Michigan water trail access. A 680-foot carry from the gated road to the concrete shoreline and then 200 feet on a grassy path to the beach shore—yup, that would make it an alternative for me.

Next up is Sheridan Park. Literally. Amazingly, almost all of our paddle today has been along parkland, and the tradition continues. Sheridan Park has almost the next two miles of shoreline! Inland, o'er the top of the cliff, the park has a War Memorial, picnic areas, a playground, pavilion, and benches overlooking the panorama. There is even a fishing pond in the park. The Oak Leaf bike trail meanders the full length of the park. The bluffs are one hundred ten feet high with exposed glacial stratigraphy. There is a steep paved path down to the beach shoreline. We stop for lunch between the dozen concrete jetties protecting the sand, mixed with pebbles and sea worn stones beach. Perfect dream day picnic area almost all to ourselves!

Sheridan Park continues along the shoreline, with the Oak Leaf trail above the bluff. Even as we pass two deluxe apartment buildings with incredible views. Anywhere along the cliff beach is public park land and we are free to stop and enjoy the shoreline, although much of it is a natural rocky coast. The hillside is a mostly green with dots of white and colored wildflowers.

Stay close to shore to enjoy the wave protection that the breakwater spillway provides a thousand feet off shore. As we investigate the coast line, there is a large brick and white striped structure with the round tower on the northern end. This is the FBI—the Federal Bureau of Investigation building. The black fence around it has razor blades at the top. "Don't even look at it, they have cameras everywhere" my sister Becky says, as if a senior citizen on a bike or in a kayak is a concern! But. . .of course, I take her advice and turn my head away—wait, don't believe that! I take a picture, "I have a camera too" I retort.

As soon as we pass the FBI building, we are back to parkland! Above the headland is Bay View Park with its share of shoreline—three quarters of a mile. From the top of the bluff, is a tremendous seascape and skyline of Milwaukee in the distance. Bay View Park also provides a sandy beach to explore by kayak. And folks have used the Oak Leaf trail to stop and swim and play in the water, or for a quiet picnic on the shore.

Just as we pass the FBI building, there is an opening in the breakwater. Just 130 feet outside the opening is the Volunteer shipwreck in 15 feet of water. She was a very powerful steamer that was capable of towing large rafts of logs. But in 1914, she was wrecked and burnt at this location.

But don't stop looking down now! Stay close to the inside of the breakwater for more shipwrecks. The Sebastopol shipwreck lies about 2/3 of the way off shore to the breakwater rock pile 15 feet down under. She was another steamer and during her very first season, carrying a full crew and passengers. It was a fateful voyage in 1855, a very dark and stormy night. . . The captain mistook lights on shore for the pier lights and came too close to shore and struck ground hard. Large quantities of her goods washed ashore with parts of the ship as she broke up. There was a hazardous rescue but all of her sixty passengers were saved and "most of her crew". What, most of her crew? They forgot to mention that four crew members lost their lives—kind of important if you were one of the lost. . .

And just north of the Sebastopol shipwreck lies the Alleghany. A large propeller cargo ship that dragged her two anchors in heavy winds, then her smoke pipe broke and she could not use the boilers to propel her. She lies buried mostly in mud inside the breakwater too, again in 15 feet of water.

Ah, thankfully, our day is bright and cheery. A groin of white limestone shoreline protection rocks line the lake front, with the bike trail following along with a small half wall protecting the path. Although there are homes atop the cliff, we can't really see them behind the shrubs and trees. A tiny square peninsula known as "Texas Rock" juts out from shore with a grassy square and patio.

South Shore Beach arrives shortly after. You can slide up onto the sandy shore and head just south to the South Shore Terrace. Located in the 1930's brick bathhouse with lovely arches, the outdoor beer garden serves Milwaukee pretzels, beer breaded cheese curds, Hoan Bridge burgers, and Klement brats or polish sausages. They only serve Milwaukee Miller beer, and the best part is that the proceeds go back to the community!

South Shore Park includes a blue padded playground south of the bathhouse and an upper park over the hill which offers a Saturday Farmers Market including live performers. Wisconsin farmers and local food producers offer their products in a great community gathering. Have to admit, the market sure smells appetizing!

We tour through the South Beach harbor, appreciating the sailboats, yachts and dinghy's in the harbor. Love the ingenuity of naming each boat such as Caribbean Soul, Sail La Vie, and my fav—Surface Tension. I'd probably name mine, "Babs' Boat". . .oh so original. Maybe I should name my yellow kayak "Banana Split", or my blue water fabric covered kayak "Pool Cool". What ya' think?

On shore is Cupertino Park. A small park along the harbor. There is a fishing pier at the south end by the marina. This is the northern end of the Oak Leaf paved trail, at least the portion that follows the lake south of the Milwaukee River. The park offers ample benches to bask in the summer warmth and the lake scene. What makes this park special is the killer view of the Milwaukee skyline, which we truly get to relish from our kayaks!

Tucked into the corner of the harbor at the north end of Cupertino Park, is the remains of the Lightship 57 shipwreck. She was built in

1891 with white oak and iron spikes with two masts. Designed purely for use only during the navigational season as a temporary light "house", just to avoid the cost of a true lighthouse on land. She was stationed at Grays Reef, eighteen miles west of the Mackinac Bridge and moored in place by a sinker and chain. The Lightship was illuminated by a cluster of three oil burning lanterns hoisted up to each mast head. Retired from duty in 1923, she was brought to South Shore Beach and used as a clubhouse until she was wrecked by a storm in 1924. She lies in barely six feet of water and is the solitary known example of a lightship in Wisconsin.

We duck between the narrow breakwater opening flanked by the stone pile pier and the outer breakwater. On shore is the Milwaukee Coast Guard Station. The station is responsible for Lake Michigan safety from Port Washington to Wind Point in the south. The Coast Guard does boat safety, and reminds us the average temperature for Lake Michigan is 65 degrees on the warmest days of Summer, and dips to 50 degrees in Spring and Autumn. Also, cold water shock kills 20% of people within the first minute of immersion. Perhaps,

just a small hint to wear our wetsuits. . . This station averages 120 search and rescues a year. We are eternally grateful for their service. They also enforce Maritime Law, which we appreciate when jet skiers get too close to us for our comfort. Magically, the Coast Guard appears to remind the jet skiers of maritime laws. Score one, for us little boats!

Besides watching out for Coast Guard Boats, we are also approaching the ferry dock for the Lake Express Ferry. The Milwaukee Ferry was the first high speed auto and passenger ferry in the United States, when they re-established the ferry route to Muskegon Michigan. The crossing takes just 2.5 hours coast to coast, allowing one to totally skip the traffic jams on the Chicago turnpikes. In summer, the ferry leaves Milwaukee in the early morning, lunchtime, and evening, and arrives back at mid-morning and afternoon, so keep a watchful eye out for her as you paddle past.

The next mile and a half are past the industrial terminal area, so be mindful of other large ships besides the ferry boat. This, combined with all the pleasure boats, creates jumpy seas, even inside the breakwater zone. Hence, we are now in an area of at least intermediate skills needed for paddling. The award for more difficult kayaking, is the opportunity to appreciate the lighthouses.

A half mile out on the end of the northern breakwater at the river opening, is the white Breakwater Lighthouse. Built in 1926 the lighthouse stands guard as a beacon to our heritage. Although from a distance it looks small, the lighthouse is actually five stories high and sits on a concrete base that is 20 feet tall. The Art Deco styled lighthouse is built of steel framework and plating with a flat concrete roof. The square tower rises two more levels and initially used a fourth order Fresnel lens in its cast iron lantern room. As proof of how dangerous being a lightkeeper was, the chief lighthouse keeper fell to his death from the top railing of the lighthouse.

Turn towards the golden arch bridge and the Milwaukee River. As we approach the river entrance, on the north pier is Milwaukee's Pierhead lighthouse "the red lighthouse". When the natural Milwaukee River was moved north to this location and the piers were extended, a lighthouse was needed for ships coming into the North Cut of the river. This lighthouse was built in 1872 of steel tapered cylindrical circles to form a tower with a round cast iron gallery and a ten-sided lantern room. The original Fresnel lens was a large fourth order lens, but when the Breakwater lighthouse was built, that lens was needed further out and a smaller fifth order Fresnel lens was placed in the Pierhead lighthouse. A perfect pretty lighthouse as we look up at her from the river, and an easy to access by land on the Hank Aaron walkway path with the red railing to match the lighthouse.

The golden Hoen Harbor Bridge greets us. It is the gateway into Milwaukee's inner harbor and downtown that bridges Milwaukeeans together. It is a tied arch designed bridge that was used as a car chase scene in The Blues Brothers movie.

After the bridge, the river forks, the Kinnickinnic River to the south, and the Milwaukee River and downtown to the north. Just a half mile into the Milwaukee River, the Menomonee River joins it. So, we are at the confluence of all three of Milwaukee's Rivers. Not one to pick our favorite, we bee line it straight ahead, to the Milwaukee County Boat launch with its two busy boat ramps.

We quickly, carry our boats to the side, where there is a small short wall lined green space. This gives Chris and I time to rest and, while Rick hops on his scooter to go get the car back at Bender Park. Time for us to choose our downtown entertainment on this sun shiny dreamy day!

Logistics:

Milwaukee County Boat Launch on the convergence of the Milwaukee Rivers:
43.0249, -87.9040. 600 S. Water Street, Milwaukee. Fee, port-a-potty. Very busy boat ramp with limited parking.

Cupertino Park, Milwaukee:
42.9999, -87.8867. 2000 E. Iron Street.
Not a launch site. Street parking on S Shore Drive.

South Shore Beach, Milwaukee:
42.9958, -87.8819. 2900 S. Superior Street. Parking area by beach.

Bay View Park, Milwaukee:
42.9853, -87.8665. 3120 S. Lake Drive. No launch site (high bluff), on a calm day, may use the shallow beach. Street parking only.

Sheridan Park, Cudahy:
42.9595, -87.8448. 4800 S. Lake Drive. Long steep paved hill to the jetty at the lake shore. No fee, restrooms in the park.

Directions to Pulaski Avenue Access, Cudahy:
442. 9509, -87.8434. 151 E. Pulaski Avenue. Parking on street.

Slip through gate and carry boats down a long steep hill to a rocky shoreline. Alternate access, no fee, no restroom.

Warnimont Park, Cudahy:
42.9478, -87. 8438. 5400 S. Lake Drive. No launch site, but perhaps a rest stop underneath the large bluff on a shallow beach.

Grant Park, South Milwaukee:
Seven Bridges Trail beach area: 42.9235, -87.8442. Not a launch site, nice rest break area. Parking area on Grant Park Drive.

Grant Park Beach: 42.9076, -87.8408. 100 Hawthorne Avenue. Parking lot for the beach.

Bender Park beach, Oak Creek:
42.8677, -87.8395. 4300 E. Ryan Road.
No fee for beach launch and nice restrooms.

Shipwreck locations:

Lightship 57: 43.0015, -87.8855. A light house ship, lies just 6 feet under in the South Shore Harbor north corner.

Allehany: N 42 degrees 59.160, W 87 51.768. A propeller ship, lies off shore of Bay View Park inside the breakwater.

Sebastopol: 42.9863, -87.8633. Lies off shore of Bay View Park 330 feet inside the breakwater rock wall in 15 feet of water.

Volunteer: 42.9852, -87.8582. Lies .3 miles off shore of Bay View Park just 210 feet outside the breakwater opening in 15 feet of water.

Kayak Wisconsin, Lake Michigan Water Trail

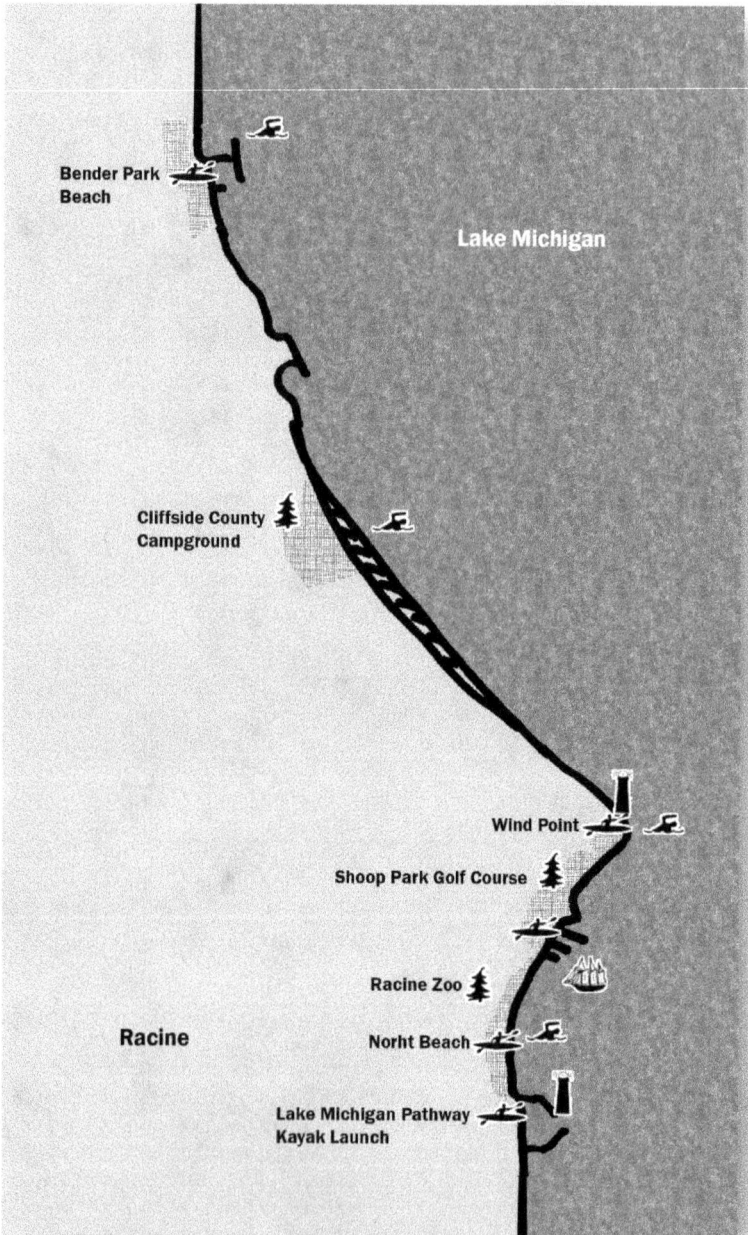

Bender Park Beach

Lake Michigan

Cliffside County Campground

Wind Point

Shoop Park Golf Course

Racine Zoo

Racine

Norht Beach

Lake Michigan Pathway Kayak Launch

Leg 17

Wind Point

Oak Creek to Racine

With Wind Point Lighthouse and
Racine's award-winning beaches

11 miles

A wonderful Wisconsin touring day. Classic colossus freshwater sandy beaches in Racine, followed by the timeless traditional Wind Point Lighthouse. Then staggering sand bluff shorelines.

The problem with shortening the paddle? The straight up sandy bluffs in the middle, where it is possible to rest under the cocoa colored cliffs, but launching a kayak—not so much. You could start at Shoop Golf Course, south of Wind Point, and paddle to Bender Park for an 8-mile paddle, if you are OK with skipping Racine's award-winning beaches.

We have a light, from the south wind, so we choose to launch in Racine and paddle north to Bender Park. So many choices of sandy beaches to choose from in Racine: North Beach, Zoo beach, or even Parkway Beach in north Racine. We park on Michigan Boulevard and roll our kayaks down the paved Lake Michigan pathway to the famous Racine North Beach to launch.

North Beach is incredible. Over four hundred feet of deep, white, groomed sandy beach, no difficulty finding a quiet area to launch.

Kayak Wisconsin, Lake Michigan Water Trail

This is the crown jewel of the many Racine beaches. Certified a National Blue Wave clean beach. North Beach is a Family Friendly Beach winner by Parents Magazine with its large sand box sand beach and shallow waters of Lake Michigan, and one of the largest playgrounds in Wisconsin with a pirate ship and rope swings at Kid's Cove. Also awarded a top ten Freshwater Beach by USA Today, the beach sponsors several events including a Beach Volleyball tournament, and Bikes Boards 'n Beach—a skateboard and BMX bike competition. But don't worry, the beach is a half mile long, so it is easy to find a quiet picnic area all your own.

Amazing sunny day as we glide off the sandy beach and head north. Slightly ruffled water, shimmering in the sunshine. The lake a clean, clear aquamarine color, with sand rippled patterns on the lake floor. Powder blue sky with soft wrinkles of white clouds streaking through the sky. A wonderful Wisconsin day.

North Beach flows into Racine's Zoo Beach. So named, because up on the crest of the bluff is Racine's Zoo. Lions and tigers and bears, oh my! Listen for their roars. Rhinoceros, orangutans, and kangaroos too. Listen for the grunts and squawks. You can explore the aviary, the barnyard safari, the giraffe encounters, or ride the Zoo Choo Express. Zoo beach continues past the zoo where there is a row of old jetties jutting out into the lake.

The bluffs continue under Michigan Boulevard for a quarter of a mile with sandy beach spots between the now dilapidated docks. Then lake homes are on the headlands with a sequence of rock pile jetties with private beaches between. We are entertained by an armada of sailboats out on the lake enjoying the light breeze.

Parkway Beach arrives at Vincennes Circle road. A small creek and bridge with steps down to the beach. Nice sandy beach connects to a stone wall at the bottom of the hillside, a grassy hill, then a plateau on the top with a bench to enjoy the vista. This is the last of the beaches of Racine to launch a small watercraft.

Another mile of nice lakeshore homes, some with stairways down to the shoreline. A half mile north of Parkway Beach, start searching underwater, because the H.L. Whitman shipwreck is nearby! A two-masted schooner with an interesting history, got struck twice by other schooners and was grounded another two times. Perhaps they should have hired a new captain? In 1869, the H.L. Whitman was heading south and got too close to Wind Point, struck the reef and sank. She lays perpendicular to the shore about 500 feet from shore in 7 to 10 feet of water. Look for parallel beams of her frame.

As we follow Lighthouse Drive, we arrive at Shoop Park Beach and Golf Course. Unmistakable due to the three concrete piers: wee baby sized, medium sized, and long sized, all in a row. I'm sure you'll find one just right for you! Sand and cobblestone beaches between. Gorgeous view toward Wind Point and the lighthouse as you stroll out on the docks. The golf course is a 9-hole course, and all the fairways are truly in the shadow of the lighthouse, with several the edge of the bluffs. One more secluded beach and jetty with missing portions are around the mini point. The park extends all the way to the large Wind Point and lighthouse.

Wind Point is the farthest east we have been since Sheboygan. She got her name from sticking out into Lake Michigan and collecting big winds. We were lucky on our day, we had just a gentle wafting breeze and could fully relish Wind Point and her lighthouse. Wind

Point is the remnant of a prehistoric reef from when the lake was a sea. The natural point once had a T shaped pier and the remains do extend under the water line, so be careful of large boulders just underneath the lake surface. I almost ram into one as I am enjoying the view. . .opps.

And a view it is. A charming, classic lighthouse. The lighthouse tower stands over one hundred feet high and has been continuously lit since 1880. Her light shines over 19 miles eastward. She is one of the grandest, tallest and oldest still working lighthouses on the Great Lakes. Her light is a distinctive flashing pattern that initially used a mechanism of weights, and pulleys to rotate her enormous third order Fresnel lens. Unlike most lighthouses, the Wind Point lighthouse also had a second smaller light with a red lens that glowed from the window lower in the tower. This light was a fifth order Fresnel lens and was used to warn mariners of the Racine Reef.

The lighthouse grounds are cozy, peaceful gardens with paved walkways, and picnic tables. A delightful rest stop on our paddle. The lighthouse is open to tour on the first Sunday of each summer month. However, the gardens and picnic area are free to enjoy every day. Another wonderful spot to sojourn and swim at their beach, and bask in the glory of this gorgeous lighthouse.

We paddle further northwest along the sloping shoreline. Past sprawling homes with extraordinary views of the lake. Mini rock pile jetties signify private beaches. However, a series of eleven of these stone piles is the quiet campus of the Siena Center. The facility and grounds are a religious retreat center to renew hope, peace, and harmony. A perfect time to stop, and refresh our bodies and spirit. Their guiding vision encourage us to "come to where the spirit stirs the waters". The Siena Center offers retreats that include solitude, the wilderness of loss, and soul searching. The natural prairie, woodside paths, and the beautiful cobblestone beach of Lake Michigan presents us an opportunity for some tranquil meditation and to thank our higher power for this wonderful day.

Just past the Siena Center, is the old Western Publishing building. Remember reading Little Golden Books as a child? The Poky Little Puppy, Scuffy the Tugboat, and the Little Red Hen, were some of the original titles. Over a billion of these inexpensive books were printed right here in Wisconsin. After over 50 golden years, the books are still being printed, but by Penguin Random House now.

A series of condos, Waters Edge, are located along the shoreline bluff. Then high sandy clay bluffs that are tree lined with home set back and often not even noticed. As we near Chapla Park, there is one home right on the edge. Its patio is already hanging out over the abyss, with one corner of the home with the foundation exposed. Yikes! I'm sure you could get a good cheap deal on that home. . .

Chapla Park is a quarter mile long park up on the hillside highland. Nice green grass parkland with benches for folks to appreciate the panorama of Lake Michigan. However, under the hill there is a rock pile groin, which means no ability to land on shore.

But don't despair, right after Chapla Park is Cliffside County Park and campgrounds. The park itself is situated on the plateau above the sliding bluffs. For three-quarters of a mile, there are short sand and cobblestone beaches under the bluffs. Cliffside was our last planned rest break area. It would be a difficult climb down from the park above, so we are pretty much guaranteed our own private picnic beach. Lovely vista as we chill out, and grill out. After lunch, time for a splendid swim. Again, a wonderful Wisconsin day to wander down the Lake Michigan coast line.

Don't go too far and pass Cliffside Park, as next to the park is the Rohner Law Enforcement Training Center. You know, the guys with guns. Yup, this is where they train. Not only do they train with guns here, they also have an explosive training area. Yes, where they set off explosives. Now, all of that stuff is up on the bluff and not down by the lake. But yup, too close for my comfort. As the land makes a small zigzag out into the lake, you are approaching the Racine County Line Rifle club. Yeah, more guns shooting area. Again, it's up on the plateau, but I for one, would skip landing on this beach area too.

The big industrial area is the Oak Creek WE Energies Plant. It is two, two plants in one. The Oak Creek Power Plant and the Elm

Road Power Plant comprising almost a mile of Lake Michigan shoreline. Both are coal-based power plants that operate twenty-four hours a day. They have a total of six steam turbines combined with four large chimneys that discharge water vapor only. The largest chimney is 550 feet tall!

The Oak Creek Power Plant, does share their land with us. On the north end is the WE Energies Fishing Pier with the emerald green railing. Great place for fishing and picnicking. Fisherman catch Coho and Chinook salmon, along with lake, brown, and rainbow trout. The fish are attracted to the slightly warmer lake temperatures in the discharge channel—a great place to see if we can find the large fish! WE Energies also offer access to the north beach for walking and for dogs, but no boat launching or swimming. The beach runs for a third of a mile.

North of the WE Energies beach is the Oakwood Cliff and Trails. An open field on the plateau with a rock pile groin on the coast line for a half mile. The old closed, Fitzsimmons road borders the Oakwood Cliff and Trails area. The walking trail follows the supposedly haunted old drag strip road, with rumors of cars flying off the bluff at the end into the lake. Ooooh, eerie. . .

We arrive at Bender Park. The harbor is to the three-lane boat ramp, but we choose to go around and land on the north side at the beach. Small sandy beach, but nicely nestled with a little protection by the harbor wall. Patriotic flag flapping in the breeze at the end of the wall flanked by the boat ramp and beach. Easy carry of the kayaks through the cream-colored deep sand. Diving into the flawless beach water, we relax, loosen up, and stretch out after our paddle. Truly, a wonderful Wisconsin summer day! Can we stay a little longer, can we?

Logistics:

Bender Park beach, Oak Creek:
42.8677, -87.8395. 4300 E. Ryan Road.
No fee for beach launch and nice restrooms.

Cliffside County Park, Caledonia:
42.8247, -87.8141. 7320 Michna Road. No launch site, due to high unstable bluffs, but shallow beach for a rest break on a calm day.

Wind Point Lighthouse, Racine:
42.7811, -87.7576. 4725 Lighthouse Drive. This is listed as an emergency launch site. No fee, restrooms available.

Shoop Park Beach, Racine:
42.7766, -87.7612. 4510 Lighthouse Drive.
No fees, but no restrooms either.

Parkway Beach, Racine:
42.7644, -87.7772. 1 S. Vincennes Circle. Steps down to the beach.
Parking on the shoulder of the road. No fee, no restrooms.

Racine Zoo Beach, Racine:
42.7802, -87.7813. 2075 Michigan Boulevard.
Street parking, and then carry boats down the paved Lake Michigan
Pathway to the beach. No fee, no restrooms.

Racine North Beach, Racine:
42.7401, -87.7779. 1501 Michigan Boulevard.
Busy parking lot, but there is some parking along Hoffert Drive also.
Restrooms at the beach house. No fee.

Lake Michigan Pathway Kayak Launch, Racine:
42.7367, -87.7786. 1 Barker Street.   At the end of the road, what
looks like private area for the RYC (Racine Yacht Club), there is
public access to follow the Lake Michigan Pathway road around the
Club to a whole new parking area! Nice kayak launch in the Racine
Harbor! No fee, no restrooms.

Shipwreck location:

H.L. Whitman: 42.7703, -87.7707. A two-masted schooner lies 7
to 10 feet deep about 500 feet off shore, .5 miles north of Parkway
Beach in Racine, or .5 miles south of Shoop Park.

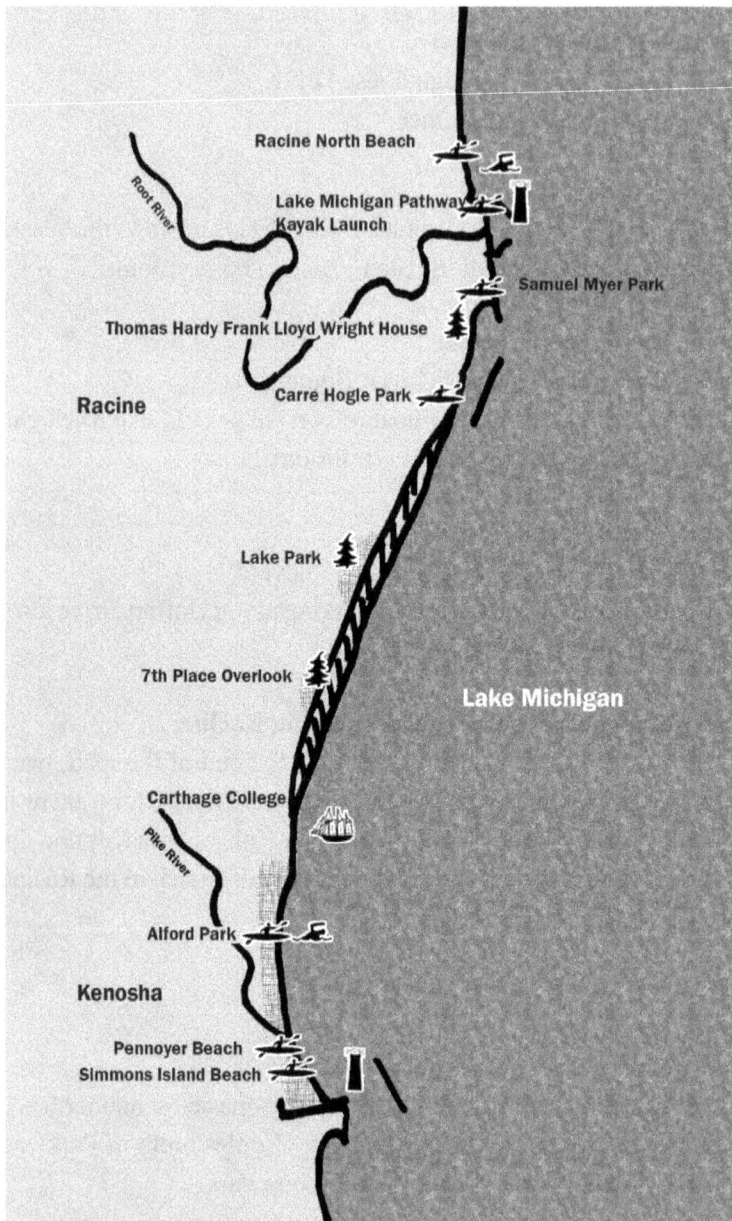

Racine North Beach

Lake Michigan Pathway
Kayak Launch

Samuel Myer Park

Thomas Hardy Frank Lloyd Wright House

Carre Hogle Park

Root River

Racine

Lake Park

7th Place Overlook

Lake Michigan

Carthage College

Pike River

Alford Park

Kenosha

Pennoyer Beach
Simmons Island Beach

Leg 18

Overlooks

Racine to Kenosha

*With Racine's Top Ten beach, Overlooks,
and Kenosha beach*

10 miles

Tour radiant Racine, by her coastline, "she's cooler by the Lake". Racine is famous for her top ten Great American beach, and a Frank Lloyd Wright masterpiece home, best seen by the lake. Then lofty Lake Michigan cliffs between Racine and Kenosha. Which brings us to Alford Park in Kenosha, a serene beach on the northside of Kenosha. Bluffs and beaches, what else could you ask for?

The only way to actually shorten this paddle is start at Samuel Myers beach in south Racine, which will decrease the paddle to 8 miles. But, in doing that, you also cut out the best beach. Between Racine North Beach and Kenosha's Alford Beach is high bluff overlooks and lots of rip rap shoreline—a mumble jumble of huge rocks.

A little nervous about this day, forecast is for 75% rain, and on our drive to Racine, it pours so hard we have to slow way down. As I groan, Rick said "this water is not going to fall again today", I reply "being a bit optimistic aren't we. . .". But as luck would have it, he is correct with his glass half full sunniness, the day turns into a 75% sunny day!

As we launch our kayaks, the sky is considering clearing up and creates a delightful canvas. Both north and south, dark storm clouds still broil, whereas, in the middle a hole opens and the sun begins to filter through. A hopeful start to our day.

Racine offers a lot of choices for a launch beach. Racine Zoo Beach is the most northern beach. You can park on Michigan Boulevard and roll, or carry, your boats down the paved path to the nice beach. This is a quieter beach area, and perhaps if you listen hard, you'll hear the zoo animals up on the bluff. The Raptor Roost and the Bear Ridge areas are closest to the beach. But the zoo also has rhinos, zebras, giraffes, kangaroos, tigers, and monkeys, so you may hear a whole chorus of jungle sounds emanating from above.

A third of a mile south, is Racine's North Beach. This beach is special. North Beach has been named a Top Ten Family Friendly Beach in Parents Magazine, with a Kid's Cove, huge playground with a really fun nautical theme. Also, North Beach is a Certified Blue Wave Clean Beach with over a third of a mile of soft groomed sand beach and crystal-clear water. It was voted a Top Ten Best Freshwater Beach in USA Today, and a Great American Beach by Midwest Living magazine. A Caribbean equal, the Beachside Oasis actually has potted palm trees in summer. Tables with umbrellas for drinks and munchies, and hammocks or colored beach chairs. Lots of sand volleyball courts. Truly a slice of paradise.

Just north of Racine's breakwater pier with the Lake Michigan Pathway trail, is another beach area with a parking lot behind it. To get to the Lake Michigan water trail small craft launch site, drive behind the Racine Yacht Club. There is a little parking lot with a matted launch area—made just for us! We would have missed it,

but an incredible park employee pulls up and tells us about this hidden launch that "no one knows about". From here, you can paddle west into the Root River, or out towards the Racine lighthouse.

Going around the north breakwater, almost to the end, is the Racine Breakwater lighthouse. The light is an insignificant small red square light tower, up on stilts with a hexagonal lantern room. Initially built of wood in 1924, in the typical style for a pier light, the tower was covered in steel plating for protection. It had a fourth order Fresnel lens. Now decommissioned, it is lit only by floodlights at night, and the official pier light is a single tower on the south pier.

The real lighthouse story of Racine is the story of the Racine Reef Lighthouse located a mile off shore south of the mouth of the harbor. After many disasters with ships hitting the Racine reef, the town built a castle lighthouse on the reef. Honestly, a castle, who does that? Constructed with a steel frame, the Victorian castle was two stories with double hung windows, and four taller gables on each corner with a decorative oval window in the top triangle of the gables. In the center was an octagonal tower with windows on every other side, then topped with a round lantern room with a circular walkway around it. Sounds gorgeous right? Perfect for the city known as the "Belle City"—beautiful in French. But. . . don't bother kayaking out to the castle lighthouse. It is gone. After it was automated, it fell into neglect and demolished in 1961, this unique picturesque lighthouse, lost to history. Thankfully, the Fresnel lens was saved and is in the Racine Heritage Museum.

Kayaking around the harbor's entrance and down the south side of the breakwater is the Racine Overlook and the Christopher Columbus Causeway. Tucked into the corner is another small harbor for the Festival Park boat launch. There is a concession stand here, Smoke'd On the Water, if you are in need of substances. The large orange roofed building is the Racine Civic Center Festival Hall, a venue for symphonies, shows, weddings, and concerts. Behind that site, is the Harris Rotary Park with a large outdoor park with covered shelter for events and a large white Genesis tent. Just south of the buildings is a sprinkling fountain, Racine's Splash Pad for tots, and wild grownups (but I'm not naming names. . .oh the heck, of course it's me), to play in on hot summer days.

As we follow the shoreline of protective boulders is an extended grass and tree lined park, Pershing Park. There are wide open green areas for soccer and picnics, then a bunch of brown curves, loops, and half-pikes of the B3 Skate Park for use by skateboarders, inline skaters, and BMX bikers. The tan buildings behind the park is Gateway Technical College. One of the largest of the state's technical colleges, it has over 25,000 students serving three counties.

Following along the shoreline with us, is the Lake Michigan Pathway. This ten-mile bike and walking trail started in north Racine at Melvin Avenue following the Michigan Boulevard past the Racine Zoo, North Beach, the harbor area, and now continues along the shoreline with us along Pershing Park. At the end of Pershing Park, the shoreline rock wall continues, but the shore behind it does not. This is the Samuel Myer Park. We can see the small emerald green hexagonal roof of the gazebo pavilion. This park is another easy launch site for small non-motorized watercraft with a short carry. Or just a gentle rest break beach.

This hidden beach area, has another surprise, the Thomas Hardy Frank Lloyd Wright house. Wright designed two buildings for the S.C. Johnson Company in Racine, and this house. The Hardy house is considered to be Wright's masterpiece house, a classic Frank Lloyd Wright prairie school design. Built in 1905, it was intended to fit the site—a dramatic sloping hill, with the home joined with the bluff. This two-story home has an unassuming front; terra cotta stucco with narrow square windows on top. It is a private home, so no tours. Lucky for us, the best view is from the protected waters of Lake Michigan where the back of the house has long, tall, high windows connected to a walkout terrace with an expansive view of Lake Michigan. It is the last home before the green grassy hillside, so it is hard to miss viewing it from the water, although there are some trees for privacy.

When the breakwater ends, we spy what looks like a rock island in the lake, this is just the continuation of the breakwater. We choose to stay closer to shore and appreciate the calmer waters. On shore, the uninterrupted grassy hill lingers above the pile of limestone sarsen boulders. At the conclusion of the shoreline protective groin is the last of the shoreline parks of Racine, the Carre-Hogle Park. A pleasant picnic area with tables and shade trees, with a little spit of land providing a mellow landing spot.

As the breakwater ends, the rocky shoreline continues, this time with houses on the bluff. After about a dozen homes, the lawn covered hillside continues over the rocky shoreline, along with our biking friends on the Lake Michigan Pathway. The pathway turns inland around the Racine Waste Water Treatment Facility. The tanks, pools, and the ball shaped structure are all needed to clean a lot of water, about 20 million gallons of water a day. It only takes approximately twenty hours to clean the 20,000,000 gallons of waste water before it is discharged, clean, back into Lake Michigan.

Kayaking along the coast as it gradually slopes to the east, we follow the bluff past an old industrial site with a steel fortification and walled canal. Then tall sandy bluffs with homes in Mount Pleasant perch above. As Sheridan Road nears the edge of the bluff is Lake Park. All we see is an insurmountable heap of jumbled rocks with a wildflower and shrub lined cliff. It is a narrow strip of a park with a small playground on the cap. The neighborhood kids, have cleared a single-breasted trail down to the mass of giant stones on the shoreline. Definitely not a rest area for us on the coast.

So instead, we sneak into a little belly of a bay under the bluff below the homesteads above. A pebble beach with the looming clay cliff with holes in sandy top. Made by cliff swallows with square tails, or perhaps Kingfishers? The birds never hang out with us long

enough for a photo op, the sneaks stay secreted in their nests. We lounge on a drift wood log, snacking on sandwiches and vegies. A beautiful view. Our quiet lake in front of us. Strolling the beach, finding multicolored stones and beach glass pebbles. A rock retaining heap with a tiny tree growing as it leans on the hillside. The sky, still working on clearing, with clouds just above the horizon coloring the lake a deeper aqua hue. We steal a quick swim off our forbidden beach. Fresh and clean, invigorating.

Then onward we go, paddling south along the cliffs. Two miles of homes resting over the bluffs. The sloping precipices, almost always with a layer of rocks on the shoreline to protect their craggy hill. Sometimes, each home has defined their property with an outpouching of the rocky pile to protect their shore. Infrequently, the homeowner has defied nature and added a stairway or path down to the shore. On occasion, a deck will dangle out above the overhang, offering an incredible view showcasing Lake Michigan.

We surprise a couple of teenagers in their skivvies, jumping off a cement jetty. Perhaps they thought we couldn't tell they were in their underwear. I was just happy we hadn't surprised them in their birthday suits! On the shore, they had built a lovely trellis with drift wood, providing a sun shade over rocks aligned as chairs—flat on the bottom, with a straight up boulder behind for the back rest. A perfect natural beach cabana.

After another row of lake homes, we spot it. Our favorite residence. Sitting above a natural rock and pebble beach. A sloped hill wrapped completely in brilliant green shrubbery, then a tree lined lot. Sitting high above the shrubbery is our preferred lake home—a true tree fort! Nestled in a huge maple tree, resting in the crook of the large branches, with limbs actually shooting through the outer walls. A simple unpainted timbered tree fort. We can imagine, unwinding in "our" fort, the tree gently swaying in the breeze, surrounded by windows to revel in the Lake Michigan view. Ahh— and it might be in our price range.

As we cross the county line at 1st Street, we enter Kenosha County. The Pottawatomi Native American name was Kenozia, "place of the Pike". Lake Michigan is one of the homes of the Northern Pike, whose average size is 20 inches long and can weigh more than 30 pounds. Sporadically, when kayaking, we'll get a glimpse of a huge pike swimming below us.

We pass a grassy plain above the rocky coast with a large structure with a red patio awning. This is the Hob Nob Restaurant, which is an upscale supper club with an incredible view of the lake. There is, however, no lake access. They do offer outside patio seating to relax and enjoy the stunning vista of Lake Michigan after kayaking.

Just three quarters of a mile later is an easily missed 7th Place Overlook. A meadow plateau atop the straggly bluff. A really timeworn old stone fire oven is the most interesting feature at the park. Easy to vision some great barbecue coming out of this stove. Drooling just at the thought. . .

A few country family hotels and inns intermix with homes as we enter the city of Kenosha. The Surfside Bowling Center is a square building up on the ridge obscured by pickle and cucumber green leafy trees.

As the homes peter out after 17th Street and where Carthage College campus begins, start looking down, the M. Courtwright shipwreck looms below. She was a two-masted wooden schooner that had previously collided with another schooner, but lived to tell the tale. However, in a November gale of 1871, she was not so lucky. The M. Courtwright became waterlogged and was abandoned. The crew was rescued by life saver volunteers.

Then large glass fronted school buildings loom on top of the bluffs. They are part of Carthage College, the ala mater of Rick's daughter. The Science Center, Library, Café, and dorm halls, along with the spire of the Chapel are located on the shoreline. Carthage is a private liberal arts and science college. They are so fond of their location; it is designated a wildlife sanctuary and arboretum. Besides the breathtaking views of Lake Michigan, the petite Pike River winds through their grounds, both of which offers freshwater research courses. Carthage boasts itself as "Midwest nice" and celebrates their lake shore with classes on the beach, lake views from the labs, sunrises from the dorm rooms, and studying to the sounds of the lapping waves.

We follow the lapping waves, to the beach at Alford Park in Kenosha, situated right after the breakwater rocky shoreline of the college. We gently land on our own slice of beach with a huge drift log to lay out our wet PFD's, and cockpit skirts. Rick follows the beach trail to the parking area where his scooter awaits. As he completes the shuttle, I have time for surveying the beach. The beach is three quarters of a mile long, traveling all the way to the mouth of the Pike River. And after the mouth of the River, the beach continues along Pennoyer Park for another quarter mile. The sand beach is 250 feet deep with a few rocks and pebbles along the shoreline. Even on this charming sunshiny day, it is a quiet and peaceful area. A pleasant beach for a lovely afternoon swim.

Logistics:

Racine North Beach, Racine:
42.7401, -87.7779. 1501 Michigan Boulevard.
Busy parking lot, but there is some parking along Hoffert Drive also.
Restrooms at the beach house. No fee.

Lake Michigan Pathway Kayak launch, Racine:
42.7367, -87.7786. 1 Barker Street. At the end of the road, what looks like private area for the RYC (Racine Yacht Club), there is public access to follow the Lake Michigan Pathway road around the Club to a whole new parking area! Nice kayak launch in the Racine Harbor! No fee, no restrooms.

Festival Park, Racine Civic Center, Racine:
42.7284, -87.7792. 800 Pershing Drive.
Fee to launch, restrooms available.

Samuel Myers Park, Racine:
42.7185, -87. 7787. 1 11th Street.   Parking lot, no fee.

Thomas Hardy Frank Lloyd Wright House, Racine:
42.7164, -87.7819. 1319 S. Main Street. The home is private, please respect their privacy and view the home from the water or walk or drive past it.

Carre-Hogle Park, Racine:
42.7101, -87.7821. 1729 Main Street. Parking area, no restrooms, no fee. This is considered an emergency access due to a rocky shoreline.

Alford Park Beach, Kenosha:
42.6127, -87.8196.   Alford Park Drive, Kenosha.   No fee, no restrooms by beach.

Pennoyer Park and Beach, Kenosha:
Pennoyer Park Pike River access: 42.6068, -87.8193.
Pennoyer Park Beach: 42.6045, -87.8178.   3601 7th Avenue. Parking area to access the mouth of the Pike River.   No fee, restrooms!

Shipwreck location:

M. Courtwright: 42.6265, -87.8171. A two-masted schooner lies 10 feet deep, 450 feet off shore by Carthage College campus, just south of 17th Street.

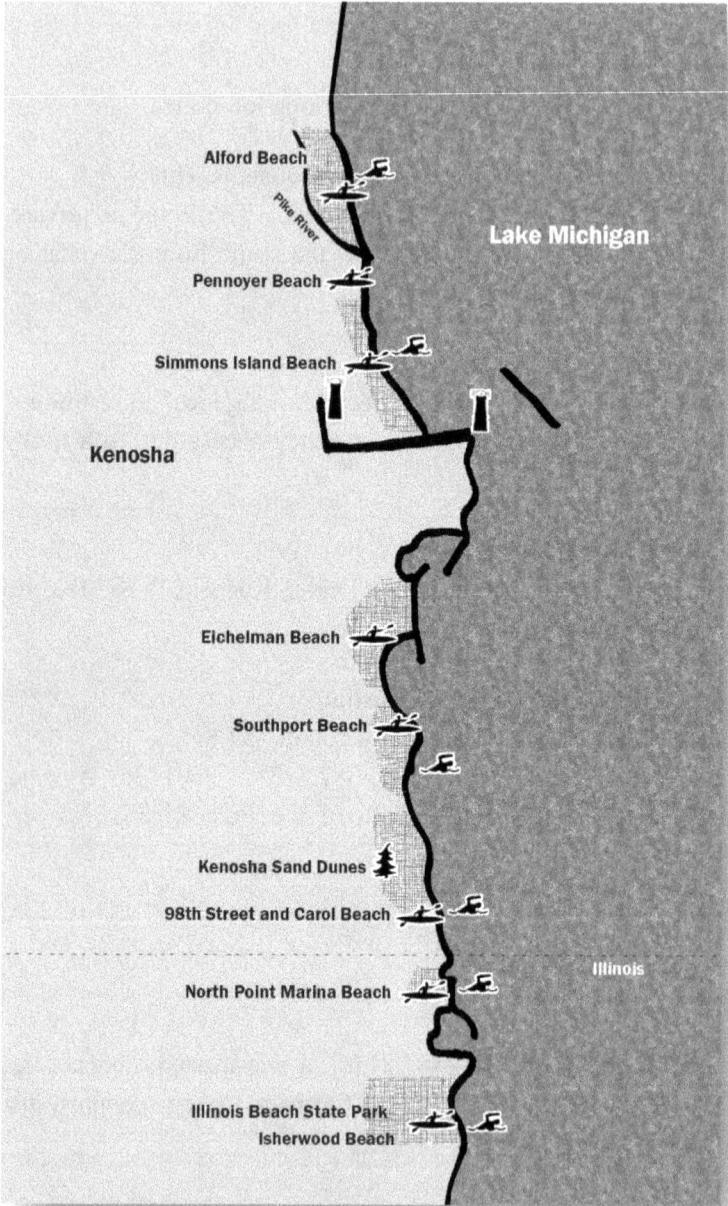

Leg 19

Into Illinois

Kenosha to North Dunes Beach, Illinois

With Kenosha harbor, lighthouses, and beaches to Illinois

11 miles

Into Illinois! Fun exploration of Kenosha, a vibrant city with a great harbor area and two landmark lighthouses. A spattering of beaches almost every mile as we paddle to Illinois. Then, into Illinois and North Dunes Nature Preserve, the beginning of six miles of parkway and beaches in Illinois!

The midpoint of our paddle is Wisconsin's 98th Street Lake Michigan's water trail public access with about a 100-feet of sandy beach smooshed between beach homes. Another mile south brings you to the more frequented Prairie Shores/Carol Beach. Another way to shorten the paddle, would be to start south of Kenosha at Eichelman Park beach and kayak to the Illinois line at North Point Marina beach for a 6.5-mile paddle.

Rick and I woke up so excited to start the day's paddle. "We are going to Illinois today!" It has been several years of paddling, starting in Green Bay and going first north up the coast of the Door County peninsula about 100 miles. Through Deaths Door we paddled into Lake Michigan proper. And now, the almost 300 miles south. . .and finally we will enter Illinois! Hip, hip hurray!

Forecast is for a perfect sunny day with light winds and up to one-foot waves. Simple, dimple! We chat excitedly as we drive to North Dunes Nature Preserve in Illinois to drop off the chase "car" Rick's trusty scooter. We walk the beach path to the shore line. . .and our jaws drop. Intense noisy crashing breakers greet us. "Oh, my gosh, those are big waves" I shout over the clamor. "We can handle them" Rick replies. "Oh. . .my gosh, what happened to the one-footers?" I retort. Rick rechecks the forecast, it is sticking with the light wind for all day. "Those are big white caps" I again remark. "Yeah, two to four footers" Rick accounts. "Oh. . . my gosh" is all I can come back with, my enthusiasm waning.

We drive up to Alford Park beach in the northern section of the city of Kenosha. The stunning sandy beach is a wonderful for swimming and relaxing. Sometimes a quiet and peaceful beach with occasional rocks and cobblestone. Quiet? Not so much today. Crashing waves here too. . .what a surprise.   "Well", Rick surmises, "a good example of Lake Michigan making its own weather". Thanks for sharing Rick, did I mention, "Oh. . .my gosh, those are big waves!"

Evidently, Rick agrees, as we decide to go back to Pennoyer Park, just south of the mouth of the Pike River, at the southern end of Alford Park beach. Rick's ingenious plan: put into the delta of the Pike River, skirt up, and then challenge the "oh my gosh big waves". Have to admit, I was still a little apprehensive about this whole paddling plan, wondering about renting bikes instead? But nope, there I was, skirting up and facing the lion's mouth of the surf waiting to eat me up. Off we go, side by side, partners in crime through the wall of waves, one crash, second wallop, third collision of a white cap over my head, and then we are through. Not so bad, if you attack head on. Fine then. . .onto Illinois!

Pennoyer Park offers another quarter mile of sandy beach shore. More of a laid back, quiet quality time at the lake, type of beach. Me, however, I was riding the waves, getting a feel for the sloshing back and forth, big wave, pause, whopping whitecap, and then a short lull. Feeling more comfortable with every stroke. I got this!

J F Kennedy Park follows immediately after Alford and Pennoyer beaches. Rock pile groin that I don't want to crash into, then a bright green grass area for a half mile. Pretty much most of Kenosha's lakeshore, 90% to be more exact, is public parks, beaches, and trails.

The Pike Bike Trail is following us along the shoreline. It traverses the length of the Alford beach and north through Carthage College. The bike route also goes south through Pennoyer Park, JF Kennedy Park, Simmons Island Beach, up and around the Harbor and Park, Eichelman Beach, Wolfenbüttel Park, and south to the Kemper Center historic site and art center. The bike path is over 10 miles long, mostly along the Lake Michigan shoreline.

For us, as the rock pile shore line ends, the Simmons Island Park beach begins. A half mile of groomed soft sand beach all the way to the North Pier. Another Lake Michigan pearl. This park offers frequent community events and the beach has a historic olde bath house. Built in 1934 as a Federal Works Project during the Depression, the landmark bath house is in the Tudor style with rock walls, and half timbers and stucco in the gables.

Simmons Island also has our first Kenosha lighthouse, although it is difficult to see from the lake. The Southport Lighthouse sits 1000 feet behind the shoreline, hidden by the Kenosha Water Utility building. It is called Southport, as it was the first port north of

Illinois in Wisconsin. Built of yellow Milwaukee cream brick, it is conical in shape with a replicated lantern room. Originally it housed a fourth order Fresnel lens, but was decommissioned when the lens was transferred to the lighthouse on the north pier. This lighthouse, had several unique keepers. After one of the lighthouse keepers died, his widow and daughter were the pioneering female lighthouse keepers. The last of the Southport lightkeepers was a one-armed man, having lost his arm in a Civil War battle.

We head out to the end of the north pier, which to our delight has a 600-foot breakwater barrier. Ahh. . .a lull in the swells. Time for Rick to take a swig of his coffee. Who brings a coffee cup on a whitewater Lake Michigan paddle? Rick does. All smiles, I lift my water bottle to toast his coffee thermos and our day to paddle.

The breakwater gives us the opportunity to peruse the newer Kenosha lighthouse. In 1900 the pier finally culminated in its full length, and this lighthouse was erected. It has twelve circular tapered rings topped with a cylindrical lantern room and has the old Southport lighthouse's Fresnel lens. The color of the lighthouse was

painted brilliant red. Although the lighthouse is now an automated electric beacon, it still is the primary light for Kenosha. The lighthouse tower itself was sold and is now the Kenosha Lighthouse Art studio, and offers an artist in residence program with free admission to tour the artist's work during special events.

Welcome to Kenosha's fun and flamboyant harbor. If you head into the harbor, the south wall is the epicenter of Kenosha's Lake Michigan shoreline with Harbor Park and Celebration Place which hosts community events throughout the season. Activities include the Wisconsin Marathon, Taste of Wisconsin, Beer Border War Fest, Jazz and Blues Fests. There is a fountain and statue of Columbus, by a Kenosha artist. A trolley with restored streetcars, loops through the park on a two-mile circlet. The vintage streetcars, each have their own color and style. They offer a land based scenic tour of the Lake Michigan shoreline.

Following the south wall is the Art Walk Promenade, with a dozen sculptures. Every two years, the sculptures are switched and new ones brought in. My two favorites were the "Window" where you can frame in the red north pier lighthouse, and "Night in Tunisia" which reminds me of the sails of a schooner in the wind. During the sailing season, Kenosha's own authentic wooden tall ship, the Red Witch, docks on the south harbor wall. With a red mahogany hull, she is a two-masted Great Lakes working schooner, a replica from the mid-nineteenth century. When in full sail she has 2500 square feet of sail blowin' in the wind.

At the end of Harbor Park are two museums, the northern museum is the Civil War Museum which focuses on the perspective of the war from the folks in the upper Midwest states. Over a million men from this region served in the Union Army. There are personal stories, photos, and narratives, including three letters from Caroline Quarlis, the first known fugitive slave conducted through the Wisconsin Underground Railroad to freedom in Canada.

The southern museum is the Kenosha Public Museum. One exhibit is "The Wisconsin Story" where you can experience the change in climate from the Ice Age, and the lives of Native Americans in Wisconsin. One of the mysteries at the museum, is the story of their two mammoths, both found in Wisconsin in Kenosha County. They are the largest and most complete mammoths excavated in all of North America. Both of the mammoths have been carbon dated to be 14,500 years old. There are marks made by tools on the bones, indicating both of the mammoths were butchered by humans. Thus

demonstrating, that humans were in Wisconsin and the Western Hemisphere, a 1000 years earlier than previously thought.

The western end of the harbor is the Navy Memorial Park. The interesting artifacts here are an anchor and a large deactivated—thankfully—torpedo. The white building with red roofs on the east side of the marina harbor, just past the Southport Lighthouse, is the Kenosha Coast Guard Station. It was first established in 1879. It received the first motor driven lifesaving boat on Lake Michigan.

Paddle back out of the harbor, and head south past Celebration Place and Harbor Park, and at the south end of the rock pile wall, is a circular patio on land, for folks to enjoy the lake panorama. A quick wave as we pass by.

Masses of masts stick up from the Southport Marina. It is a public marina with over 200 boat slips. They offer many amenities, but no boat launch. However, the Kenosha Splash Pad and Lakefront Park offers fun for the kiddos. There is an interesting feature in the playground, the Kenosha Harbor Chimney.

Adjacent is Wolfenbüttel Park. Gorgeous emerald green lawn and a crescent shaped enchanting gazebo with European flower beds. This park, flows into the Eichelman beach park, which has a partially protective breakwater rock wall. The groomed sandy beach would be a nice launch site for our Lake Michigan paddle. Interestingly, there is a World War I Howitzer cannon pointed out to sea at the beach park—are they expecting a pirate attack?

We paddle past the Kenosha breakwater and are back into the swirls and swells of Lake Michigan. On shore, is the beautiful Kemper

Center, popping up as we top each wave. The oldest building, is the Durkee Mansion, home of a Wisconsin United States Senator. Charles Durkee initially was a member of the Free-Soil Party, but switched to the new Republican Party that was founded in Wisconsin. In 1865 the home became a boarding school for young women. More school buildings were added and the Kemper School celebrated 100 graduating classes. After it closed, the Center was transferred to Kenosha County for a park and is now an Art and Conference Center. As we paddle past, we can see the Chapel and the Observatory dome. The chapel has stunning stained glass windows and a hand carved altar. The old auditorium has ornate windows and wrought iron railings on the balcony. Above the Conference Center is the Observatory dome, that houses an automated telescope and is used by Carthage College for astronomy courses. Along the coast, are flower gardens, a delicate white gazebo, and a walking/biking trail under the tree canopies. Many of the trees are ancient, as each graduating class planted a tree.

Onward we bounce amongst the seas, feel like I'm jumping on a trampoline. Past beautiful older lake homes, each with their own character. In a mile, we arrive at Southport Park beach. The 400-foot long beach is a mix of sand and cobblestone. It is unprotected from the waves and we decide it is "too much work" to attempt to land. The Southport Beach House is a stunning Art Deco colossal edifice. Built during the Depression as part of the New Deal to get the country back to work. They used recycled bricks creating a patchwork quilt look. Two Tudor style large chimneys grace the sky on either end, as two sets of matching stair case stepped windows bookend the gentle arches of the covered patio that faces the beach. Inside, the ballroom is beautiful marble with geometric ornamentation, a perfect setting for the frequent wedding events. I try to get a photo as I bob up and down in the swells, attempting to frame Rick against the picturesque backdrop. Mostly, I end up with wonderful pics of a wall of turquoise water. Finally, I give up and do a short video, with Rick occasionally popping up atop a swell. Great video. . .if you'd like to get a bit of sea sickness.

Southport Beach park also offers playground equipment, benches along the Pike Bike Trail, and an open-air covered picnic shelter. Just south of the park, is the Kenosha Waste Water Treatment Plant, with its domed recycling pond.

Bordering Southport Park from the trail that follows along the lake, is the Kenosha Sand Dunes. These give you a flavor of what the original shoreline was like. The dunes are part of the Chiwaukee Prairie State Natural Area that was created when glacial ice receded and Lake Michigan's water level was lowered in stages. This formed a series of ridges and swales along the shoreline. A trail runs the full length of the half mile shoreline dune. The glorious golden sand bluffs attract us, but there is great danger, especially today. To control erosion and protect the dunes, there is a large pile of rocks along the coast. One portion seems to have less boulders, but there are hidden rocks below the water surface. Might be possible to land on a very calm today, but not today.

 Just south of the Kenosha Sand Dunes, off of 86th Street is a Lake Michigan Water Trail public access. Nice bench with a great view, but the shore is rock lined. We paddle on, springing up and back down, vaulting up, and retreating back into the low of a swell. Rows of nice lake homes, many with their own rock jetties to protect their private beach shore. Rick is bob, I am bobble, challenging to stay within vision of each other.

A dozen side streets later, we get the drift (catch the pun?) of the 98th St Pleasant Prairie water trail access. This one is a keeper. Off street parking, short carry, nice sand and cobblestone beach. 200 feet of your own paradise. Rock pile on the north end and a stubby concrete jetty on the southern end. Love it!

Less than a half mile later we arrive at Edithton Beach. Truly a misnomer. Old cement steps angle out into the lake. Perhaps when the lake levels are low, there is sandy beach after the steps. But it is a nice, quiet grassy area to enjoy the shore and the lake vista from land. And the steps are pleasant to relax on. . .on calmer days. At the southern end of Edithton Beach is Barnes Creek.

Just a couple of homes south is another public access at 102nd Street, but this again is a rocky shoreline. Just after a few more paddle strokes, is Lakeshore Park. Another nice viewing spot, with organized concrete steps and rocks, with underwater cement strips skirting out from the shoreline. Lakeshore Park is a quarter mile long and culminates at Carol Beach, in Pleasant Prairie.

Carol Beach is a sandy beach with a rock lined edge when it abuts the grassy area. The sign at the beach is now listed as Prairie Shores Beach. The depth of the sandy beach is dependent on Lake Michigan water levels, but should be navigable on most days. This is the largest sand beach along this day's paddle, and you should be able to find your own beach spot to relax and have a picnic.

Chiwaukee View and Phil Sander Park are the next public parks along our paddle. They are intersected by 116th Street. Both offer a grassy area with impressive views of Lake Michigan, but from the water, all I see are concrete steps with crashing waves crushing the shoreline. Yup, we'll steer clear of those today... There is however a short section of concrete-less, sandy beach at the southern end of the Phil Sander Park.

And the very last of the Wisconsin Lake Michigan water trail accesses is 122nd Street in Pleasant Prairie. Our last opportunity to touch the Wisconsin shoreline. Nope, the beach is huge crumbled concrete slabs and rocks. The shore continues to be pounded by white caps. We wave goodbye to Wisconsin.

The Illinois line is just a half mile south of 122nd Street. On the Wisconsin side, is Runaway Bay with the Prairie Harbor Yacht Club. This is an exclusive private club with a protective harbor entrance. As we are paddling past, three large sailboats motor out of the yacht club. Noisily pounding on each and every swell and white cap. As Rick watch the boats join us out on the lake, he calls out to the sailboat "Hey dude, are you sure? It's a little rough out here". I give him a "I can't believe you said that" look. Looking surprised, Rick jumps and shrugs "Oh yeah, we're out here!"

Yup, here we are dancing and grooving, swishing and swashing in the waves. Certainly, the lake swells had not gotten any smaller during the day. Into Illinois! Winthrop Harbor marks the Illinois line, with a public sand dune beach protected between the Wisconsin and Illinois harbor walls. This probably would have been a calmer exit spot for us on our wild water day. Winthrop Harbor, North Point Marina is the largest marina on the Great Lakes, with 1500 boat slips, and a large boat launch area. They have a passion for boating, in a serene lush setting. The restaurant, The Tropics, has been featured on the food show WGN's Chicago's Best, and has a large patio deck seating with delightful views of the marina.

We can see it; we can see it! The North Dunes Nature Preserve! Actually, the nature preserve starts right after the marina, but we have chosen to land one mile later at Isherwood Beach, the largest depth of sandy beach. Rick is on his own as he heads in to challenge the two to four-foot crashing waves, twists sideways and slides onto the beach. He jumps out and waves me in. Deep breath, and here I go "just ride the waves" I whisper to myself over and over as I hear the booming of the surf as I head into the beach. Doing good, doing good, then suddenly I'm breached by the waves and slide into shore, leaning into the wave to prevent capsizing. Doing good, I keep sliding south along the shore. . .straight towards children lounging at the edge of the water line enjoying the splashing waves. A wave of terror attacks me as I realize the speed I'm still moving at, straight towards their legs. I quickly climb out of the cockpit to stop my boat. Right in the nick of time!

Quickly we move the kayaks up onto shore, away from the crashing waves. We hug, paddle lift, high five, and celebrate our safe landing and kayaking into Illinois! I offer to empty our holds of all our safety gear, dry out everything, and encourage Rick to head back with the scooter to retrieve the car. "I'll take care of everything". As Rick kicks through the sand heading to the parking lot, I realize what I just said. Yup, my kayak has three inches of water in the cockpit, but Rick's has about six inches with at least half of the beach sand loaded down in the bottom of his cockpit.

After pumping out the water from both our boats, and scooping out the buckets of sand in Rick's boat, I hang all the gear to dry on a large drift wood drying rack. Finally, all my work is done, and I can swim and play! I love body surfing waves. I wade out into the surf, ready to dive into the next white cap, when the high wave scoops me up, down, and under and slides me up the sandy beach. I jump up quickly to avoid the next rip tide. A baseball size clump of sand in my hair and a three-inch stone in the top of my swim suit. Scoop the sand out of my swimsuit, trying to be discreet. . .as I dig deep into the butt of my swimsuit. Dang—now I gotta' get back into the surf, just to wash out my swimsuit. This time, I kneel down and dig my back foot into the sand under the water and lean into the wave, I'm washed around like in a washing machine, but manage to stay upright. Now to lean in and wash my hair out on the next white cap. Good enough. I give up, the waves are stronger than me, and I go to dry off on my drift wood seat. Down to picking sand and pebbles out of my hair, swimsuit, and brushing off the sand on my legs.

Logistics:

Alford Park Beach, Kenosha:
42.6127, -87.8196. Alford Park Drive. No fee, no restrooms.

Pennoyer Park and Beach, Kenosha:
Pennoyer Park Pike River access: 42.6068, -87.8193.
Pennoyer Park Beach: 42.6045, -87.8178.   3601 7th Avenue.
Parking area, no fee, restrooms at the beach!

Simmons Island Park Beach, Kenosha:
42.5909, -87.8128. 5001 4th Avenue.
Nice beach house with restrooms, no fee.

Eichelman Park Beach, Kenosha:
42.5797, -87.8131. 6125 3rd Avenue. Street parking, or use the
parking lot for Wolfenbuttel Park, with a long carry to the beach.
No fee, no restrooms.

Southport Beach, Kenosha:
42.5621, -87.8120. 7501 2nd Avenue. Parking area, restrooms.

1st Avenue Public Access to Lake Michigan, Pleasant Prairie:
42.5500, -87.8125. 8608 1st Avenue. Sign marks this emergency
access, recommend avoiding it due to rocky groin.

98th Street public access, Pleasant Prairie:
42.5303, -87.8134. 100 98th Street. Nice sand and pebble beach
for launching. Park on the grassy area. This is considered an
alternative access. No fee, no restrooms.

102nd Street public access, Pleasant Prairie:
42.5219, -87.8121. 10303 Lakeshore Drive, at the intersection of 102nd Street. Emergency access, due to a very rocky shoreline.

Lakeshore Park, Pleasant Prairie:
42.5201, -87.8119. 10510 Lakeshore Drive. Pull off parking area. Old rugged cement steps, so it is an emergency access, not recommended for launching.

Carol Beach, Pleasant Prairie:
42.5165, -87.8111. 10800 Lakeshore Drive. Off street parking. Mostly rocky groin, but sand beach past it into the lake (dependent on lake levels). No fee, no restrooms.

122nd Street public access, Pleasant Prairie:
42.5001, -87.8061. 108 122nd Street. Last possible Wisconsin launch site and it is an emergency access due to a rock and pebble beach. Unfortunately avoid this one. Bummer.

North Point Marina Beach, Winthrop Harbor, Illinois!
North Point Beach: 42.4877, -87.8039.
North Point Marina boat ramps: 42.4877, -87.8039. 701 North Point Drive. Spring Bluff Drive has closest parking to the beach.

North Dunes Nature Preserve/Isherwood Beach, Zion Illinois:
42.4751, -87.7981. 17th Street. Parking lot at end of road. Long carry to the very nice sandy beach! Outhouse restroom.

Kayak Wisconsin, Lake Michigan Water Trail

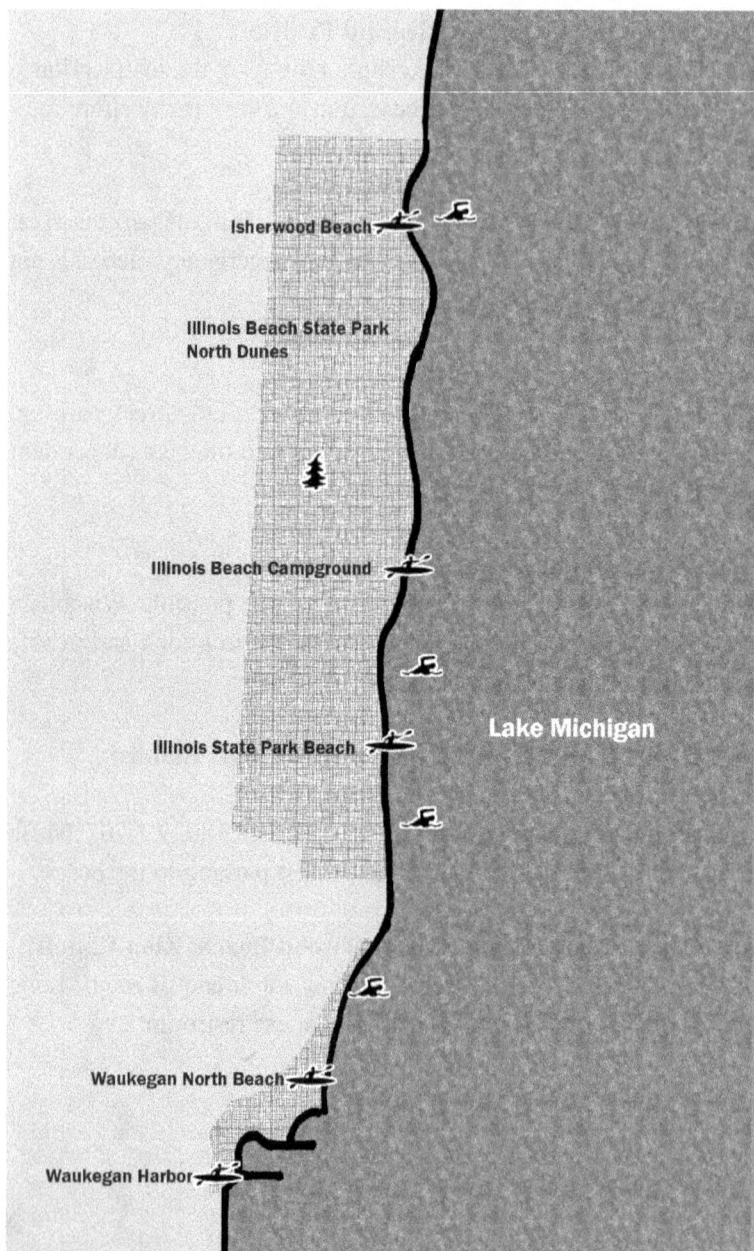

Isherwood Beach

Illinois Beach State Park
North Dunes

Illinois Beach Campground

Illinois State Park Beach

Lake Michigan

Waukegan North Beach

Waukegan Harbor

Leg 20

The Illinois Beach

Illinois Beach State Park to Waukegan

With Sand Dunes and more Sand Dunes

8 miles

This is it. This is it, if you want sandy beaches. These are the best sand dunes on Lake Michigan, in all of the state of Illinois. If we lived in Illinois, this would be our "home beach" to paddle. This is it, a cool impressive paddle!

And, you can absolutely and easily divide this paddle into two shorter paddles. South Beach is 5 miles north of Waukegan, with a nice parking lot and superb sandy shoreline to launch off. Since it is a decent long drive to Illinois—I know, I know, Illinois folks like to escape to Wisconsin and don't fret the drive "up north", but we have decided to skip the two-car drive and try Ubering or Lyfting for the shuttle. Umm, we'll see how that works. . .

We are so excited to return to complete our adventure, onto Chicago! We get up early for the drive south to Illinois and arrive at the beach at a perfect time. Perfect time for a thunderstorm that is. We have unloaded the kayaks when the storm blows in. "We'll give it a half hour to pass over" Rick says. "We'll give it another half hour". I am wet and cold, and both Chris and I vote to go buy a board game, go to the hotel and call it a day. "It is going to blow out to sea, honestly", Rick begs. "See, it is getting better already".

Not really, when I am looking at the radar. Long group discussion on which way that long skinny red blotchy radar storm is actually heading. Just saying, Rick is quite persuasive. "You are going to regret it, if we just give up today, it is going to turn into a nice day". Yeah, sure. . . "We can just start paddling and if it looks dice-y we can turn around, or get out at South Beach". Well, the lake is still fairly calm—even after the storm, the lake has no whitecaps, and what little waves there are, are less than one footers. OK, we'll give it a try. . .

Still, damp and cold, we push off of shore at Waukegan Municipal Beach. It's a lovely beach, great parking. Seems kind of iffy, as we drive in past industrial parks, but then it turns more marine-y, as we turn north on Seahorse Drive. Honestly, are there seahorses in Lake Michigan in Illinois? As we drive past Larsen Marine and drydocked sailboats, the beach opens up before us. Beautiful. You have your choice, North Beach Park, a natural sand dune beach, or on the south end of the parking lots, Waukegan Municipal Beach in the harbor. Actually, you have a third choice. You could drive straight into the Waukegan North Harbor, and just south of the US Coast Guard Auxiliary Station. There you will find a fine, free, canoe and kayak launch that is listed on the Illinois Lake Michigan Water Trail. Thank you, welcoming Waukegan!

At the harbor, there are also several concessions stands, Dockside Dogs which serves Chicago hotdogs and burgers, Dockside Ice Cream, and Dockside Deli. No picnic lunches needed!

The Waukegan Municipal Beach is inside the harbor walls, making it a safe sandy beach for children of all ages. We choose to launch close to the north harbor wall, where it is a little more natural with a bit of sand dunes and sea grass. Of course, there are only a few die-hard beach goers left on the beach when we launch with cloudy, still threatening skies, and a light drizzle. Bikini girl has waited out the storm in her red car, still being very optimistic—like Rick. The only other couple has walked out to the small north harbor light. The Waukegan Municipal Beach, is one of the locations for Stoke Riders, a kiteboarding instruction company. The kiteboarders are not at the beach today, since it is a damp, but calm day.

We launch and head out past the little green and white north lighthouse and harbor wall. Great surprise! No increase in waves out in the real Lake Michigan past the harbor after the storm. Waukegan's North Beach park is a gorgeous sand dune area with a large sand beach for a quarter of a mile after the north harbor wall, and a skinny beach that continues another quarter mile. The peacefulness of the beach gently lulls us into a relaxed mode. And already, I am whipping off my raincoat as the drizzle ends and breaks in the clouds begin. Rick gives me that knowing, smirky look. I growl back at him, not quite ready to admit he may have been correct in his weather prediction. . .

At the end of the beach are three cream chimneys, part of the Waukegan Generating Station. It is one of the oldest coal-burning plants in the nation. The spit of land with the white metal light tower at the end, is the harbor wall for the station. Stay further out on the lake as there are discharge pipes that can create churning waters.

After that, the Illinois Nature Preserve begins with over two miles of shoreline with no road access! This is a spectacular natural wildlife area where you can play on the shore for miles. How fun is this in Illinois! It is a dune savanna that was created thousands of years ago when Lake Michigan—then called the glacial Lake Chicago (how fitting is that for our paddles to Chicago?) was formed. The glaciers advanced and retreated, repeatedly causing dunes with swales or marshes between. These are the only remaining beach ridges left in Illinois and have the greatest plant diversity in all of Illinois. On top of the dunes are black oak trees mixed with pines. The dunes also support prickly pear cactus, perhaps a barefoot walk on the dunes should be avoided! In the marshes you may see big bluestem grass with purplish finger like spikes, and blue joint grasses with delicate pink flowers—who names these things? Deer and coyotes traverse the preserve along with owls and cranes. This worthy place was Illinois' first nature preserve and is now a national natural landmark.

We enjoy the windblown oak trees by the Dead River. Ahh, it is a perfect secluded beach for a stop for swimming, only shared with the lake gulls. The Dead River area is definitely not dead, but is so named because the river normally dead ends at the lake. Only during high water and lake surges is the dune overrun and the river flows out into the lake. I suppose it is time to admit Rick was right. . .as no storm are nearby and filtered blue sky joins us. We need to stop

and look for sun screen lotion. To Rick's credit, no bragging is heard.

After the Dead River, a trail comes to the shoreline. The southern portion of the Illinois Beach State Park offers 5 miles of trails, including the gravel Dead River Trail which is a tad over 2 miles. There is parking with a nature center 1000 feet inland. No one has ventured to the lake today, so we continue to have Lake Michigan and the Illinois Beach to ourselves. Is this the best kept secret in Illinois? We pass by Farnum Point, we see no cape coming out into the lake. Maybe when the lake water is at a lower level. . .

In the Illinois Beach State Park, the Three Fires of the Algonquin, Potawatomi, Chippewa, and Ottawa Nation's first lived here. By the 1600's the French explorers surveyed this part of the Northwest Territory. Then during the Civil War, the Northern section was Camp Logan, a Union prisoner of war camp. It was converted into an Army basic training camp during World War I and II. A perfect location for tank training, yup I can see why. On this day, we first spot beach goers and civilization as we approach the first structure, we've seen for over two miles—the southern unit of the Illinois Beach State Park and the Illinois Beach Hotel Resort.

The Illinois Beach Hotel Resort is snuggled right on the shoreline with grand views from the hotel rooms. Our view from the lake is all windows, the windows of the banquet hall and restaurant, with outside eating on the patio. This is where my sister, Becky, and I made our headquarters as we scouted the beaches from here to Chicago in prep for kayaking. Hard job, checking out all the beaches. . .but someone had to do it! We loved that you could walk out of the hotel and stroll immediately to the beaches.

As we pass the hotel, there is a small private beach for hotel guests. Then the next building with the flag flying, is the Illinois Beach State Park Office. After that, is a large sandy beach, a thousand feet long. This is the Southern Unit Beach of the Illinois Beach State Park. The beach is fine sand and pebbles. But when you have your pick of untouched beaches for miles, why stop at the established beach and share paradise? This is the beauty of kayaking; we can find our own quiet beach nirvana. This is our midpoint kayak launch site.

There is a rocky groin with some beach in front of it for the next mile. But behind the rocks is the dune, and behind the dune is the Illinois Beach State Park campground. This means that you could camp on your paddle to Chicago! The wooded sites of 302-330 are right by the dune, and there are natural trails leading to the shoreline. You can land on the beach and carry your kayaks over the rocky groin and to your campsite just 360 feet inland.

Along this stretch of shoreline, there are two nearly identical abandoned beach houses. Built in a mid-century modern style, they still look lovely. The have an eight arch roof line, some of the original pink paint, and vertical cement air flow walls to compliment the style. They are also important for us, because the southern beach house has a narrow cement ramp rather than the rocky groin, and the northern one, has a small sandy beach trail access. Both of the old beach houses have established trails that lead to the campground sites for easy access.

The hiking and biking trail of the Illinois Beach State park follows us along this shoreline, but now turns inland. You can bike from the southern section of the Illinois Beach State Park to the northern section by going inland and following the Zion Bike Trail.

The reason the trail detours inland is because the Zion Nuclear Power Plant sits smack dab between the southern and northern units of the Illinois Beach State Park. The nuclear power plant closed in 1998 due to rising costs. It previously served Chicago and northern Illinois. It is in the process of being decommissioned and getting the many spent fuel rods out of Zion safely. Some of the last buildings are the two twenty story high green capped concrete containment silos, which are being slowly dismantled.

Hosah Park is immediately north of the nuclear power plant. The North unit of the Illinois Beach State Park trail rejoins us by the shore with a boardwalk trail coming to the beach with an observation deck. You can land on the sandy shore and follow the trail inland for just 300 feet to a small shelter. There is a parking lot for the start of the trail by Fulton Avenue, but is a third of a mile to carry the boats to the water. So, I recommend this area as a nice resting beach stop rather than a put in.

From the boardwalk north there is almost a mile of beach that follows the old Burnett Avenue dirt biking trail. What is nice, is that there is again no car access to this area, so the beaches are generally ours to explore and enjoy. We have not seen a single biker or hiker on our day, just maybe, the huge storm this morning has kept them away...

We pass 17th Street with a rocky outcropping and a fenced industrial electrical cream brick building. Straight Kellogg Creek seeps out to the lake next. The next half mile of the shoreline is a mix of cubed rock groin. There are however a couple of trail accesses to the water's edge. Also, several small shelters and parking areas are inland. This is listed on the Illinois Lake Michigan water trail as a launch access, but I would skip it due to the stacked rocks on shore. Soon, we see a variety of metal walls. Close to the metal walls, there are obstructions out in the lake, so stay further off land.

As we 'round the metal wall, we arrive at Isherwood Beach. A pretty sand and pebble beach. We relax and have a snack. Then the moment comes to try out Uber or Lyft. But, Illinois Beach State Park, the northern unit, is kind of in no man's land. Even the road in, after 17th Street turns east, is marked as "unnamed road". A little difficult to tell a driver where to find us. Rick marks where he is standing when he requests a ride. . . and it works! The driver finds him! His driver has lived in Zion for several years and never knew the beach park was here. Oh, no, we have created a new beach goer!

As Rick enjoys having someone to tell our story to, as he shuttles back to get the car, Chris and I pack up and bring the kayaks and our equipment little by little to the parking area 550 feet inland. Whew! It has turned into a spectacular sunny day without a cloud in the sky! And hot. By the time, Rick arrives back and we load up boats and supplies, I am ready for another swim break. Rick and I wade into

the water. What? It is now freezing cold; the storm seems to have blown in ice water. It's too cold to swim. . .too hot not to try! Rick squeals "I'm a baby, I'm a baby", I laugh so hard I might wet my pants, but I too only make it thigh deep. Chris sits on the beach giggling at our antics!

Logistics:

Waukegan Harbor canoe and kayak launch, Illinois:
42.3599, -87.8243. 55 South Harbor Place, Waukegan. Free parking on street. Carry your boats to the boat ramps. On the south end by Government Pier is the free canoe/kayak ADA launch! Several concession stands are at the harbor.

Waukegan North Beach and Municipal Beach, Illinois:
42.3642, -87.8157. Sea Horse Drive, Waukegan. North Beach has a 1000-foot carry over the sand dunes. Or drive to the southern end of the parking lots for the Waukegan Municipal Beach. Stay north, close to the north harbor wall to avoid beach goers.

Illinois Beach State Park Southern Unit Beach access, Zion:
42.4306, -87.8046. 39101 Illinois Beach State Park, Zion, Illinois. Parking lot. Short carry to the beach (if you can park close!).

Illinois Beach State Park Northern Unit Beach access, Zion:
42.4715, -87.7977. End of 17th Street, Zion, Illinois. Parking area for Isherwood Beach. At least a 500-foot carry to the shoreline.

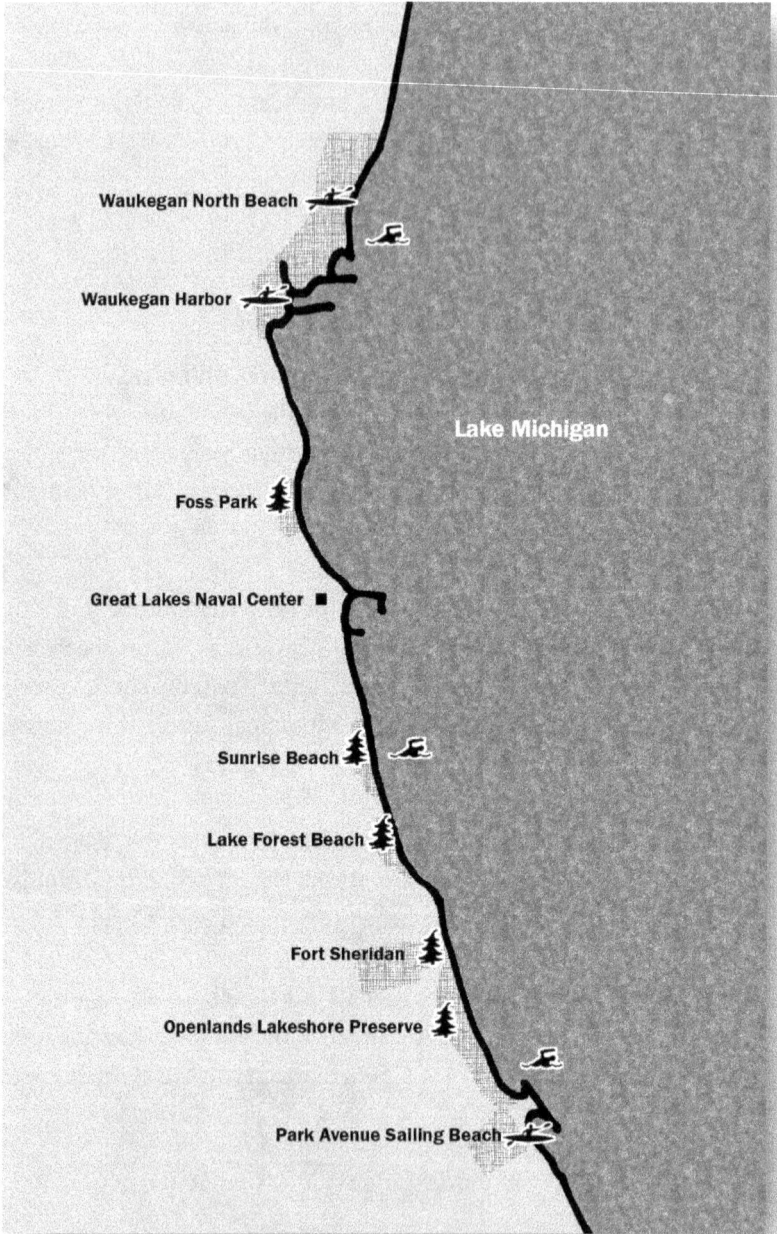

Waukegan North Beach

Waukegan Harbor

Lake Michigan

Foss Park

Great Lakes Naval Center ■

Sunrise Beach

Lake Forest Beach

Fort Sheridan

Openlands Lakeshore Preserve

Park Avenue Sailing Beach

Leg 21

Having a Ball

Waukegan to Park Avenue Beach, Highland Park

*With Great Lakes Naval Center and
Openlands Lakeshore Beach*

13 miles

An unexpectantly delightful paddle! A quiet and calm lightly textured lake surface. Turquoise clear water. The Openlands Lakeshore beaches has wonderful natural beauty for us. And gently bobbing playful balls floating on the lake, just waiting for us to scoop them up! Unexpectantly silly and delightful!

Paddling to Chicago takes some planning and preparation. Good news, there are lots of beaches along the way. Bad news, we can't use them, they aren't public—they are owned and physically guarded by each of the towns. Even if they are listed on the Illinois Lake Michigan Water Trail, you may not necessarily to be able to use their beach. Therefore, you need to make prearrangements to be sure you can launch or even land at the beaches. We launch at Waukegan Municipal Beach and paddle south. We are able to get permission to land at Sunrise Beach in Lake Bluff, 6 miles south from Waukegan. We also have special arrangements to land, launch, and park from Park Avenue Boating Beach, which is 6.5 miles south of Sunrise Beach in Highland Park. Unfortunately, no half way launch site.

Early start. Launch in welcoming Waukegan; Waukegan Municipal Beach. We launch inside the harbor, by the north harbor wall. Quiet, perfectly peaceful. We could launch a speck farther north on Waukegan's North Beach or a bit more south, by the boat ramps with a canoe and kayak launch for free! In Illinois no less!

We cross the harbor entrance that is serene this morning. Inside the harbor, is the Coast Guard Auxiliary. This civilian volunteer crew, an arm of the US Coast Guard, assists in education, safety, and search and rescues. Thanks for helping keep us safe.

As we pass the marina and harbor and head closer to shore, the shoreline is actually green! We are following the Metra train line and the shore is all tree lined. Very pleasant and tranquil for over a mile. Over the trees, the Abbvie company buildings dominate the skyline. Abbvie is a biopharmaceutical company that is a spinoff of Abbott Laboratories that develops health care technologies.

Foss Park and beach is up next. Named after a congressman from Illinois. He spearheaded the efforts to get the naval training center located to Illinois. Some folks have launched from Foss Park beach, but signs in the park indicate dangerous currents and no swimming. However, the beach is listed as a good place for searching for sea glass! Worn by waves and recycled by Lake Michigan, old bottles and jars that were carelessly discarded (hopefully in bygone days) are tumbled in the lake to form rounded colorful gems. These are fun to search for as you go beachcombing.

At the end of Foss Park, next to the beach, is the North Chicago Water Treatment Plant. The plant works every minute of every day to exceed EPA regulations using energy efficient equipment.

Next up is the huge Great Lakes Naval Training Center. This is the only Navy training center in all of the United States. Surprisingly, they chose this site, miles away from any ocean! Situated on over 1600 acres with 1,153 buildings, it has over 1.3 miles of shoreline. First, we can see the RV campground located on shore, followed by the teal roofed (matches the lake color) Navy Gateway Inn. Then it is Nunn Beach which offers recruits and personnel a wonderful Lake Michigan playground. No, we civilians cannot land here.

The Great Lakes Naval Training Center, the "Quarterdeck of the Navy" was founded in 1911. 40,000 recruits train here annually, with about 7,000 on base at any given time. During World War II, that numbered swelled to over 100,000 sailors training at the Center! Our Dad was one of them. He was one of the one million sailors that trained at Great Lakes throughout World War II.

It is exciting to see Building One, the Clock Tower building. It is one of the original buildings from 1911. Dad would have marched and prepared for service in the war in the Sea of Japan right here! The clock tower is red brick and stands over 300 feet high. The four, thousand-pound clock faces with the arches above, have Roman numerals and half-inch thick glass plates. It is easy to see why this is the Great Lakes Naval Training Center's iconic landmark. The Great Lakes Marina is next, which offers sporting equipment and boat rentals to Navy personnel. As we pass the Marina, we are now away from the restricted district of the Naval Academy.

We have been kayaking for four miles, and I want to swim. It is another two miles to one of the few beaches we are allowed to land on. But I want to swim! The lake is crystal clear, exquisitely calm, and is calling my name. Chris suggests we slip out of our boats and

swim right here. Great idea! Gives us the opportunity to practice the safety techniques of reentry into our boats. Rick paddles up next to me, and steadies my kayak so I can easily slip into the lake. With my legs dangling into the water, I realize it is a bit chilly! I hesitate. Rick says "I can't hold the boat for-ever, you need to commit!" OK. I let go and submerge like a submarine quickly. And just as hastily, I torpedo straight up and out of the water and try to land back into my kayak! Cold! Did I mention chilly? Chris laughs, and states "perhaps we should reconsider". "Nope, you have to commit! Jump in!" Rick and Chris join me in the refreshing dive. Really, really, crystal clear, I can see my toes! Rick admits, "I can see the hairs on my toes". Yeah, not so much for me Rick. . . but I swear I can see at least ten to twenty feet down. Amazing—and refreshing!

Our fun is not over, shortly after our stimulating swim, I spot a golden ball bobbing on the lake. I detour the slight way to capture my find. Matches my boat, a perfect banana yellow, knobby, toy ball. I wish I knew its story of how it found its way to my kayak.

Rick and I play catch. Well, I play catch. Rick appears to be intentionally spiking the ball to splash me! Just like a little brother.

The rest of the way to Sunrise Park Beach, are attractive homes situated on the hillsides. They sit on the shores of one of the greatest lakes in the world, but many of the huge homes also have swimming pools overlooking their views. We pass past the private Shoreacres Golf Course clubhouse with its perch above Lake Michigan. It is known for a soothing atmosphere with multiple ravines and creeks.

Along this stretch we notice two blue bobbing balls on the lake. Rick replies, "no, I think they are markers for a fishing net". Nope, just two more blue balls afloat. One was slimed and obviously living on the lake for quite some time. Rick offers it to Chris, who politely declines, and we save it for trash. The other is a delightful ball with cartoon characters on it—a keeper! How fun is this!

Multiple metal and rocky outcroppings to protect the shoreline jut out into the lake. Then the sandy coves of Sunrise Park Beach in Lake Bluff are in view. Our lunch site! It is on the Illinois Lake Michigan Water Trail, but you must make prior arrangements to land on the beach. There is some parking up on the narrow streets above. Then there are oodles of steps down to the beach. Would be a difficult place to launch. Depending on which day we choose to visit, we were instructed to use different coves. There is a total of four bays, two for swimming, one for dogs, and a fourth inlet, is the sailing beach for the Lake Bluff Yacht Club, a sunfish sailing and racing club. We can only land there on a day that they do not have an event going on. All quite confusing. We land on the north cove, the dog beach, but since there are no dogs swimming, seems like the most out of the way from swimmers and sailors, to land.

Once on the beach, it is quite serene. Pebble and sand beach and a pleasant stop for a rest. There is no swimming—except for dogs, on this beach cove. I offer to do the doggie paddle. . .

Belly full, we are nicely rested, and ready to return to paddling. About one quarter of a mile south of Sunrise Park, is Ravine Park. A narrow slit of a park that follows a ravine. Pleasant hiking trail that crisscrosses a winding creek with multiple bridges and steps. The stream ebbs and flows as it curves its way down to Lake Michigan. Ahh, that is the part that is interesting to us. If you haven't made prior arrangements, there is a charming cove by the ephemeral creek that could be discreet bay a to sneak into for a secluded swim and rest break. Shh. . .

Lake Bluff is a village with enchanting manors on manicured hillsides, mostly nestled down curvy quiet lanes. Each unique with compound roof lines, and built with a variety of bricks and stones. There are snarly metal shore containments sticking out into the lake, many times the distal ends are hidden underwater.

Then the affluent city of Lake Forest greets us with unceasing sharp bluffs. Does Lake Forest have more trees than bluffs? It is designated as a Tree City by the Arbor Foundation. Lake Forest Cemetery towers over the bluff with its cap of green trees. A secluded sandy beach under the cemetery could offer another sweet spot for a swim and respite, but there are no trespassing signs. Another mile of beautiful abodes. White or cream brick prevail with many gables and arches. Impeccable manicured lawns, and sometimes even the hillsides are landscaped down to their private shores. Various homes have sequestered rocky berms, or metal walls to make their own coves.

Lake Forest Park Beach with four defined rocky coves with striking curved sandy beaches beckons us. But so sad, it is not to be. We are prohibited from landing on the beach. Residents only. If you walk in from above, there is a non-resident swimming fee, but we kayakers, are not allowed to land, not even on the cove where there is a sailing beach. We can only stare longingly at the spectacular sandy beach with the brick path that loops the coves.

Two more miles of magnificent mansions that amuse us. Are they getting more opulent? Is that possible? More and more of the homes have manicured cliffs. Luxurious homes and lavish pools. Where do these people work? On an incredible wonderful weekend day, no one seems to be on their beaches. Maybe, they work too much?

We arrive at Fort Sheridan. First, the Fort Sheridan Cemetery which was established in 1889. Army personnel from the Civil War to present conflicts are buried here. Three soldiers who served with General George Custer in the 7th Cavalry are interred here. Even World War II German POW's that were held at Fort Sheridan are entombed in the cemetery. Quiet grassy grounds with a ravine leading to the bluff and the Lake Michigan shoreline.

Next up, is the Fort Sheridan Nature Preserve. On top of the bluff is a prairie savannah with fields of wildflowers, and over four miles of hiking and biking trails and a new overlook of Lake Michigan. Deep ravines that meander down through the seventy-foot high bluff to the natural beach. A three-quarter mile long unpretentious beach—and yeah, no, we are not allowed to land here either. The reasoning for no swimming or landing of water crafts? The "potential for unexploded ordinance from past military training exercises". Risky? Do you feel lucky?

Following the native beach, is the Fort Sheridan Reserve Center. The original Fort Sheridan, a real army fort, was established after the Civil War, and was a training center for the Spanish-American War, World War I and World War II. The fort was closed in 1993, and many of the historic homes were converted to private residences. George Patton once lived here. All the homes were built in the cream-colored bricks molded from the clay mined from the Lake Michigan bluffs. These homes are much more modest and unpretentious. You just might be able to glimpse the historic water tower barracks from the original buildings over the tree tops.

And we arrive at the gem of this trip. The Openlands Lakeshore Preserve. It extends from the Fort Sheridan Preserve to Highland Park. With the Fort Sheridan Beach, that is almost two miles of protected, public natural beach under the olde Fort Sheridan homes! The beach is undeveloped with flowing sands, banked by towering precipitous bluffs. The ridges have oak trees, while the ravines have sugar maples, birches and junipers. A hiking and biking path follows most of the lakeshore, with beautiful bridges over the ravines and several beach accesses down flights of steps. This moraine topography was created by the receding glaciers carving out the ravines and cliffs. We land between two of the repetitive metal shore protector walls that give us the sandy beaches sandwiched between them. Groups of beach combers sprinkle the beach. A rare natural community, spectacular!

Shortly after our beach break at Openlands, Chris spots a floating orb. Really? No way! Chris finds a ball too! A rainbow striped globe with black stars. She outshines us with our basic balls. Way to go girl! The last ball is the best ball. Now we each have one. Anyone missing a ball?

The old white mansion on top of the bluff at the end of Openlands, is the closed Congregation B'nai Torah. The snowy white lodge with the unique arched gables is quite striking.

Then comes Moraine Park, a two leveled park on the grounds of the long gone, fabled Moraine Hotel. The upper park has sculptures woven amongst a path, great for bird watching and meditation. The lower level goes down to the beach. If you stay close to shore, you may get a view of the remnants of the original stone steps and a moss-covered bench dating back to the 1898 hotel. The beach is listed as a non-swimming beach, without lifeguards. Which means no one would notice if you land there, right?

And then we see the Park Avenue wharf extending into the lake. There is an 800-foot natural beach before the metal peninsula. We meet a group of stand-up paddle boarders coming north from the boating beach. The instructor propels herself over to us, "are you the Door County kayakers?" She welcomes us to the Park Avenue boating beach!

We go around the southern end of the metal quay, past the motor boat ramp, and land at the North Shore Yacht Club sandy sailing beach. Hop out of our kayaks and are greeted by local kayakers. With our special permission to use the private beach, word has spread that long-distance kayakers are coming to the Park Avenue Boating Beach. It appears, that kayaking is very popular in the Chicago area, but everyone seems to use their own reserved local sailing beach, paddle around a few miles, and always return to their home beach. No one seems to say hello to their adjacent city beaches. I think it is time to expand their horizons and stop and say hi to their neighbors!

As Chris and I start heaping our equipment on a small tarp, Rick makes the Uber/Lyft call. He waves goodbye to head up the third of a mile up the Park Avenue hill.

Chris and I finish packing up the gear and sit on the small hill to watch the commotion of motor boats coming and going. Our fav, is the young man learning to launch the motor boat with guidance from Dad. Took a few tries, but the son keeps his cool well, as Dad gave instructions. I'm sure having an audience was so helpful. . . hence we give him kudos for a job well done, and off they go to enjoy their afternoon on the lake. A lady and her SUP arrive back on beach, I offer to help lift the board up on top of her car, but she is a pro and doesn't need any assistance, obviously she's done this before!

Chat with a couple of kayakers who heard we were coming, and we share stories of Door County paddling. As Rick arrives back, Chris and I are yakking with Maureen, the Commodore of the North Shore Yacht Club. Appreciate the welcome that was given us by the folks in Highland Park, thanks for sharing your beach with us!

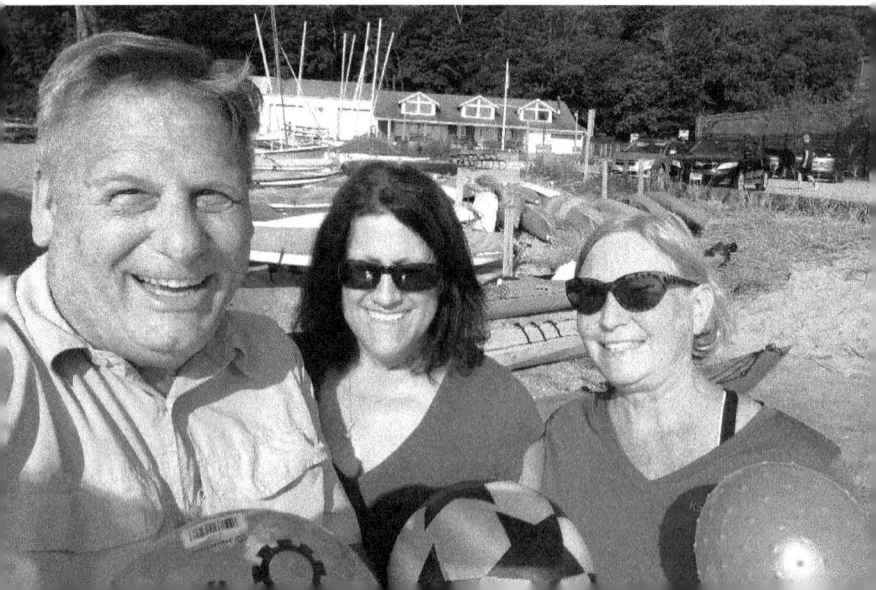

Logistics:

Waukegan North Beach and Municipal Beach, Illinois:
42.3642, -87.8157. Sea Horse Drive, Waukegan. North Beach has
a 1000-foot carry over the sand dunes. Or drive to the southern end
of the parking lots for the Waukegan Municipal Beach.

Waukegan Harbor canoe and kayak launch, Illinois:
42.3599, -87.8243. 55 South Harbor Place, Waukegan. Street
parking. Carry your boats to the boat ramps. On the south end by
Government Pier is the free canoe/kayak ADA launch!

Sunrise Park Beach, Lake Bluff, Illinois:
42.2782, -87.8292. 1 Sunrise Avenue. Must have prior
arrangements to use this beach. Please contact Lake Bluff Park and
Recreation Department at 847-234-4150. Listed on the Illinois Lake
Michigan Water Trail. Fee to land on the beach or to launch if you
are a non-resident. Long carry down steep steps, if you can find
parking on the lanes above the bluff.

Park Avenue Sailing Beach, Highland Park, Illinois:
42.1901, -87.7874. 8 Park Avenue. Must have prior arrangements
to use this beach to launch. Please contact Highland Park; Park and
Recreation Department at 219-838-0114. If you make special
arrangements, you may be able to obtain a daily parking pass. All
paddlers may land and use the public restrooms on the north side
of the North Shore Yacht Club.

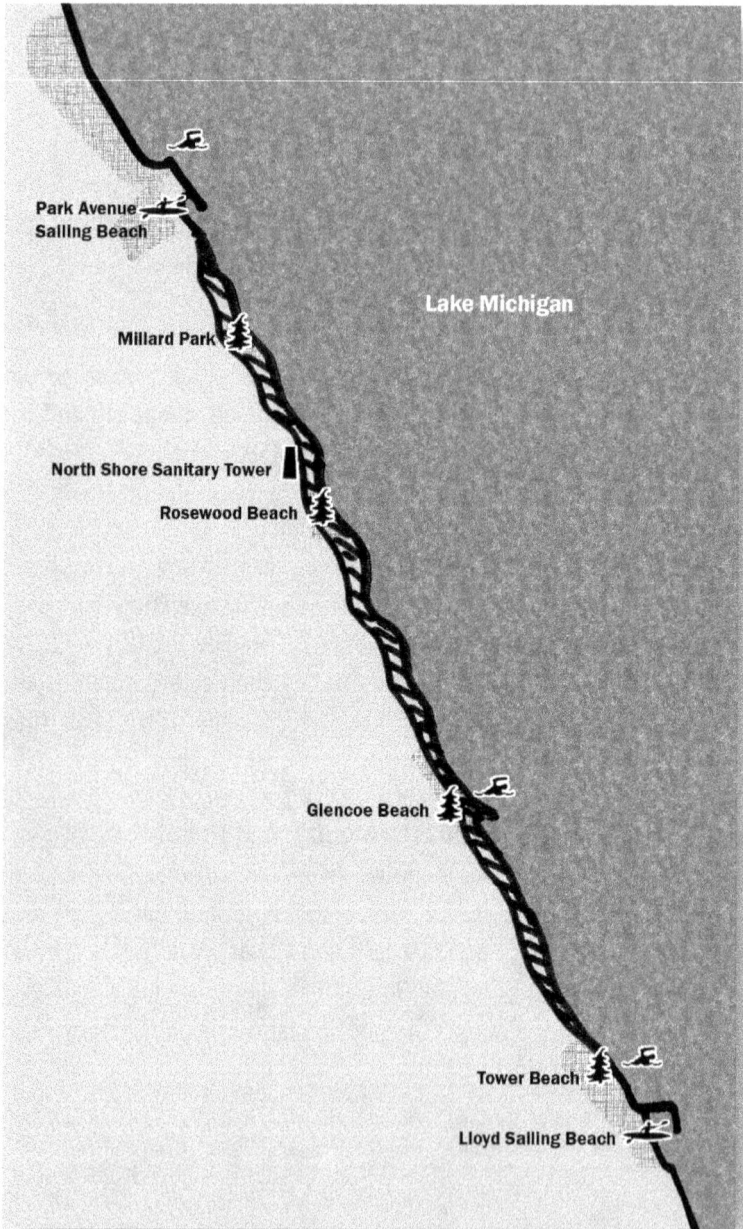

Leg 22

Magnificent Mansions

Highland Park to Winnetka

With Park Avenue and Lloyd's Boating Beaches

6 miles

What do I remember about this paddle? The homes. How immense can mansions get? This whopping big! Stay close to shore and just sit back, drop your paddle, and let your jaws gape. The homes, drop dead gorgeous!

We planned to paddle longer on this day, but with the forecast predicting big bad storms later in the day, so we choose to play it by ear. . . or rather sight, in this case. "Eyes on the sky", Rick always says. This plan works really well when you are Ubering/Lfyting for the shuttle—no car to drop off, so we have options for landing and ending our paddle.

We launch in the morning at Park Avenue sailing beach, on an exquisitely quiet morning. We have special permission to park and launch at Park Avenue North Shore Yacht Club beach. Works well to make the prior arrangements, as the northern suburbs do not generally share their shoreline well. . . However, when paddling, Park Avenue is available for all non-motorized water craft to land for rest breaks, and to use the restrooms on the northern side of the club house for the North Shore Yacht Club.

Give a friendly wave good bye to our hosts as we gently launch on the sandy shoreline in their protective cove. Almost immediately we pass by the Highland Park Senior Center up on the bluff.

Two interesting half-moon homes up on the precipice. Several estates with landscaped winding paths down to private beaches. Another option that is employed, are personal trams, for an elevator ride down to the beach, amazing. And plenteous pools abound— rectangle, oval, or even more unique, you name it, you will see it. I'm guessing the pools are kept warmer than Lake Michigan's summer average temp of a balmy 62 degrees!

After just a little more than a half mile is Millard Park with a thousand feet of sand and pebble beach between six metal ramparts as shore protectors. But they don't want anyone to swim here. There is a rock garden on the shoreline with large boulders of local stones engraved with their geologic names: basalt, granite, quartz, sandstone, and limestone. On a very calm lake day, you could step out of your boats in knee deep water, hold your boats on a leash as they float off shore, to enjoy this wonderful unique garden. Ravine Drive, winds through the park and down to the southern end of the park with a nice parking lot. Would be a really easy kayak launch site, but no. You need a parking permit to park in the lot, and they are not on the Illinois Lake Michigan Water Trail. So, shucks. . . There is a historic garden above the bluff. Flowering rock walls, ponds, wild flowers, and benches overlooking Lake Michigan.

The city of Highland Park is home to the Ravina Festival with classical, pop, and jazz concerts during the summer, along with being the home to Chicago's Symphony Orchestra. Highland Park is another wealthy suburb. They pride themselves as being a green city and are designated a Tree City USA by the Arbor Foundation. The trees shield the bluffs and provide a natural environment for the marvelous manors with multiple turrets. For over a mile, massive mansions, each looking like a country club, but are in reality spreading residences. Expanding estates of red brick colonials flanked by vast sunrooms, or Georgian style homes adorned with symmetrical tall narrow windows on each level. Homes are built into the hillsides, first two, then three, and later even four stories tall! Some with their sailboats buoyed and bobbing off shore, or power boats sitting on their secluded beaches. They launch their boats with a beach launcher—a powered boat trailer than maneuvers by itself on the sandy shoreline, pretty cool.

A comely cove comes in view. Actually, it's a trio of horseshoe bays, the golden sand seems to summon us. Chris asks, "can we land?" No Chris, we can't stop at Rosewood Beach, no public launches are allowed, and no landing on their beach. They have three coves; a nature bay, and two swimming and recreational beaches. A fetching teak boardwalk follows the length of the triplet inlets. Lake Michigan is an American miracle, and we, non-residents, are allowed to pay to park and swim at the beach—but don't try landing.

Wonderful wooded bluffs are above the creamy sand beach. A very cool tower sits amongst the foliage, the North Shore Sanitary Tower. A white brick, art deco tower with a trio of narrow windows in a singular vertical column facing the lake. Three metal crowns top the tower. Built in 1931 it is now on the National Register of Historic Places, and was featured on the cover of the Smashing Pumpkins album Oceania.

Underneath the tower, is the Rosewood Beach Interpretive Center. It is a flat-roof, modern teak wood shelter lined with floor to ceiling glass windows. As we paddle by Rosewood Park Beach, a morning yoga on the beach class is in session. We stop paddling for a moment, and stretch, reaching up in unison with the group. A deep breath in to fuel our spirit, and a full breath out to salute the sun!

Another mile of stunning impressive homes. Mediterranean stucco villas with sloping roofs with wide overhangs over fabulous patios. Midcentury modern homes with open floor plans with giant glass windows overlooking the lake. And chateaus with steeping pitched hipped roofs, oodles of dormers and colossal chimneys. Each luxury home is unique and interesting, exceptionally entertaining!

The Lakeshore Country Club is next for us to paddle past. An exclusive club for the elite to relax and socialize. Amenities include a golf course, tennis courts, a regulation size pool with a screened cabana. Luxury at its best. The 1910 club house is a timeless red brick beside vivid white paned glass windows. The Lakeshore country club house has a grand entrance, formal dining room, card

rooms, guest rooms and is topped with a central spire. The lodge overlooks the sprawling prim lawn scanning their restricted beach.

But next door is the North Shore Congregation, the Aitz Hayim Center for Jewish Living. Their large iconic sanctuary has a post-modern architecture with a dramatic soaring roof, and lily shaped windows. We sneak onto the shoreline for a short rest break. We appreciate the community's religious environment, are quiet and un-disturbing, and respect their shoreline.

We are now in the village of Glencoe. It has a German and English heritage, and is the home of the Chicago Botanical Gardens. Glencoe is one of the richest towns in Illinois, with homes that average 6,000 square feet. And the average price of a home on the Lake Michigan shoreline? $5 million dollars! Maybe, I can afford a boat house? May be their dog house? We paddle past a mile of unbelievable homes, mostly historic, by famous architects. Elegant gothic style homes with grand tall halls, and pointed arch windows with ornate details. Many in the Arts and Crafts style, with ageless, simplistic features with local natural materials. And there is prairie school architecture with symmetrical clean lines of brick, stone and wood. Several Frank Lloyd Wright homes, but they are generally on the ravines, rather than the bluff overlooking Lake Michigan.

As we approach Glencoe's only beach, we first see the huge white stone two-story Perlman Boating Beach House. An exquisite edifice with stone arch windows. Then a deep sand beach with a lovely shaded trellis picnic area and a dock on the south end of the beach with sea side tables with blue umbrellas. They offer a beach café and sand volleyball courts.

Chris says "can we land here?" "No Chris we can't." Although the beach is on the Illinois Lake Michigan Water Trail, we can't actually land here or launch here. The Boating beach does offer sailboat, kayak, and SUP's for rental, and non-residents are allowed to swim here, but kayakers can't use their own kayaks to stop here. I called the city park department, and my sister and I actually stopped here when we were scouting beaches for kayaking. Chatted with the Boating Beach manager about our predicament of limited safe rest breaks in paddling. And his explanation was, "the lifeguards might need to rescue us, and then not be there to protect Glencoe's own swimmers". Are they trying to keep the riff raff out? Are we riff raff? Is that like pretty ricrac zig zag lace trim? What. . .no? Glencoe is the "Queen of the Chicago suburbs", if I would wear a sparkly crown and do a princess wave, would they let me land on their beach? When my sis and I were at the beach, a nice friendly Glencoe neighbor did offer her driveway for us to park and roll our kayaks to the beach. Aww, sweet. . . I did have to explain that I was writing a book, and all my readers might take her up on her offer!

Just another 1.75 miles to the next beach and our take out site. But man, oh man, the mansions seem to be getting even bigger! Our favorites? The Greek columns, not only on the Parthenon manor, but by the boat house, and the swimming pool with a shaded cabana! An absurdly large boat house castle with turrets, arched windows, stone chimney, and topped with a copper roof. Dude—it's a boat house! But bar none, our top choice for the over the top mansion is, drum roll please. . . The gigantic four storied circular tower home that is so amazing we all grab our cameras. But, as we paddle past it, we realize that isn't the whole house, on the southern side is an

alcove with another three-story turret! We actually burst out laughing! Gees, I'd need a map just to find my bedroom. . .

While we are still cracking jokes about the mansions, we approach the Tower Road Beach. A fairly deep beach that is six hundred feet long, it offers soft sand and pebbles on the beach. The beach is cleaned and raked daily and gives beach goers a playground, foot paths and a bath house with concessions. Free non-resident parking is above the bluff with the winding road or staircase to the beach. My sister, Becky, and I enjoyed this beach on our beach scouting vacation to Chicago. While I enjoyed splashing in the waves, Becky sat on the beach and searched for sea glass. . . Lake Michigan glass. Geologic gems are made by nature and polished by man, whereas sea glass are opposite gems, made by man but honed by nature to be smooth, frosted beach discoveries. Becky did her best gem collecting here and came away with several fun finds! We met a bag lady, well she did carry a bag, and with her head down, obviously searching for sea glass too. She had lots of curved lake glass in her collection—in a rainbow of colors! We had a pleasurable chat with our new friend. And while we were relaxing on the beach, a larger wave came ashore getting Becky's butt wet. Made me laugh, until I realized my flip flops were floating away, and Becky got the last laugh!

And yes, there is a tower at Tower Road Beach. As Chris, Rick and I paddle past the beach we look up to see the 300-foot high smokestack of the Winnetka electric and utility company. But this isn't actually the tower that Tower Road is named after. There used to be real water tower in front of the smokestack. It was a brick, octagonal steeple, originally filled with water, with a viewer's platform under the low-pitched tile roof. The view was said to be legendary, but with the advent of high-pressure pumps, that tower became obsolete.

The Tower Road Beach is only a swimming beach, not a sailing beach, so. . . we paddle on. But no worries, Lloyd Boating Beach is literally right around the pier. Becky and I scouted Lloyd's too. After so many "no, you can't launch here", "no, you can't land here" from so many of the northern suburbs of Chicago, we were getting discouraged. I actually called Rick and with tears in my eyes, said "our plan to kayak to Chicago may not be possible!" But then, Becky and I stopped at Lloyds. Almost immediately, a young male staff worker came over and said in a friendly tone "can I help you?" I asked if we could launch kayaks at Lloyds and "certainly" was his response. I was so excited; I gave him a big hug as I said "I love you"! He seemed a bit mortified. . .

So, Rick, Chris and I paddle hesitantly into Lloyd's sailing beach. Very busy, motor boats unloading and launching from the boat ramp in a dizzyingly circle. Nervous, that we may take up too much room. Nope, the kind, professional staff again welcomed us. No problem, if the Uber/Lfyt driver drives down to the beach for our shuttle. No problem if Chris and I sit, relax, lounge, and swim, while we wait for Rick to return with the car. Wow, the team even asked if they could help us load up the kayaks! Go to Lloyds! Welcoming Winnetka!

Logistics:

Park Avenue Sailing Beach, Highland Park, Illinois:
42.1901, -87.7874. 8 Park Avenue. Must have prior arrangements to use this beach to launch. Please contact Highland Park, Park and Recreation Department at 219-838-0114. If you make special arrangements, you may be able to obtain a daily parking pass. All paddlers may land and use the public restrooms on the north side of the North Shore Yacht Club.

Glencoe Beach, Perlman Boating Beach, Glencoe, Illinois:
42.1904, -87.7870. 55 Hazel Avenue. This beach is listed on the Illinois Lake Michigan Water Trail, but only residents may use the beach to launch, non-residents are not even allowed to land on the beach. Fee to swim, restrooms.

Lloyd Boating Beach, Winnetka, Illinois:
42.1146, -87.7304. 799 Sheridan Road. This beach is on the Illinois Lake Michigan Water Trail and they are incredibly warm and welcoming! Small parking area with a fee, after you unload, drive back up the hill to park in Lloyd Park. Reasonable launch fee, restrooms available.

Kayak Wisconsin, Lake Michigan Water Trail

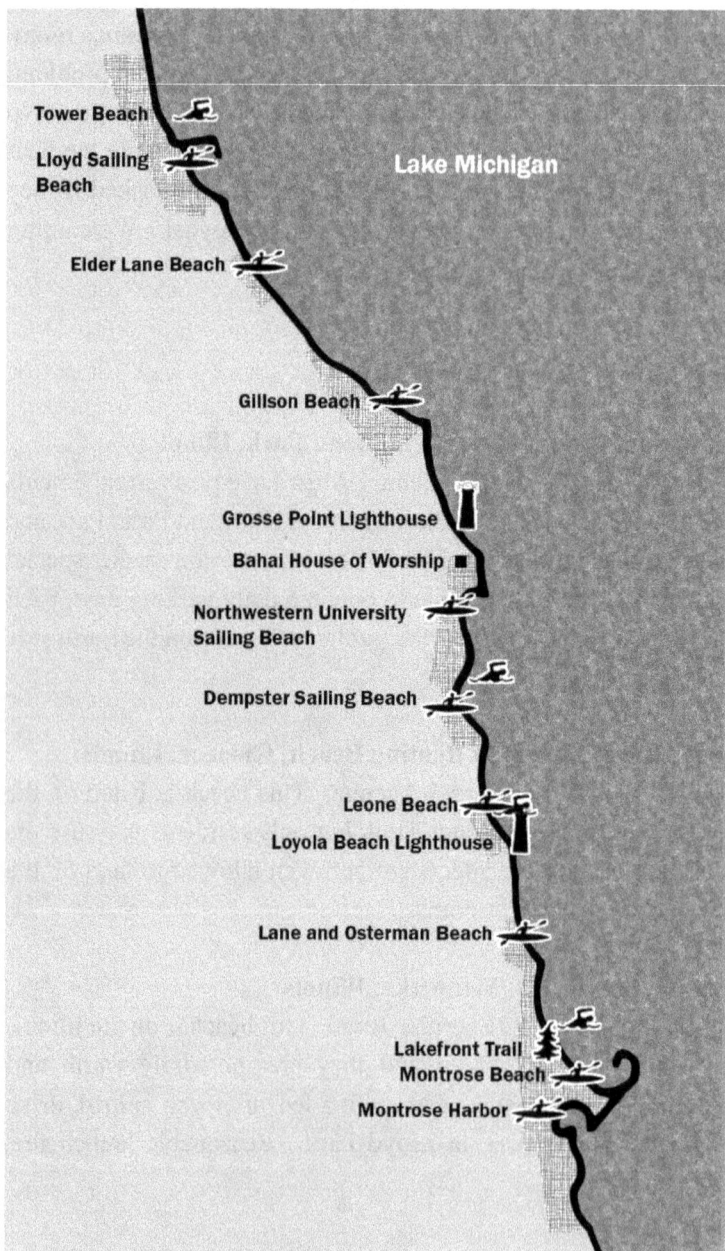

Tower Beach

Lloyd Sailing Beach

Lake Michigan

Elder Lane Beach

Gillson Beach

Grosse Point Lighthouse

Bahai House of Worship

Northwestern University Sailing Beach

Dempster Sailing Beach

Leone Beach

Loyola Beach Lighthouse

Lane and Osterman Beach

Lakefront Trail
Montrose Beach

Montrose Harbor

Leg 23

Into Chicago!

Lloyd Sailing Beach to Montrose Beach, Chicago

With nice options for swimming and launching

13 miles

Summer fun paddle. Perfect paddle for your own personal pleasure paradise. Best to do on a wonderful warm sunny summer day, so you can stop and enjoy all the beaches we can land on and relish!

Hey, we have options for shortening this paddle! Smack dab in the middle of the paddle, are the Northwest University Sailing Beach, and Greenwood Beach's Dempster Sailing Beach. Both would be perfect if you wish to do this long paddle in two separate days. Another option would be to paddle a little further south on our last paddle (Leg 22) and kayak to Elder Lane Beach which makes the last paddle 7.25 miles from Park Avenue Sailing Beach (need special permission) to Elder Lane Beach. Or you could even keep going to Gillson Beach for a 10-mile paddle. That would shorten this paddle to a 12 or a 9-mile day—which had been our original plan. On our last leg, we shortened the paddle day due to a storm that was forecasted to hit the Lake Michigan shoreline. Limiting our previous paddle was certainly a good idea, as the storm was furious, and we were really, truly happy to be warm, dry and safe in the car before the thunder and wind storm hit.

Now, might be the time to mention the Skokie Lagoons, as an alternative to Lake Michigan if the wind and waves look daunting to you. They are only 2 miles west of the lakeshore. There is a kayak launch at Tower Road which gives you access to the Lagoons for 4 miles of paddling. To get to the south Lagoons, you need to portage over a dam, but this also gives you access to the Skokie River which flows down to the North Branch of the Chicago River! Portage a different dam, to access the north Lagoons, which brings you to the ponds of the Chicago Botanical Gardens. The Skokie Lagoons were once a large bay of the ancient Lake Chicago. As the geologic Lake Chicago receded, the bay was transformed. Skokie means big wet prairie, as named by the Native Potawatomi Tribe.

However, today is good, safe day to kayak Lake Michigan. And since we love Lloyd's Sailing Beach, we were ecstatic to return to launch there again for this paddle. Lloyd's charges a reasonable launch fee, and the professional young staff are cheerful, and quite willing to assist in unloading the kayaks for us! Today, the lake has texture with one-foot swells that are expected to switch direction and increase during the day. After researching the forecast, Rick felt that most of the day, the wind and waves would be coming from the north and recommended that we paddle north to south.

So, off we go, pushing off on the gentle, protected bay at Lloyds Sailing Beach. Lloyds actually has a nice swimming beach which continues past their shelter for over five hundred feet. I prefer the southern end of the beach, past the shelter, for a quieter swimming experience. There is only one other couple lounging on the beach— umm, I'm not sure that they appreciate having to share their beach with me!

Immediately, we spy, another swimming beach with a delightful white and gray beach house and an arch above the door. Maple Street Beach offers a small beach that is protected by a fishing pier. Free parking up above the bluff, but no launching allowed.

We are paddling by Winnetka, an affluent picturesque village that ranks fourth in the United States for highest income. The homes demonstrate this. A boomerang shaped house and a red colonial with Babylon hanging gardens through steps down to their pool and boat house. Or a sleek modern, all glass house, with a pool above the beach house. The mansions average six or more bedrooms, with even more bathrooms, with over 10,000 square feet in size! One home is worth $10,000,000, (as I place my little finger by my mouth Mini Me style)! Yikes! But, then again, amusing to marvel at. And at least I don't have to clean all those bathrooms. . .

In a mile, we are already arriving at our third beach in Winnetka. Elder Lane Beach has a small beautiful soft sand beach., snuggled between two shore protector walls, and a walkable pier. This beach does have a sailing beach and we can launch kayaks! Lovely upper level park with a sun dancer statue with wrought iron railing steps or a winding paved path ramp that would allow rolling kayaks down. Nice size parking lot, with a reasonable fee to swim and launch. The beach house is stone brick with arches above the windows.

Just one home later, is Centennial Park with just a dog beach. Picturesque paths line the beach. Then we enter the village of Kenilworth. The only Kenilworth Beach has s a red brick castle right on the shoreline. Rows of kayaks line the private sailing club. But at the sandy beach, no kayaks are allowed.

A tiny third of a mile later, is the Mahoney Farm Preserve Park. It is a wildflower preserve and bird sanctuary with walking paths above the shoreline, a bird bath, and a babbling brook. We paddle past a trio of the first multi-level condo buildings we have seen in Illinois. A sign of skyscrapers to come? We are now in Wilmette, as we go past Langdon Park Beach. The beach is a small natural beach with no facilities and we are not invited to land here.

A few gorgeous houses later, and we arrive at Elmwood Dunes Preserve. A tiny sanctuary lovingly restored by community volunteers, with a landscaped dune, native flowers and grasses, and a staircase down to the sandy beach. This hidden gem is nestled between two lakeshore estates. We are allowed to land on the beach and appreciate the quiet natural beach.

Because, next up, is the busy Gillson Beach. Can't miss this large beach! First from the north, is the sailing beach where you can rent kayaks, paddleboards, and sailboats. Next is the buoyed and life guarded swimming beach. Gillson Beach does have a nice changing room shelter and concession stand. Further south is a natural beach, designated wading area only, where non-motorized boats may launch at the very southern end by the breakwater wall, but only if you have beforehand obtained a park permit through the park department. The fees here are more expensive than the other northern village beaches. Parking is free for non-residents only on Middle Drive—if you can find space, and then you need a kayak wheeled cart to roll your boat down to the lakeshore.

Between the two break water stone piled piers is the dog beach. Then there is the Wilmette Harbor entrance. It is here, that the North Channel leads to the North Branch of the Chicago River! Inside the harbor, is the private Sheridan Shore Yacht Club, and the U.S. Coast Guard station. The Coast Guard station averages about 100 search and rescues each year in their area. Twice, they have assisted in plane crashes, in 1951 a plane from the Naval Center crashed, and in 1965 a United Airlines plane crashed into Lake Michigan.

You can't miss the incredibly beautiful Bahá'í House of Worship Temple! The beach area on the shoreline does belong to the temple complex. All are welcome for quiet contemplation on their grounds, gardens, and in the house of worship. There are nine sacred gardens with reflecting pools surrounding the temple, signifying unity in diversity. The majestic dome, a symbol of oneness, embraces natural light during the day, and illuminates at night, representing light and unity. As we gaze on the Bahá'í House of Worship's stunning architecture, we take a moment to join in quiet reflection.

Another little bit of paddling into Evanston, one of largest north of Chicago towns. We travel past multi-million-dollar homes with compound rooflines, numerous chimneys, various dormers, and round turrets. One home has a green grass patio above their beach house which is connected to the main home!

We arrive at Grosse Point Beach with the lighthouse above. Previously my sister and I toured the lighthouse, and had a fascinating tour with the passionate tour guide. Built in 1873, the Grosse Point Lighthouse was needed to mark the northern approach to Chicago. This region was explored by Father Jacque Marquette and he actually camped here. When this lighthouse was built, Chicago was America's busiest port—more ships arrived in Chicago than New York City and San Francisco combined!

The lighthouse has a brick tower linked to the keeper's house. The tapered tower sits on a 25-foot high bluff and is 113 feet tall (and has 141 steps, which I can attest to. . .). It has a second order Fresnel lens—the largest size on all of the Great Lakes. As she aged, the brick tower needed a reinforced concrete skin. . .can I have a new un-wrinkled skin too? The view of the Grosse Pointe beach from the lighthouse is awesome! And that is as close as we got to it— Becky and I were not even allowed to look at the beach without paying. And as Rick, Chris and I paddle past, Rick wants to stop at the beach. "Rick, we can't". Rick replies, "Let's just land on the far north end where there aren't any people". "Good luck" I shout, as Rick heads into shore. I twiddle my thumbs, waiting to see if he can land. Just when I think he is going to be successful, the lifeguard on his stand, picks up his megaphone and barks out, loud enough for all of Illinois to hear "Kayakers—you—can—not—land—here. Go—back—to—your—point—of—origin!" I almost jump out of my kayak with fright, and then wished I had paddled into shore with Rick. Lake Michigan is public! We could go into shore, stand in two inches of water with our kayaks, and we would be legal! Rick cautions, "nah, let's just go to the next beach".

But the next beach is the Northwest University Beach, and it is private. But not a soul is swimming, just the lone lifeguard on his chair. Rick paddles in again, doesn't get yelled at, but no, we can't land on the empty beach here either. . . We paddle on, past the gorgeous Northwest University Sports Pavilion with its giant dome sticking out into the lake. Northwest University is renowned as a leading research and teaching university. We paddle on, past the campus lakefront green peninsula, where we get our first glimpse of the incredible Chicago skyline. We play tourist as we all grab our phones for photos. We are getting close!

Around the peninsula is Northwestern's Sailing Center. All are welcome here! Everyone can rent sailboats, sailboards, kayaks, and SUP's. They offer instructions for catamaran sail boating and windsurfing, along with SUP yoga classes. It is OK to land here, and then walk over to the neighboring Clark Street Beach to swim.

After the beach break water wall is Centennial Park with picnic areas, horseshoe pits, and a model airplane airport for remote control planes! This park evolves into Dawes Park with a fountain, pond and hiking paths. The Church Street boat ramp is here for motorized watercraft and power boats. Time to be aware and on the lookout.

And right next door is our new goal. The Greenwood Street Beach and the Dempster Sailing Beach. This Evanston beach is the one we are allowed to land on. We head towards the south end, for the Sailing Beach. Ahh, time to stand and stretch! I head into the water to dive in, but I'm whistled at, not by cute boys, but by the lifeguard.

I must walk 20 feet north to the Greenwood Street swimming beach. Geez, I'm not good with rules. . . but it feels wonderful to swim and play in the water. Rick keeps his shirt on, "I don't have to put on sunscreen then" and swims with his new bright red, heart shaped goggles. "Such a nerd" as I roll my eyes. But it is an awesome day for swimming! Then lunch, wow, didn't realize I was so hungry!

Greenwood Beach with the Dempster Sailing Facility would be a launch point if you wish to cut this paddle in half, although it is expensive, and parking is limited to hard to find street parking only. You are allowed to launch close to the water and then park.

As we pack up and climb into our kayaks, we head south, past Burnham Shores Park and Elliot Park with green lawn above the rocky protected shoreline. At Elliot Park is a mosaic sculpture— "when one tugs at a single thing in nature, one finds it attached to the rest of the universe". Then it is Evanston's Lee Street Beach, a swimming beach only. Nice houses with private pools and condo buildings, interspersed with the quiet tiny Clark Square Park, Garden Park, and then South Boulevard Beach, the last of the Evanston swimming beaches.

We made it! We are in Chicago! Yeah! Juneway Beach is a terraced steps beach, our first of eighteen street end beaches in Chicago. Launching is not permitted at these small neighborhood beaches. Several condo buildings are literally on the water's edge, only a shoreline metal wall protects the buildings. Followed by a series of more street beaches interspersed with condos.

Right after some beach side buildings, we arrive at the "L" beaches, Leone Beach is the spot for stopping with our kayaks and for launching or take out. It is the northern most part of the beaches, where there is a parking lot and a short carry in to launch. Leone is the quieter, smaller beach, and is immediately followed the larger Loyola Beach. Loyola Beach is a half mile long, and the sand beach is wide, much easier to spot from the lake. At the southern end of the beach is a natural dune habitat and the concrete break water wall with the rusty metal Loyola Lighthouse at the end.

The beaches just don't stop, without delay we have another series of neighborhood beach, all within a quarter of a mile. One of the beaches is named after Tobey Prinz, who led a "Save the Beaches" campaign that was successful in protecting these small neighborhood beaches. Thanks Tobey!

The stone protective shoreline indicates we are passing Loyola University. It is one of the largest Jesuit Catholic Colleges in the nation. The jewel on campus, is the Madonna Della Strada Chapel. Built in an Art Deco style with creamy stone and red roof tile, is has an amazing rose stone stain glass window designed from a snowflake set in a cross. We stop to gawk.

After the college, behind the rocky shoreline and nestled between condominiums, is Berger Park. It offers a pirate ship themed playground, and a historic mansion. The park is followed by six mid-size condominiums, all on the Lake Michigan shoreline. There is a tiny little Chicago Park, named "559 Park" between the condos. What? No one has had this park named after them? Let's just name it the "Babs Park", since I did kayak past it. . .

Then we arrive at Lane and Osterman Beaches. Both are on the Lake Michigan Water Trail! Yeah, we can stop to swim again!

Small Lane Beach is behind a rocky shoreline protective berm. Access at Thorndale Avenue to launch. Between the two beaches, is the condo that was pictured as the home of Bob and his wife Emily in the 1970's show, the "Bob Newhart Show". Then, we are at the third of a mile-long Osterman Beach. Nice sandy beach, but again only street parking, so we didn't choose this as our take out site.

We paddle out past the fishing pier and another metal pierhead lighthouse at the south end of Osterman Beach at Hollywood Avenue. The wind and waves have switched direction in the afternoon, and we do have one to two footers fighting our progress. And the Chicago skyline doesn't seem to be getting any closer!

Thankfully, the shoreline is quite lovely with cement steps with green parkland behind it. Chicago's famous Lakefront Trail, joins us in our quest to downtown Chicago. Foster Beach is just a half mile south of Osterman Beach, with a deep soft sand beach, volleyball nets, beach umbrellas, bike rental and a concession stand. Foster Beach has a breakwater pier with a metal lighthouse. They even have a Trapeze School at Foster Beach, you know, like trampolines, acrobatics, and actual flying on a trapeze! But, no landing for kayaks—so no swinging on a trapeze for us today.

The concrete steps shoreline shadows us all the way to Montrose Beach. We are here, we made it! Time to land! Wait, why is Rick still kayaking, "stop Rick!" "How far is he going?", Chris and I moan. . .to the south end, where he is supposed to go. Dang. The north end of the long beach is the dog beach, then the long swimming beach, and finally tucked into the curve of the pier is the sailing beach, where we can land. Made it! Paddle lift!

I dive in to swim. Ahh, I needed that. Then, its time pack up and carry everything up to The Dock, the beach bar and restaurant, where Chris and I will wait while Rick Ubers back to Lloyd Beach to retrieve the car.

"Why is there a pond in my way"? Due to a storm surge, there is a pond where beach used to be. Montrose Beach has added a narrow floating bridge over the pond. Now, we have to navigate our boats over the bridge where hordes of beach goers are pulling wagon loads of beach supplies. "But I'm tired!" I whine. But there is no choice, so off we go to pilot our carts across the makeshift bridge.

Whew, we make it to The Dock Restaurant and park our kayaks next to the raised patio. Chris kisses Rick goodbye as he makes his way to meet his Lyft driver. Chris and I, climb through the rope railing and sit down next to our boats. . .and order margaritas! "How long does it take to drive 13 miles through Chicago traffic and back?" I better start slowly sipping my second margarita. . .

Logistics:

Lloyd Sailing Beach, Winnetka, Illinois:
42.1146, -87.7304. 799 Sheridan Road. On the Illinois Lake Michigan Water Trail and they are incredibly warm and welcoming! After you unload, drive back up the hill to park in Lloyd Park. Reasonable launch fee, restrooms available.

Elder Lane Beach, Winnetka:
42.0994, -87.7154. 301 Sheridan Road. Not listed on the Illinois Water Trail, but signs posted in the park and on their webpage, state

it is non-motorized boat launch. Paved path to carry/roll your kayaks down the hill to the beach.

Gillson Park Canoe and Kayak Launch, Wilmette:
42.0786, -87.6816. Sheridan Road at Michigan Avenue. On the Illinois Lake Michigan Water Trail, very pricy to launch and park. Restrooms. No swimming at the kayak launch beach. Parking is free on Middle Drive but long carry/roll to the kayak launch beach.

Northwestern University Sailing Center, Evanston:
42.0503, -87.6723. 1823 Campus Drive. On the Illinois Lake Michigan Water Trail. Pricy launch fee, free parking weekends only, parking permits at the parking office.

Greenwood Beach/Dempster Facility, Evanston:
42.0416, -87.6702. 1251 Lakeshore Boulevard.
On the Illinois Lake Michigan Water Trail. Expensive launch fee, restrooms, parking only for daily pass users on the public streets.

Leone Beach, Chicago:
42.013, -87.6616. 1222 W. Touchy Avenue. On the Illinois Lake Michigan Water Trail. Parking fee, no launch fee.

Lane and Osterman (Hollywood) Beach, Chicago:
41.9880, -87.6532. 5800 N. Lake Shore Drive. On the Illinois Lake Michigan Water Trail, access at Thorndale or Ardmore Avenues, street parking only. Restroom at Osterman Beach, no launch fee.

Montrose Beach, Chicago:
41.9664, -87.6352. 4400 N. Lake Shore Drive. On the Lake Michigan Water Trail, fee in parking lot, limited free street parking. Windy City Watersports rents kayaks. No launch fee, restrooms.

Kayak Wisconsin, Lake Michigan Water Trail

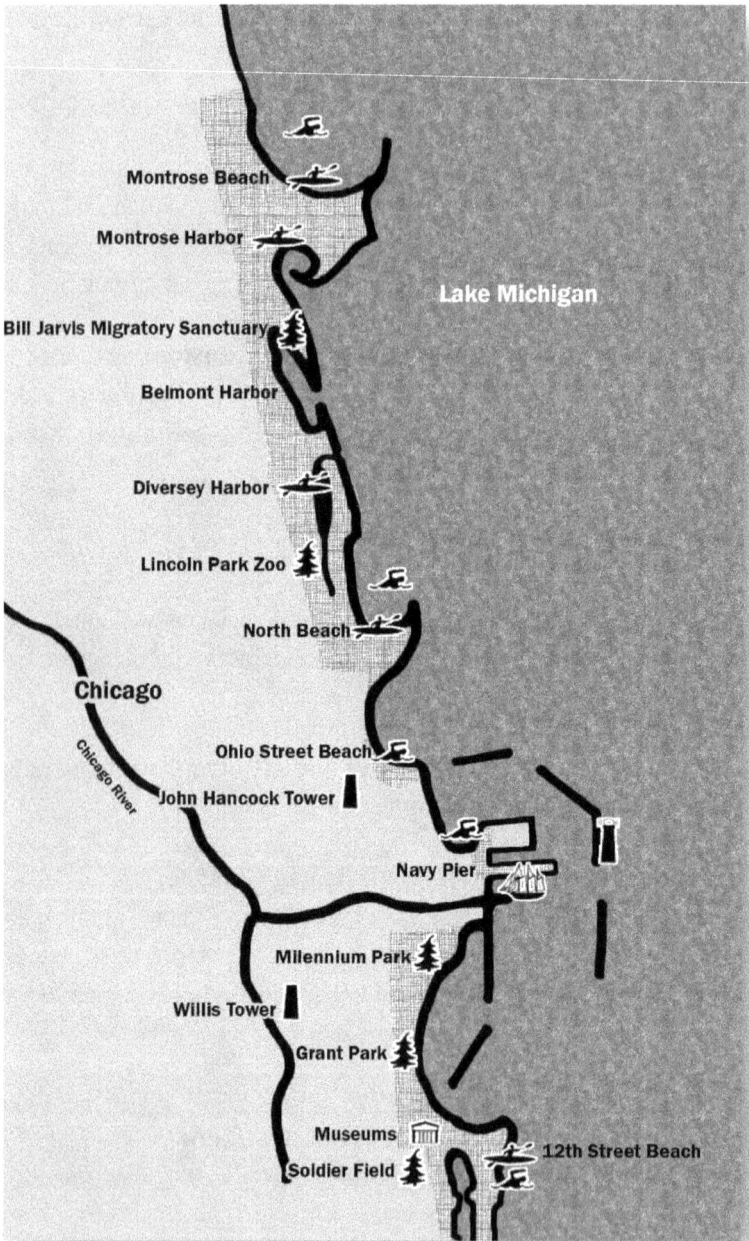

Montrose Beach

Montrose Harbor

Bill Jarvis Migratory Sanctuary

Belmont Harbor

Diversey Harbor

Lincoln Park Zoo

North Beach

Lake Michigan

Chicago

Chicago River

Ohio Street Beach

John Hancock Tower

Navy Pier

Milennium Park

Willis Tower

Grant Park

Museums

Soldier Field

12th Street Beach

Leg 24

Chicago Skyline

Montrose Beach to 12th Street Beach

With the Chicago skyline and North Avenue Beach

9 miles

I'm so excited, I just can hide it! We paddle the Chicago Skyline. Quadrillion dollar views, the museum campus, Navy Pier, the Chicago Harbor Lighthouse, and a beach with a jaw dropping view. Wow, Chicago by boat!

We launch at 12th Street Beach and paddle north to Montrose Beach. It is possible to cut the paddle in half by using North Avenue Beach which is on the Illinois Lake Michigan Water Trail. Another option would be to use Diversey Harbor for a midpoint, making a 6- and a 3-mile paddle. You can shorten the paddle by a half mile, by using the Montrose Harbor fishing dock. Using Montrose Harbor would be quieter water if the lake is a little rambunctious.

Up early with eagerness, we head down to 12th Street Beach. The Adler Parking lot is closest and we score early bird parking rates to get close to the 12th Street Beach Access. The parking lot is also used for the Adler Planetarium, Shedd Aquarium, Soldier Field, and The Field Museum of Natural History. If you miss out on being able to park in this lot, then you'll need luck and good carts to roll your boats to the beach.

12th Street Beach is located on the manmade Northerly Island, which was the site of Chicago's second World Fair. The causeway from the mainland was added later. Besides a huge concert pavilion, the island is a natural area with a pond, hiking paths, and the Daphne Garden with three fairy sculptures entwined with lush flowers.

We only have to carry our boats 300 feet to the beach, using the paved path with a circle, and a few steps down to the beach. Two ladies are at the beach with their dogs, and I play catch and retrieve for a few minutes while I wait for Rick to recheck the forecast. I consider jumping in for a quick swim, but wet swimsuit syndrome gives me hesitation. The 12th Street Beach is 1000 feet long, with a beach house, restrooms, and a taco stand. The beach is protected a little on the north end as we slide off from shore.

The Adler Planetarium is the huge dome building that we angle around to head north. There are cement steps to the water's edge surrounding the observatory. Above the steps is green lawn and a spiral circle of large granite blocks, symbolizing an ancient celestial

observatory. The Adler Planetarium's dome theaters offer shows including the night sky over Chicago—what is hidden by the city lights. On Saturdays, you can do yoga with a sky show. At the planetarium you can touch a meteorite, a moon rock, and a piece of Mars! The little round building with the angled roof is actually a very large telescope.

If you head west into the harbor the Shedd Aquarium is in the south corner. The exhibits at the Aquarium includes the Caribbean Reef with sea turtles and sharks. The Oceanarium shows off sea lions, dolphins, and white beluga whales. The Polar Play Zone offers a touch pool with starfish and stingrays, and a penguin colony. And the At Home on the Great Lakes, has fresh water fish including the sturgeon. Sturgeons are Wisconsin's largest fish and are generally bottom browsers—until they come to spawn! Sturgeons live over 100 years, and lived with the dinosaurs. . .and the Shedd Aquarium offers us the opportunity to touch a sturgeon!

Inside the breakwater walls is Monroe Harbor, with boats jetting out, along with the Shoreline Water Taxi running from the Museums to Navy Pier, making this paddle an intermediate paddle. Green parkland, the Lakefront Trail and the continuation of the steps down to Lake Michigan are along the shore. In the middle, is the Queens Landing, since England's Queen Elizabeth sailed down to here for the opening of the St. Lawrence Seaway in 1959. Buckingham Fountain is in Grant Park across Lake Street and is one of the largest fountains in the world. Built in a Palace of Versailles, Rococo wedding cake style. The fountain's center jet shoots up 150 feet hourly, and at night is choreographed with music and lights.

We stay out past the harbor seawall to be entertained one of the best views of the Chicago skyline. The tallest buildings to the south behind the Adler Planetarium are newer skyscrapers; One Museum Park and One Grant Park, both have a step designs of various heights. South of the red brick Hilton is the 1000M condo building, a high-end skyscraper.

After a gap of midsize buildings is a cluster of really tall skyscrapers. First up is 311 S. Wacker Drive, locally known as the "white castle" because its top crown is brightly lit at night. Dominating the skyline is the Willis Tower, previously named the Sears Tower, at 110 stories, one of the tallest buildings in the United States. The unique step design was out of necessity due to Chicago being the "Windy City". The observation Skydeck is on the 103rd floor, and you can step out onto the glass floor Ledge. . .if you dare! The little building with the triangle top in front of the Willis Tower is the historic art deco Chicago Board of Trade. When it was built in 1930, it was the tallest skyscraper in Chicago, and is topped by a Roman goddess statue. The Franklin Center is the one with two antennas on top. The really obvious red painted building is the CNA Plaza, it occasionally lights up its rooms at night to display messages such as "Go Bears", don't believe they've ever lit up with "Go Pack Go".

Continuing with the massive bunch of skyscrapers of the Chicago Loop, is the whitish Chase Tower, distinctive for its vertical curve, wider at the base and skinnier at the top. In front, is the historic Metropolitan Tower, and kind of blocked in our view, is the Three First National Plaza with its unique saw tooth and step up design, giving its office tenants many more corner offices. The gray black Mid-Continental Plaza is so massive it covers an entire city block. Above the historic buildings, rises the residential Legacy Tower, a tall slender glass skyscraper.

We can't resist, as we stop to take a selfie with the Chicago skyline! Behind us, the white building with the slanted top is the Grant Thornton Tower, which is luminously illuminated at night. At our angle of view, the Pittsfield building is next with the pyramid at its Top. A Chicago landmark, it has an art deco gothic architecture. The building with a classical triangle on top of each of its facades with an aqua roof is 77 West Wacker Drive. Closer to us is the Heritage apartments, its shorter section is concave, and the taller tower is convex. In front on the lake shore is Millennium Park with an outdoor music pavilion, gardens, fountain, and the humongous mirror kidney bean that you can walk under!

You can't miss the Crain Communication building with its slanted top angled towards the lake resembling a sailboat, not a woman's body part. . if all the tall skyscrapers represent a man's body part. The building that says "Prudential" at the top and has a huge antenna, was the first skyscraper built in Chicago since World War II. It's partner, Two Prudential Plaza with stacked arrow chevrons

and a unique distinctive pyramid peak with a spire. Lurking behind these buildings is the massive glass Trump Tower which actually sits on the other side of the river. The Trump International Hotel is sort of a curved triangle skyscraper with three setbacks. The tower is the second tallest in Chicago. The Aon Center, the tall rectangle skyscraper, looms in front and is clad in white granite. In front of that is a series of condo towers; an aqua blue glass, a black glass building with turrets, and one with stacked bow windows.

To the north, but still on the south side of the Chicago River, sit two very interesting skyscrapers. The tall skyscraper with the ripple design is a Blu Aqua hotel, the flowing ripples are actually balconies. Finishing up the skyscrapers south of the Chicago River, is the Vista Tower, with four towers of various heights that move rhythmically in and out of vertical, giving it a distinctive wave look.

Time to stop getting a kink in our neck gawking at the skyline. Look east to the Chicago breakwater and the Chicago Harbor Lighthouse! Located at the south end of the north breakwater wall, the lighthouse stands a half mile out from the end of Navy Pier. The white cylindrical cast iron tower is braced by two red roofed rooms on each side, one for the fog horn and the other a boat house. This "sparkplug" design with staggered windows is topped with a parapet and the lantern room. The Chicago Harbor lighthouse is now an automated light and the irreplaceable Fresnel lens removed. Although much smaller than the skyscrapers she protects, she is a Chicago landmark and is on the National Register of Historic Places.

We are passing the Chicago River lock, and it is time to be aware, lots of tour and speed boats coming at all directions. The electrifying Navy Pier looms before us. The long pier that stretches out into the lake, was built in 1916, then used as a naval training site for World War I, hence its name. It reopened as a tourist attraction with rides, restaurants, and family attractions. There is the Centennial Ferris wheel that twirls 15 stories high for an incredible view. Then a carousel, IMAX theatre, Chicago's Children Museum, and the Crystal Gardens, an indoor botanical garden. Navy Pier offers three outdoor entertainment stages along with a beer garden. And then Navy Pier is lined with tour cruise ships of all sizes! Including the tall ship Windy, with four masts, a gaff topsail schooner—the official flagship of Chicago! The Windy, is built with a modern steel hull, but has wooden booms, spars, and deck to create the old-fashioned charm of a Great Lakes Schooner. The Windy offers three decks, a kitchen galley and a grand salon at the stern with large windows. It is quite an experience to sail on a schooner with her sails blowing in the wind.

Immediately north of Navy Pier is another manmade peninsula for the largest water management facility in all of the United States, with a bird sanctuary lined with trees at the end. Closer to shore is a park with five stepped fountains symbolizing the Great Lakes. The park is a relaxing site with spectacular views of the skyline for land lovers. Near shore, is a park with a nice wooded area, great for lounging, for all those weary of the lights and action at Navy Pier. Then tucked in the corner is Ohio Street Beach, used mostly by locals and those training for distance swims.

Which brings us to Chicago's "Playpen", the no wake zone between the Ohio Street and Oak Street Beaches. Boats congregate here and often tie up together to party. You will find yachts, sail boats, and jet skiers, groovin' in this area where the water is shallow and sandy. The Lakefront hiking and biking trail runs the full length on the cement and corrugated metal lake front wall.

We follow the southern breakwater wall to enjoy the northern city skyline. The black concave tower near shore is the tripod shaped Lake Point condo tower, the lone building east of Lake Shore Drive. The dark gray vertical rectangle structure with a rectangle on top is the North Pier Apartments and is considered the masculine counterpart to the curvy Lake Point tower.

This is Chicago's Streeterville community. Here we see the tall notched corner skyscraper, and a grouping of midrange glassy pointy buildings on the lake shore. Behind these, the Trump Tower pokes up. There is a flat brown rectangle topped building with no windows that looks like a sideways Olympic podium. And then the Onterie Center is just north with its diagonal X braces on the exterior, a nod to the John Hancock Center.

Northwestern University's campus are the low-lying buildings with the pretty Abbott Hall with its blue topped spire along the shore. Behind the University and Lake Shore Park, is Chicago's Magnificent Mile, the "Mag Mile", Michigan Avenue. It stretches from the river to Lake Shore Drive. First up is the Olympia Centre, the red granite tower. Then the Park Tower with a pyramid as its cap, and a white rectangle skyscraper.

Then comes the focal point of our Near North Chicago skyscraper tour—The John Hancock Center, now called the boring name of 875 N. Michigan Avenue. It soars 100 tapered stories high with the giant X truss bracing, that holds the building up and resists the famed Chicago winds. Up on the 94th floor, is 360Chicago, the open aired observation deck, above the Magnificent Mile. It offers breathtaking views, up to four states for a distance of 80 miles! The deck has a theme ride, the TILT, an enclosed moving platform that tilts you out over Michigan Avenue. Or have a fancy dinner at the restaurant with killer views! We think it is a pretty killer view looking up from the water at this extraordinary skyscraper.

But we aren't quite done with the Magnificent Mile yet. We still have the vertical shopping mall, a classic look with limestone, green glass reflective windows, and topped with the towers that are especially brilliant when lit up at night. In front of this newer building, is the traditional historic Chicago landmark, the art deco Palmolive Building. This may not be tall, but it has class and spunk! Built in 1929 in a step-up design, it is topped with the Lindbergh Beacon which sweeps out over Lake Michigan in the evening! At the north end of the Mag Mile is One Magnificent Mile with three hexagonal shapes with various floors in Spanish pink granite and sloping roofs.

We paddle past the gorgeous Oak Street Beach because it is not designated a kayak launch beach. It is a golden triangle of sandy beach in the Gold Coast neighborhood of Chicago. Bike, volleyball, lounge chairs, and cabana rentals are available. If you think Lake Michigan is cold in the summer, you could come back in January for the annual Polar Plunge. . .

The Concrete Beach wall is lined with mid-size condos. Except, for an old mansion towards the north end, where you will find the International Museum of Surgical Science. It is fascinating to see the old-time equipment used in surgeries! As we head out the third mile around the hook wall that protects North Beach. We pass the Chess Pavilion—a really cool open-air pavilion with architectural significance with carvings and sculptures of chess pieces.

Curl around the breakwater captain's hook and head into North Beach. . .it'll take your breath away with that amazing skyline! The south end is the non-motorized boat area. Rick lands, and instead of turning around and assisting us as is his custom, he grabs his camera and keeps walking up onto the beach and across the sand to "Photography Point". Finally, he turns around, his mouth still gaping, and states "OMG", "this is my favorite beach ever".

Time to swim. . .but it's hard walking backwards into the water, to not miss the incredible view for even a moment. It is unbelievable to be outdoors swimming at a cool beach while relishing the city scape. Imagine, that there are amazing beaches in such a busy city! After swimming, we lounge on the beach for a picnic. Generally, we sit on our beach blanket enjoying the lake, today, we've turned to delight in the city view!

At North Avenue Beach is the Castaway Bar and Grill. It looks like a boat that was washed ashore and turned into a restaurant, equipped with red smokestacks and port hole windows! There is a snack bar and the rooftop relaxed patio restaurant with sandwiches, wraps, salads, and fish tacos—perfect for at the beach. North Avenue Beach is almost a mile long. The south hook, is where Chicago SUP has rentals and lessons, Kayak Chicago rents kayaks, and Windy City Watersports rents jet skis. Sun and Moon Beach Yoga offers classes, or just rent beach umbrellas and lounge chairs to relax. You can rent bikes, if you desire to do a paddle and peddle day, with the Lakefront Trail along the shore. After the main beach, there are five smaller beaches protected by short cement piers. North Avenue Beach is kind of like the Cancun of the Midwest. . . unsalted!

Back in our kayaks, we explore North Avenue Beach. There is a pedestrian path over Lake Shore Drive to Lincoln Park. Lincoln Park is huge, bigger than New York City's Central Park! Ha, so there! Known for several sculptures: Fountain Girl, General Ulysses S. Grant equestrian statue on a walk-through arched base, and the original Standing Lincoln bronze statue.

Lincoln Park is home to the Chicago History Museum. It became part of the history when it burned down during the Great Chicago Fire. Reinvented, it houses George Washington's compass, and the bed where Abraham Lincoln died. Exhibits include Sensing Chicago where you can ride a high wheel bike, hear the Great Chicago Fire, catch a Chicago baseball, and dive into a giant Chicago style hot dog! Watching the Chicago Film, you can feel the intensity of the Chicago fire, and peer down from an I-beam at the top of the Sears Tower when it was being built.

We paddle past the Lincoln Park Zoo, a world of wildlife in the shade of the skyscrapers. Lions and tigers and bears, oh my! Oh, alright, no tigers, but a variety of bears including polar bears and koala bears. Along with primates and gorillas, camels, zebras, and kangaroos, and a farm in the city. Listen for zoo sounds.

Lincoln Park also has a Conservancy with a Victorian Glass House. It showcases palms, ferns, tropical flowers and orchids. Outside has a variety of formal gardens, a Lily Pool, a Midwestern Prairie style garden with a gentle waterfall and stone paths.

Paddle by the brown roofed lakefront building that is the Theater on the Lake, with the Lakefront Restaurant. Rip rap shoreline in front, and then the Fullerton Beach concrete steps are along the shoreline and the ever-present Lakefront hiking and biking trail.

We come to a little inlet, Diversey Harbor. The beautiful bridge detail that we can see is the new Lakefront Trail bridge, with Art Deco ornamentation and gorgeous Art Deco Bridge lights. There is a designated Illinois Lake Michigan Water Trail launch in the harbor.

Lincoln Park lingers past the harbor, with an 18-hole Mini Golf Course, tennis courts, a picnic grove, and an Ultimate Frisbee field. Stay close to shore to see the Signal of Peace monument with an Indian Chief on horseback holding a staff with a peace feather. Nearby is the Big Blue sculpture. Rising behind the park is a white slim rectangle condo building, and Saint Joseph Hospital with its tripod of three wings.

A row of more condo buildings line-up behind the concrete step shoreline park as we paddle by Belmont Harbor. And Lincoln Park endures into its third mile along the lake shore. The Jarvis Migratory Bird Sanctuary is the clump of trees along the shore after the Harbor. Lincoln Park continues with a golf course where all nine holes are oriented parallel to the lake with the largest water hazard possible— Lake Michigan!

Keep near shore to head into Montrose Harbor if desired. On the Lake Michigan Water Trail, the launch site is the fishing dock, just past the star docks on the north side of the inside harbor wall. Climbing out of your boat may be a one to two-foot scramble.

We head out around Montrose Point, and past the Montrose Moonrise Observation Point. Aww, so romantic. . .and again I have to endure Rick and Chris stopping to cling their kayaks together and share a smoochy kiss. They do it every paddle—it is so sweet!

Inside Lincoln Park at Montrose is a skatepark and cricket hill. Stay quiet to hear the song birds at the Montrose Point Bird Sanctuary. Internationally known for the "Magic Hedge" which attracts an unusually large number of birds, a water feature called the dripper, and the lake dune where loons and falcons have been spotted.

We curl around the fish hook pier with its crooked finger beckoning us into the sandy beach shore. The south end is the boating beach and where Kayak Chicago rents kayaks. We land, jump out and pull the boats up a wee bit. I finagle Rick to swim and play before the work of loading up and hauling of boats. "Come on Rick", Lake Michigan is a natural spa flotation pool. We can float and let the lake's buoyancy relieve aches and pains from our day of paddling!

Montrose Beach generally has a deep sand beach, but the high-water levels of Lake Michigan have created a pond between us and the park. I try to navigate the floating bridge, but Chris takes the reins in her own hands and pulls her kayak through the shallow pond— and it works! Always knew, she was the brains of our operation. . . Rick calls the Uber/Lyft driver as Chris and I pull the boats to a shade tree and relax and watch families coming to the beach. What an extraordinary paddle day! What a mind-blowing incredible adventure this kayaking to Chicago has been!

Logistics:

Montrose Beach, Chicago:
41.9664, -87.6352. 4400 N. Lake Shore Drive. Parking lot or street parking. Kayak Chicago rents kayaks and SUP's here. Restrooms.

Montrose Harbor, Chicago:
41.9623, -87.6395. 601 W. Montrose Avenue. On the Illinois Lake Michigan Water Trail, Parking lot or street parking.

Diversey Harbor, Chicago:
41.9309, -87.6350. 2601 N. Cannon Drive.
On the Illinois Lake Michigan Water Trail parking fee, restrooms.

North Avenue Beach, Chicago:
41.9137, -87.6225. 1600 N Lake Shore Drive. On the Illinois Lake Michigan Water Trail, parking fee, restrooms.

12th Street Beach, Chicago:
41.8649, -87.6073. 1200 South Linn White Drive. On the Illinois Lake Michigan Water Trail, parking fee, restrooms.

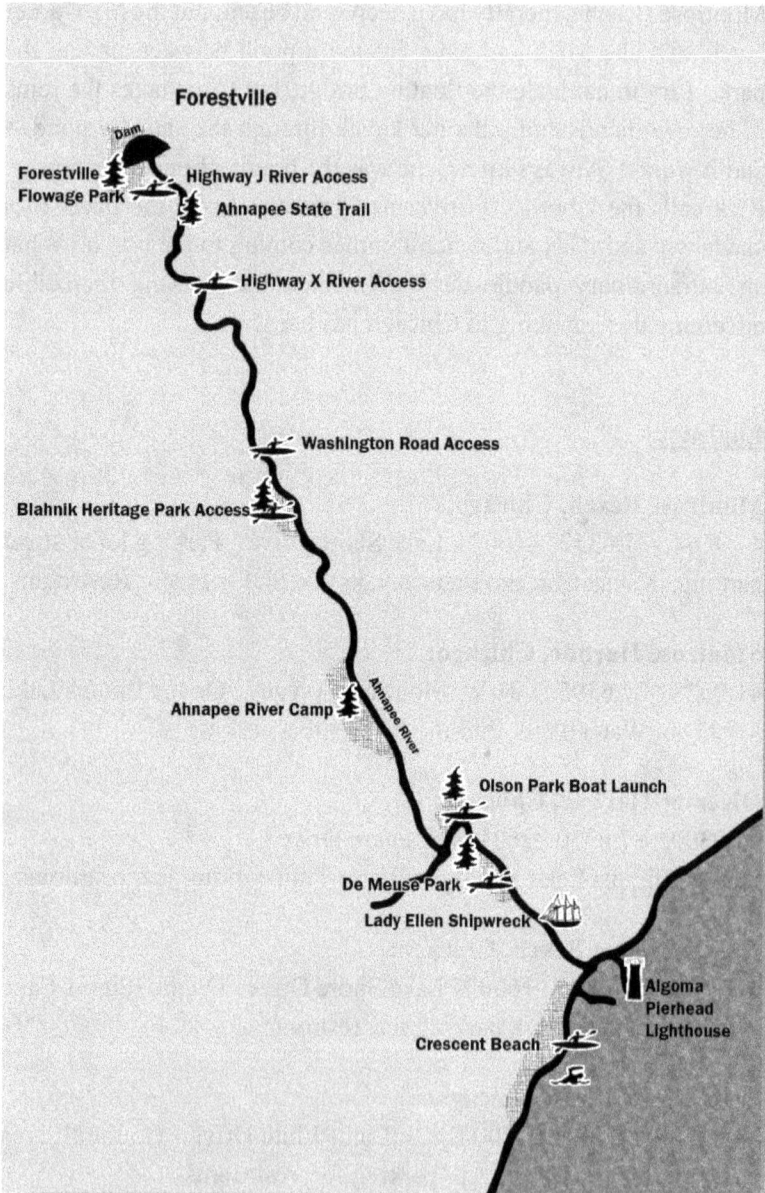

River Paddle

Ahnapee River Paddle

Forestville to Algoma

With Woods and Meadows, to Urban and a Shipwreck

8 miles

Fun friendly paddle to do with a group! We paddle from Forestville to Algoma's Olson Park and boat landing for a 7-mile paddle. You could continue through Algoma and the harbor and around the break water wall to Crescent Beach which makes it an 8.5-mile paddle. There are several opportunities to shorten the paddle such as at Highway X, Washington Road, or you could camp at the private campgrounds for river access.

Enjoyed this paddle with my therapy colleagues, bubbly Brooke did a great job organizing the event. Sharing fun outings with coworkers is a great way to build a strong team, and with this group of therapists, any little soreness from paddling is quickly healed!

We put in upriver in Forestville in the center of the Lower Door Peninsula. Forestville is a quiet hamlet with small town friendliness. From Highway J, in Forestville just west of the bridge that goes over the river, there is a little pull over parking area by the bridge allowing small crafts to unload and bring their boats to the river.

North of this bridge is the Forestville Dam Pond County Park. . . a clue that there is a dam up river. The access to the pond is actually north of the dam and is often used by kayakers and canoers for a mile-long pond paddle and then shrinks back to a river to explore further. The dam was originally built in the 1800's for a wheat mill.

My therapy team is heading down the Ahnapee River to Algoma. We have a meeting time with more colleagues at the Von Steihl Winery. Immediately Forestville lives up to its name with a tree lined river beckoning us. Most of us own kayaks, but several are borrowing kayaks and giving this paddling idea their first try. After a few giggles and grins, the whole group get the kayaks moving in the right direction.

As we paddle the twisty, turny river with chatty casual conversation, we arrive at our first bridge, County X. It's fun to call out each other's names and echo, echo, echo, as we glide under the bridge. Highway X does offer a small parking area with a path to put in from the west bound lane if you desire to shorten the paddle.

The Ahnapee Bike trail follows the river on the east side, our left side, as we kayak down the river. The trail is a "rails to trails", an old railroad track converted to a recreation trail to enjoy Wisconsin's countryside. It zigzags 48 miles from Kewaunee northwest to Luxemburg and Casco, then zigs northeast to Algoma, zagging again to follow the Ahnapee River to Forestville, before once more turning northeast up to Sturgeon Bay. Besides riveting river views and meandering meadows, there is noteworthy forest cover for even hot sunny days.

After a mile, an old train trestle crosses the river. It is the rustic Ahnapee Bike trail crossing over us, wave to the bikers as they trek past. Perhaps, we could hide under the bridge and yell "boo" as the

bikers cross the river. . .nasty girl on the loose—perhaps I've learned this from all the years of my brother's antics!

Alas, this group is well behaved. We continue gliding down the river. Serene surroundings abound with evergreen groves, prairies, and corn stalks swaying on the occasional farmland. Little streams that could be explored are scattered along the river. Gracious banter and the sharing of goodies sustain us on our adventure.

Another 1.5 miles of good times brings us to Washington Road Bridge over pass. Once more there is a small gravel area for on road parking and a slim path down to the river for another access point. Don't be surprised if an angler is there, fishing for supper. In Spring and Fall, the Ahnapee River is famous for the salmon run.

After the bridge and curve in the river, is the Blahnik Heritage Park. There is a floating fishing dock at the park that we are free to use. The dock is not a kayak launch, but is a public access spot. Take pleasure in the native wildflowers that have been planted at the park. Highway 42, angles towards the river in a mile on the east, left side of the river. On the right side, two private campgrounds offer river access, Ahnapee River Trail Campground, and Timber Trails Campground which offers kayak and canoe rentals.

One more wooded mile and a sharp left curve in the river brings us to Olson Park, our planned take out spot. There is a little stream that runs through the wooded area in the park. Two small boat launches are available. Restrooms and a picnic area are appreciated.

You may choose to continue paddling the urban view of Algoma. After Olson Park, the Algoma Hardwood Door Company is on the right of the river. DeMeuse Park is the greenery on the right bank right before the blue and white Algoma Boat Club with its private boat launch. DeMeuse Park is a possible launch site or take out spot.

Just before you go under the 4th St Bridge is Bearcat's Fish House which specializes in fresh fish (if you didn't stop to catch them yourself) and they also traditionally smoke fish using hardwoods right at their store. After the 4th St Bridge, there is green space on the left bank and two private marinas with RV camping where several fishing charter boats dock on the right.

Before the old girder, 2nd St. Bridge, lies the remains of the Lady Ellen schooner. She was a two masted scow schooner with flat bottom and a squared blunt bow, making her very stable with good deck space for hauling freight. After the Lady Ellen was towed up river to the dock in 1897, she was abandoned and never used again. At times she sits in four feet of water and other times she is mostly dry, making her framework pretty easy to explore.

The next sights are the Von Stiehl Winery and Ahnapee Brewery, both on the right side of the river, but neither has kayak or canoe access. More fishing charter services follow. If you haven't noticed by now, Algoma is an olde Great Lakes fishing port, and continues to live up to its historic roots.

Then onto the city of Algoma's Marina and Christmas Tree Point! Christmas Tree Point is where all the town folks would come at the end of the sailing season in the 1800's to watch the schooners sail past laden with thousands of Christmas trees to sell in Milwaukee and Chicago. The most famous ship was the Rouse Simmons which was decorated with electric Christmas lights and her Captain Santa. In 1912, loaded Christmas trees, she sailed past Algoma and Christmas Tree Point. However, by the time she reached Kewaunee, she was in distress with her flag at half-mast. A rescue boat was sent out, but the Christmas Tree Ship was never seen again. A message in a bottle washed up on shore by Sheboygan from Captain Santa: "Friday. . .everybody goodbye. I guess we are all through, God help us". By December, Christmas trees began washing up onto the shores. Years later, a wallet belonging to Captain Santa was caught in a fishing net. Perhaps as you paddle past Christmas Tree Point, you will see the ghost ship "The Christmas Tree Ship" as others have claimed.

Back to the now, you could turn south in the harbor and take out next to the marina by Legion Park on Lake Street. Otherwise, you need to travel out of the protected harbor, but this option does give you the opportunity to enjoy Algoma's red pier head lighthouse up close. Algoma's current round red metal tower was established in 1932. The lighthouse originally had a 5th order Fresnel lens. The new red light can be seen up to 11 miles away.

Paddle around the south pier break water to the expanse of Crescent Beach. Crescent Beach is where we stop for a quick dip and swim to "freshen up" before meeting our colleagues at the Von Stiehl Winery for free music on the green. A toast to a great day of camaraderie and sunshine!

Logistics:

Highway J river access, Forestville:
44.6899, -87.4873. 7711 W. Main Street. On road parking area. Follow the small path down to the river.

County Highway X river access, Forestville:
44.6753, -87.4831. 7634 County Road X. Park off the side of the road and follow the small path down to the river.

Washington Road river access, Algoma:
44.6465, -87.4665. E5901 Washington Road. Off road parking.
Blahnik Heritage Park, Algoma:
44.6465, -87.4713. E5843 Washington Road.
Parking area, no restrooms.

Olson Park boat launch, Algoma:
44.6171, -87.4489. 8108 N. Water Street (Hwy 42).
Restrooms are available.

DeMeuse Park, Algoma:
44.6132, -87.4415. 180 6th Street. You may launch directly off the river bank into the Ahnapee River.

Ahnapee River mouth, Lake Street/Legion Park, Algoma:
44.6065, -87.4346. 620 Lake St. There is a parking lot by the inside of the harbor and marina right on Highway 42 in downtown Algoma. Restrooms are at end of Lake Street at the corner of Lake and Navarino Streets.

Crescent Beach in Algoma:
44.6063, -87.4357. 850 Lake St. The parking lot is at the north end of the beach next to the harbor. Restrooms are at end of Lake Street at the corner of Lake and Navarino Streets.

Shipwreck Location:

The Lady Ellen: 44.6104, -87.4353. a scow schooner was abandoned at dock in the Ahnapee River in 1897. She lies in very shallow water by a small cove just west of the 2nd Street Bridge.

Kayak Wisconsin, Lake Michigan Water Trail

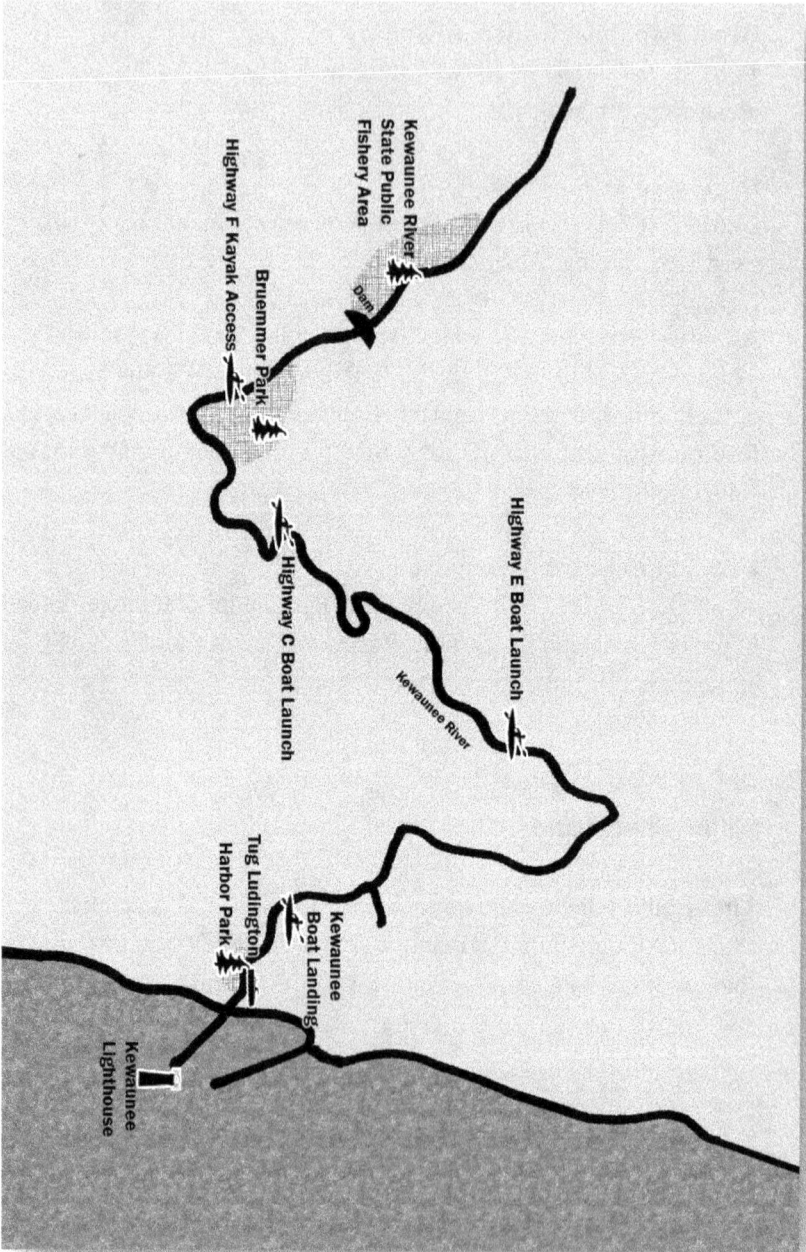

River paddle

Kewaunee River Paddle

Kewaunee and Kewaunee County

With the WOW group: Women on the Water

7 miles

For sure, a 5 mile paddle up river is possible on the Kewaunee River—maybe even more, depending on water levels. Peaceful paddle, whether you choose to do this because Lake Michigan is being boisterous, or just because you were looking for solitude. Did this paddle with the North East Wisconsin Paddlers Association, Women on the Water, the "WOW" group, yup we are wow, we even let a few guys join us (Rick included)!

It is worthwhile to head east down river a bit for a history of Kewaunee. Paddle under the Main Street Bridge with the city's Marina on the north side, and public green area with a boardwalk along the river on the south bank. Lafonds Fish Market and the Port O Call restaurant continue on the south side of the river. Then look for Harbor Park with the tug Ludington. She was built for World War II and participated in D Day. After she was released from duty her machine guns were removed. The tug was large enough to cross the ocean on her own and made her way to Kewaunee for harbor maintenance. The tug is available to tour.

Across the river on the north side is a peninsula and Harbor Point Park with fishing docks and picnic areas. Follow the south side harbor to the pier and the Kewaunee Lighthouse. The piers were first built in 1856 and the north pier has become a 1000-feet long. The present lighthouse replaced range lights and was transferred to its now location on the south pier. The lighthouse consists of a one and a half story fog signal building with the square tower lantern room on the end. The light used a fifth order Fresnel lens.

The WOW's launch our kayaks at the Kewaunee Marina boat launch, this time heading up river. Immediately, the calmness settles in and the shoreline is undisturbed. Green, very green, the fern green water, emerald green reedy shoreline, backed by the deeper pine and juniper greenery of the rolling tree line. Occasionally we rouse ducks and geese from the river's edge.

Only one mile of strokes brings us to the Ahnapee Bike Trail Bridge. An old train trestle no longer in use, now recycled for bicycles. The trestle bridge does still have its swing mechanism intact, and the ladies are beautifully framed by the bridge. The Ahnapee Trail has followed us from Kewaunee on the left side of the river and now a spur crosses the river to the north side of the city. This rails to trail

path travels 50 miles up to Sturgeon Bay. Besides bikers and hikers, the trail is used by horseback riders and in the winter snowmobiles and cross-country skiers.

Follow the river north around a tree lined peninsula. This secluded country is great for bird watching. Look for snowy egrets, teals, marsh wrens, hawks, and maybe even swans, whip-poor-wills, or bobolinks. Down below us in the river, search for bullheads, smallmouth bass, northern pike, steelhead and brown trout, and in the Autumn, the salmon start running upriver!

As we come back down around the bend, and County Road E, River Road, meets up with us, there is a small launch area before the bridge with a turn-around area but no parking. A better choice is on the west side of the river right before the River Road Bridge, where there is an unmarked Highway E boat launch.

After the paddling under the bridge, the Ahnapee Trail joins us again to follow beside the river. While we and the Kewaunee River twist and turn, the Ahnapee Trail is never far from the river for the next two and a quarter miles of quiet river wilderness with basically a nix of home or farm to be seen.

Paddle under the Ellis Street County C Bridge and then immediately under the Trail footbridge. On the west side of the river is another unmarked designated boat launch, the Highway C boat launch. Up until now, the river has been wide and deep enough to paddle all season. We have now cruised about five miles upriver. Here is our planned take out, but it is possible to continue kayaking further, depending on the season and water depth. The river quickly narrows after this point.

You can meander through the wooded areas of Bruemmer Park which offers picnic areas and restrooms and a small enjoyable community zoo. Enjoy the one plus mile of tapered river and the uninterrupted forests of the park. Before the Highway F Bridge is a parking area by the river. There is a gentle entrance off the grassy bank to the river. After the Highway F Bridge is the dam for the C. D. Besadny Anadromous Fish Hatchery which catches the salmon, spawns and harvests the fish, and then hatches salmon to restock them back into Lake Michigan. The facility is open to the public and has an underwater viewing window by the fish ladder leading to six holding ponds. Great viewing during the Fall for the salmon run!

Logistics:

Kewaunee Boat Landing Kewaunee:
44.4637, -87.5045. Highway 42 in downtown. Parking lot, kayak/canoe launch on west side. Fee, restrooms.

Highway E Boat Launch, Kewaunee:
44.4785, -87.5276. N4157 County Highway E.
Small parking area and the boat launch. No restrooms, no fee.

Highway C Boat launch, Kewaunee:
44.4785, -87.5448. 3753 Park Lane. Gravel road that takes you to the unmarked boat launch. No restrooms, no fee.

Highway F Kayak Access/Bruemmer Kewaunee County Park:
44.4578, -87.5551. E4184 County Highway F, Kewaunee. Parking off Highway F, drive way is flanked by two stone pillars.

Kayak Wisconsin, Lake Michigan Water Trail

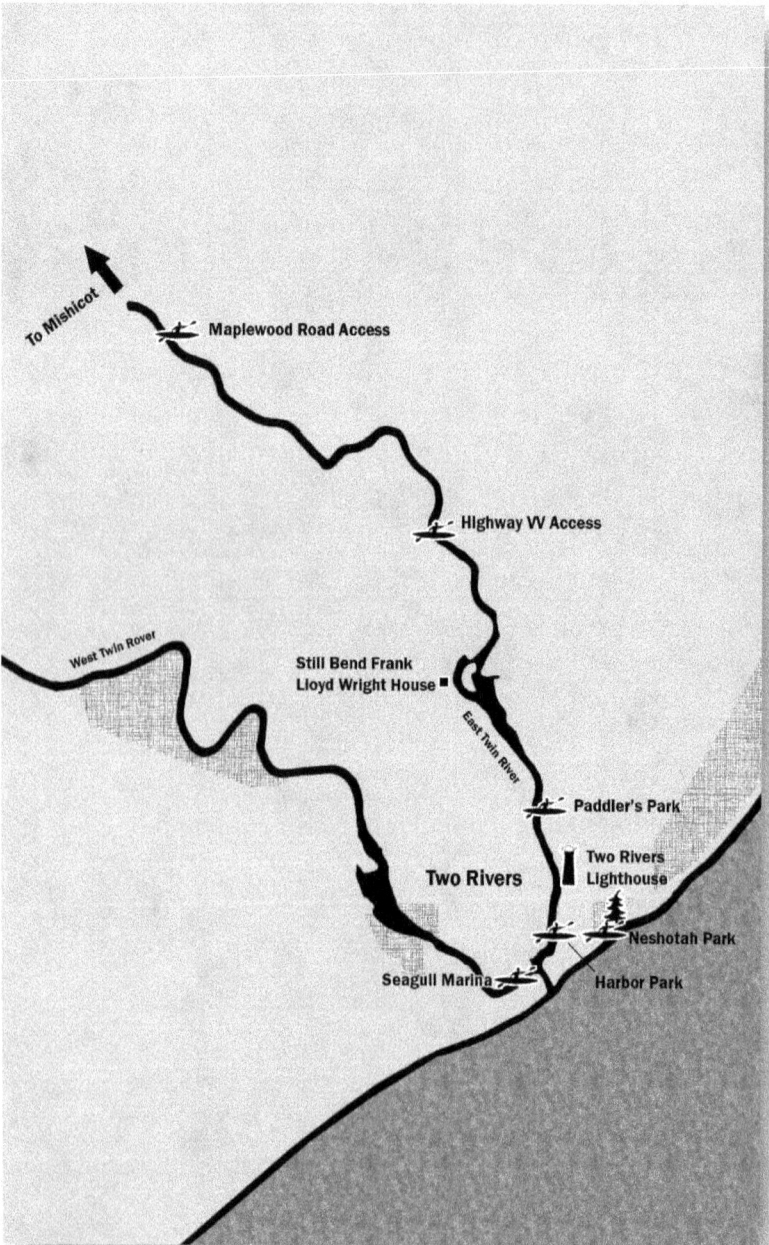

River Paddle

East Twin River Paddle

Two Rivers to Mishicot

With the Two Rivers Lighthouse and miles of nice nature

10 miles

Delightful dalliance with nature! Did this leisurely paddle with my sis' Becky, enjoying the initial urban feel with a closeup view of the Fresnel lens in the Two Rivers Lighthouse in town, and then onto quiet marsh and woods, with just fin and feather friends.

If you launch at Nashotah Park on Lake Michigan, enter the harbor and then paddling the entire East Twin River all the way to Mishicot it would be a 12-mile paddle. You could divide the paddle into two, one day paddles at Maplewood Road Bridge which is at about the 6-mile mark. Or skip Lake Michigan and most of the urban paddling and put in a Paddlers Park in Two Rivers and kayak to Mishicot for a 10-mile paddle. Going north the river narrows and you may face downed trees that you need to portage around.

For the full river paddle, put in at Nashotah Park on Lake Michigan. Might as well splash into the lake at Nashotah Park as this is a perfect groomed sandy beach!

Paddle toward the Two Rivers North Pier Lighthouse, now just a modern automated beacon, the real one is now upriver at the Historic Rogers Street Village. After following the 1200-foot long piers as you enter the mouth of the river, on the east side of the river is the pretty white Coast Guard Station with the red roof. There has been a Two Rivers Life Saving Station since 1877. This new Coast Guard Station is responsible for search and rescue, Maritime law, and provides security to the USS Badger Car Ferry in Manitowoc. Next to the Coast Guard Station at the end of Pilon Court Street is a parking area with access to the beach on the outside of the breakwater. This is a little longer carry in than Nashotah Beach—your choice a speck longer paddle or a longer carrying of the kayak—kind of a toss-up.

After the Coast Guard Station, the river forks ninety degrees right or left, decision time. . .East Twin River to the right or West Twin River to the left. . . We choose right and the East Twin River today. Paddle under the new 17th Street lift bridge, ah, don't bother to honk for the bridge master to lift the bridge.

North, we head, with green space to the west left bank and Susie Q Fish Company on the right east bank. The LeClair family has been commercial fishin' in Two Rivers for over 130 years and smoke chub, salmon, trout, whitefish, herring and carp, which is available in their store.

After some private marinas, right before the lightly arched 22nd Street/Highway 42 Bridge is the Historic Rogers Street Village. The Village has a Coast Guard Museum, commercial fishing exhibits, shipwreck displays, and the tug boat Buddy O to tour. Most importantly, look up at the Two Rivers Lighthouse with her sixth order Fresnel lens, this is probably the closest you'll get to seeing a real Fresnel lens from the water. Two Rivers has had a lighthouse since 1858. But when the piers were completed in the 1870's, the square wooden lighthouse sitting on top of the wooden framework with a trap door was built. In 1928 the lighthouse was electrified and then deactivated in 1969, and moved to its present location in 1975. The Fresnel lens light can be activated for a day in memory of a loved one—how cool is that for a tribute!

A couple of blocks up is Paddlers Park, which is a great alternate launch site as the name of the park attests to. It is only a mile from the mouth of the river with an easy slide into the river. Across the river on the peninsula is Washington Park with over a third of a mile river front greenery. The east bank is greenery also, because the houses are set quite far back giving a very secluded rural feel to the paddle. We enjoy a blue heron sitting stoically on a home dock.

Shortly after the parks, the river opens up and there is a little inlet on the east right bank that leads to the Vietnam Veteran Memorial Park, but there is no river access to the park. Back on the main river, go straight through the river channel or veer to the west and jog around the island. It is worthwhile going toward the west side of the river to see if we can get a glimpse of the Schwartz House, designed by the famous architect Frank Lloyd Wright. He named this house "Still Bend" to reflect his philosophy of building with the harmony of the environment as it looks out onto the marshy island. This home is built in the prairie school movement of architecture and if you want a very cool and unique experience, you can rent the house for the night!

The east side river channel is relaxing pleasing greenery as we are truly now more rural. The Fairview Golf Course is off to the east behind Riverview Drive. A great place to put our feet up on the front of our kayaks and do some chillaxin', settling back and sharing veggies, sandwiches, and snacks. Look down for our fin friends and watching the geese glide in for a landing.

Around a hairpin curve to the right and a gentle curve to the left comes the 45th Street/Highway VV Bridge. Stacks of condos with incredible river views are before the bridge. Then we are back to wetlands with sporadic bright white birch trees shining against the Packer green and gold reedy background.

Just around the next bend is a small stream to explore for a short distance. In less than a mile, Tannery Road and Shamrock Lane head toward the river with a few docks to give it away. The river starts to narrow and becomes more wooded. We twist and turn in a

leisurely way; the river and we are in no hurry. A crow flying may make quicker progress than us on the curvy river.

As we go around another sharp curve, an alpaca farm is on the left west bank cleverly hidden by a small forest. An alpaca resembles a camel without a hump, and with smooth fleece. The farm is off of Highway 147, Mishicot Road. The century old farm does school group tours, and has a store by appointment selling yarn, socks, and teddy bears!

A short distance through the woods we near the Maplewood Road Bridge. Before the bridge, we notice greenhouses, this is Steinie's Water Gardens which specializes in ponds, koi fish, and beautiful flowering water plants.

Paddle under the bridge, and on the northeast river bank is the public access from the road. There is parking on the side of the road. The groomed grassy shore is the Eastwin Valley Golf Course. Besides the 18-hole traditional golf course, they also offer a 9 or 18-hole Footgolf course. Footgolf is a combination of soccer and golf, where you kick off from a tee box and attempt to get your soccer ball into the 21-inch cup. How about a game after using our arms kayaking all day?

After the golf course, we again are surrounded by the peaceful forested shoreline with a few farms interspersed. The next two bridges are each about three quarters of a mile apart. First is Hillcrest Road Bridge, and then meander through the woods to Sturm Road Bridge. This bridge is right off of Highway 147 and there may be a green path to the river's edge for public access.

Variations of green continue for another half mile, where a small island is centered in the river. Take the east right side of the river as it is a little wider channel. Immediately after the island is a small farm bridge over the river. Then the emerald shoreline on the left west bank is literally green acres—Green Acres Lawn and Garden Center.

As the river narrows, watch for fallen tree logs and some of the turns in the river start to bog down. Steiner Corner Drive Bridge is next, with perhaps a green path down to the river on the northwest bank after the bridge. Here the river is shallow and narrow as it meanders into Mishicot. The shoreline is tree lined with cornfields swaying the breeze as we pass them by. The East Twin River becomes a little muddled as we try to figure out the open passage through the woods.

Through the trees on the eastern shore is Mishicot Elementary School track and field, followed by Mishicot Community School. One more twist of the river to the left and then right and we arrive at our take out site, the Safety Building parking lot before the Main Street Bridge on the south side of the river. After a nice stretch, it would be a good time to walk over to the restrooms across the street in Mishicot Village Park! Follow that by walking the Riverwalk trail along the river through the park past the dam and check out the Rockway Covered Bridge.

Logistics:

Nashotah Park, Two Rivers:
44.1524, -87.5550. 500 Zlatnik Drive. Lots of parking! No fee, nice restrooms, short carry to the water's edge.

Seagull Marina Boat Ramp, Two Rivers:
44.1461, -87.5653. 1400 Lake Street.
Listed on the Twin Rivers Water Trail. Fee, restrooms.

Harbor Park Wall Access, Two Rivers:
44.1473, -87.5640. 13 E Street. Street parking, on the Water Trail.

Rogers Street Fishing Village Public Dock Access:
44.1527, -87.5628. 2010 Rogers Street. Parking on street. Dock is off of 21st Street. Listed on the Twin Rivers Water Trail.

Paddlers Park kayak launch, Two Rivers:
44.1585, -87.5650. 1250 27th Street. Parking lot on south side by river. No fee, no restrooms. Listed on the Twin Rivers Water Trail.

45th Street Bridge/Highway VV river access, Two Rivers:
44.1758, -87.5774. 4500 County Road VV. Park on south side of road for slim overgrown path through the reeds to the river access.

Maplewood Road river access:
44.1895, -87.6058. 2300 Maplewood Road.
Park on the north side of the road. No restrooms.

Safety Building parking lot, Mishicot:
44.2367, -87.6383. 214 Willow Street. Parking lot across the street. No fee, restrooms in Mishicot Village Park.

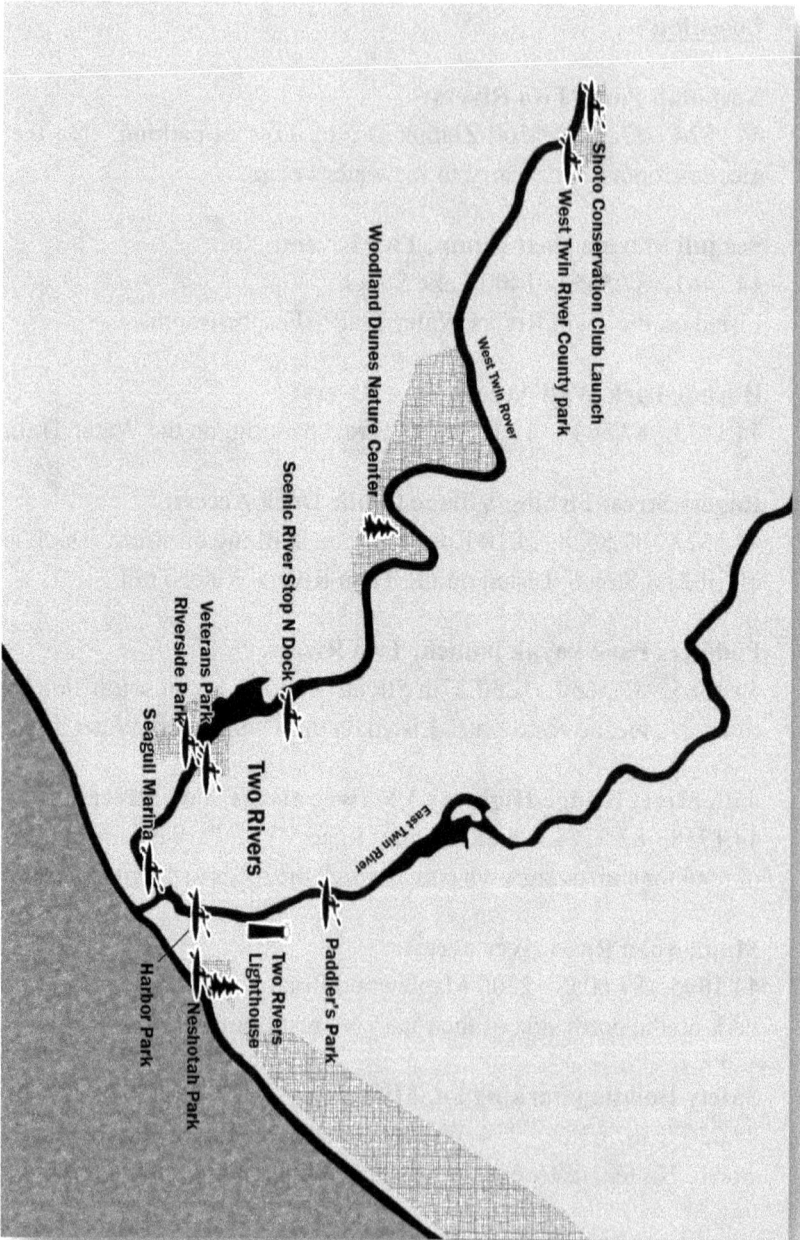

River Paddle

West Twin River Paddle

Two Rivers

With Marshes and City Life

6 miles

A fun mix of both tranquil relaxing bird watching, and several miles of the Two Rivers city life. And it was a Mom and son day! You can't do better than that, now can you!

We launch at the West Twin River County Park and paddle east. Go around the bend at the convergence of the East Twin River and the Lake Michigan harbor channel, to go west up the East Twin River to Paddlers Park, a non-motorized boat launch. A total of 6 miles, which left us time in the afternoon, on the Labor Day weekend, to catch the wind at the Kites over Lake Michigan Festival!

We drop Matt's SUV off at Paddlers Park for our shuttle car, and head over to the West Twin River County Park on County highway VV. You know you are close to the park when you spot the "crashed" airplane in the woods on the side of the highway. How silly is that prop? Always makes me chuckle. . .

As I turn into the West Twin River County Park, the road is closed. Oh, oh. The park has obviously been under water and is now all green and slimy. Opps. Able to park off on the side of the entrance road and thankfully the branch loop off the main West Twin River is now a pond and we are able to slide our kayaks into the water and paddle out to the river. Should have checked out the Shoto Conservation Club, just 1000 feet to the west. They offer free public access to the river, and have restrooms—perhaps their shoreline might not have been green and gooey. They also offer a fishing pier for the handicapped, and are part of the Twin Rivers Water Trail.

Right away on the river heading east, we get another laugh. A Jaws shark is hanging on the shoreline . . . just like they caught it on the river. Might it be the same pranksters as the crashed plane?

Then, we are pretty much in marsh field (Wisconsin's everglades, not the Wisconsin city of Marshfield). Time to unwind, breathe deeply, and enjoy the absolute solitude. A few quacks from ducks, and a trio of honks above that alert us to the V of geese flying overhead. Peaceful. A mass of tall reeds along the banks of the river. We are in our own rural utopia. A supple, graceful hawk soars above us. A blue heron standing in the shallows catch our eye, and another flapping away on the other shoreline. One lonely cormorant swims along with us, leading the way. When we get close, he frets away, swatting the water numerous times as he takes flight. Only to land a short distance ahead to continue to lead us down river.

The boggy fenland continues, even as we approach the city of Two Rivers, which lies only a 1000 feet northeast, we cannot see or hear the town. We are on our own peaceful journey down the wetlands surrounding the West Twin River. A few homes pop up along the shore, one with a glass bell tower, and three balconies— they must be bird lovers.

After 3.5 miles of peaceful paddling, the Woodland Dunes Nature Preserve is on the southern shore. This place celebrates the marsh! Created by Lake Michigan's predecessor, Lake Nippissing—when the lake was even bigger than it is now! As this ancient lake retreated at the end of the Glacier period, the ripples left 14 ridges and swales at the nature preserve. Initially formed as a bird banding research station, Woodland Dunes has grown to be a wonderful addition to Two Rivers. Many migratory birds, and monarchs, use Woodland Dunes Nature Preserve as a wayside stop. They even have a nesting platform for osprey! Osprey are making a comeback in Wisconsin with the help of man-made nesting platforms. They are large raptors, smaller than eagles, but larger than other hawks. They have slender bodies and long narrow wings, with a five to six-foot wingspan. Osprey eat fresh fish almost exclusively, therefore making the West Twin River a perfect habitat for them!

We float under telephone wires over the river. An Osprey platform nest above! We can tell he is large, with a white belly and a black hooked beak. He is too high above us to make out his white head with a brown line through his eyes. He calls to us—high pitched series of caws. He obviously is concerned with us being below him. Here's to hoping he doesn't swoop down at us. We don't want to be bombarded by him. He calms as we pose no threat and slide silently under him. A wonderful delight to share the river with him. Woodland Dunes offer seven miles of hiking trails through oaks, maple, and evergreen trees on the ridges, and bridges over the swales. Their Cattail Trail, is a 1000-foot boardwalk through the marshy reeds. It's fun to walk through them—with dry feet—on their boardwalk with the reeds taller than you! And at the end, is a kayak launch, an added bonus! Would be a great stop to stretch and tour Woodland Dunes Nature Preserve.

On the north side of the river is the Scenic River Stop-N-Dock RV Park. This is the first of a true boat launch in Two Rivers, and they are on the Twin Rivers Water Trail. We are now approaching the first bridge in Two Rivers, the Madison Street Bridge. There are two parks, the north side of the river has Veteran Park Boat Ramps, which is another possibility to launch kayaks. They offer a fish cleaning station too. Just inland is Vets park with a playground, and restrooms. Time to stop?

On the south bank of the river is Riverside Park. The most notable feature we can see, is the skateboard park half pike ramp. There are restrooms, a playground, picnic area and a hiking trail loop around the pond. Bushy shoreline, but we are allowed to land if you can find a spot, and they too have restrooms in the shelter.

We paddle under the Madison Street Bridge, a newer concrete bridge with a wrought iron railing and globe lights. On the south shore is Riverwalk Park, with a deck on the shoreline and a green lawn for picnics.

The bridge that catches our eye is the railroad bridge sitting smack dab in the middle of the river. This abandoned train trestle is locked in the open position. Built in 1899, the track previously ran from Manitowoc to Two Rivers. This train bridge is a unique design as it had a center pivot. This means that the two ends need to be perfectly balanced on the pier to safely swing. The nine riveted metal panels sit on a stone masonry and timber pier.

As we round the bend, the south side of the river has boat docks for a private marina, and then we paddle under the Washington Street Bridge. McDonalds is on the east shoreline now, getting hungry!

All in front of McDonalds are private boat docks, but at the very end is Seagull Marina with a boat ramp. And yes, we can land and launch here! On the west shore is a lovely river side park with a nice shelter and folks fishing from the river wall.

Then we are at the convergence of the East Twin River and the harbor channel to Lake Michigan. As we look up the channel, the pretty white building with the deep red roof, is the U.S. Coast Guard Station. They are responsible for search and rescues, maritime law, pollution response, and for the US Badger Car Ferry security. The Coast Guard station patrols fifty miles of shoreline.

Looking east, today, the lake looks inviting, but our plan is to turn northwest to head up the East Twin River. On the east side of the river, is Harbor Park, a lovely park area with square rock wall and a ramp down to the river's edge for launching kayaks and canoes.

A pretty bridge, the 17th Street Bridge is up next. It is a concrete and see through girder bridge with a wrought iron railing. It has a large bridge tender house with a red roof and arched windows.

We are now on the working portion of the river, with several commercial fishing vessels docked on the east side of the river, a well-worn orange and white, and two red and white fishing boats— now I'm hungry for a fish fry for some reason. . . Oh, and now I smell wood smoke, is it a campfire? Nope, it is Susie Q's Fish Market. They have perfected smoked fish with a variety of flavors. Yum! Oh dear, now I'm hungry for smoked fish. . .

Then, on each side of the river, are fishing charters. Two Rivers, nicknamed "Trivers", is in the heart of lake fishing, and wins awards for the largest salmon and trout caught. Maybe we should head out to fish for Rainbow and Lake trout, or for Coho or King salmon!

Speaking of fishing, I notice a blue heron sitting on a dock. I float close for a photo op. He doesn't fly away, that's odd—he's intently staring, at me? No, at the water. Suddenly his beak spears the water and he comes up with a fish in his mouth! And in one gulp, it is down his neck! Wow! I've never seen a heron catch a fish before!

On the right shoreline, is the Rogers Street Fishing Village with a public dock for launching, or stopping to check out the Village. It has the original 1886 historic Two Rivers Pierhead Lighthouse, which is one of only a few original wooden lighthouses left on the Great Lakes. She initially stood on the north pier, and is smaller than typical lighthouses, because her purpose was for ships to navigate into the harbor. Her restored Fresnel lens is also here. You can climb aboard the wooden fishing tug, the Buddy O, or tour a fisherman's home. Displays include artifacts from local shipwrecks—most notably, the Rouse Simmons, the Christmas Tree Ship. She sank in a blinding gale in 1912 as she was carrying a

heavy load of Christmas trees destined for Chicago. Her "Captain Santa" decorated the ship in Christmas lights. The captain and her entire crew went down with the ship, and have joined the 1,500 other shipwrecks in Lake Michigan, and the 30,000 lost souls that call the Great Lakes their final resting place. The Rouse Simmon ship's wheel is housed at Rogers Street Fishing Village. Two weeks after the ship sank, a fishman found a corked bottle that contains the chilling final entry written by Captain Santa in his log, "everyone goodbye, I guess we are all through". That too, is at the Rogers Street Fishing Village.

As we paddle under the 22nd Street Bridge, it is time to start looking for Paddler's Park on the right bank. We left Matt's bright cherry red car as a beacon to help locate it. No problem to find it, as several kayakers are loading up their four rainbow colored kayaks, making it hard to miss Paddler's Park!

Truly enjoyed our serene secluded rural paddle, and the variety of things to see in Two Rivers on the river. Now, on to Nashotah Park for the Kites Over Lake Michigan festival!

Logistics:

Shoto Conservation Club, Two Rivers:
44.1733, -87.6397. 609 County Road VV. Free to launch and restrooms! Listed on the Twin Rivers Water Trail.

West Twin River County Park boat launch, Two Rivers:
44.1741, -87.6357. 800 County Highway VV. Fee to launch. Listed on the Twin Rivers Water Trail.

Woodland Dunes Cattail Trail Kayak Launch, Two Rivers:
44.1561, -87.5866. 3000 Hawthorne Avenue. Long carry (1140 feet) on a board walk. Listed on the Twin Rivers Water Trail.

Scenic River Stop-N-Dock RV Park Boat Launch, Two Rivers:
44.1568, -87.5793. 2510 W. Rivers Street.
Listed on the Twin Rivers Water Trail.

Veterans Park Boat Ramps, Two Rivers:
44.1496, -87.5754. Marina Road. Restrooms in shelter by playground. Fee to launch. Listed on the Twin Rivers Water Trail.

Riverside Park, Two Rivers:
44.1479, -87.5754. 14th Street. Bushy shoreline, restrooms.
Listed on the Twin Rivers Water Trail.

Seagull Marina Boat Ramp, Two Rivers:
44.1461, -87.5653. 1400 Lake Street.
Listed on the Twin Rivers Water Trail.

Harbor Park Wall Access, Two Rivers:
44.1473, -87.5640. 13 E Street. Parking on street.
Listed on the Twin Rivers Water Trail.

Rogers Street Fishing Village Public Dock Access:
44.1527, -87.5628. 2010 Rogers Street. Parking on street. Dock is off of 21st Street. Listed on the Twin Rivers Water Trail.

Paddlers Park kayak launch, Two Rivers:
44.1585, -87.5650. 1250 27th Street. Parking lot on south side by river. No fee, no restrooms. Listed on the Twin Rivers Water Trail.

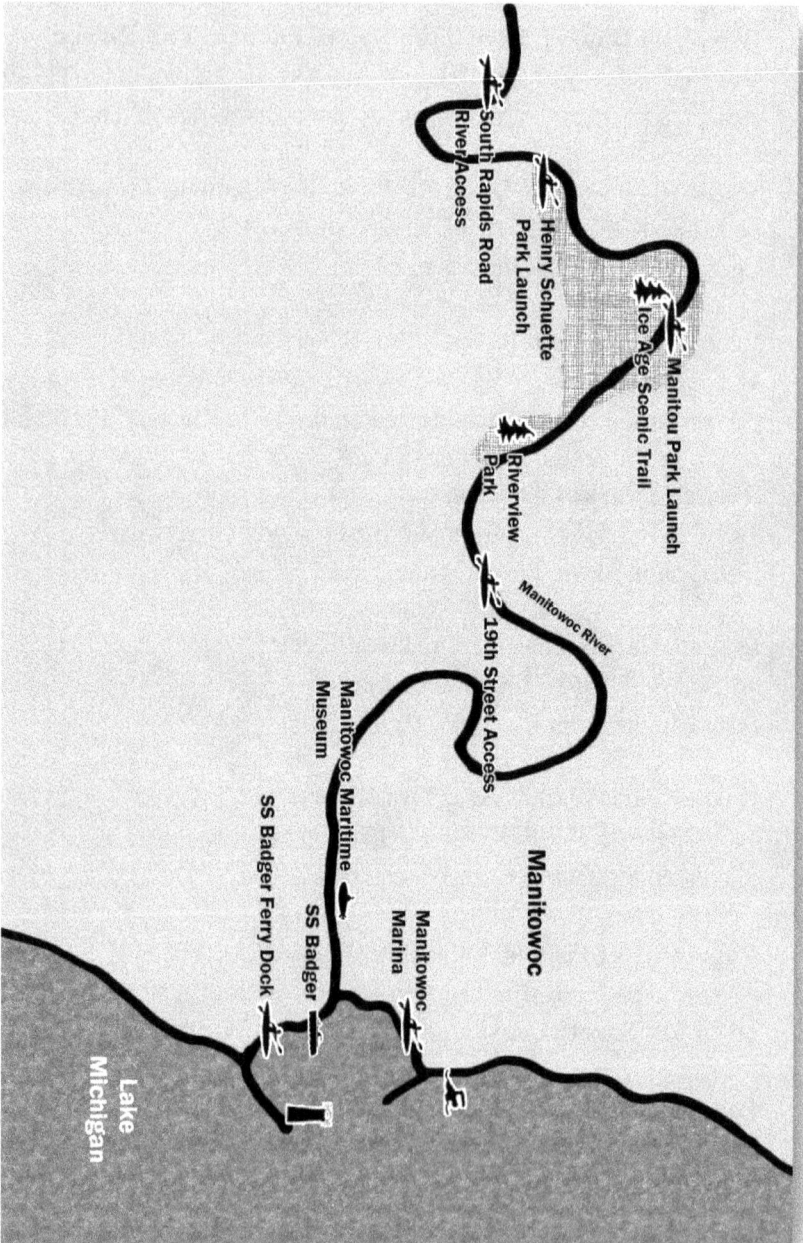

South Rapids Road River/Access

Henry Schuette Park Launch

Ice Age Scenic Trail

Manitou Park Launch

Riverview Park

Manitowoc River

19th Street Access

Manitowoc Maritime Museum

Manitowoc

SS Badger Ferry Dock

SS Badger

Manitowoc Marina

Lake Michigan

River Paddle

Manitowoc River Paddle

With the Submarine and the 7-story high Car Ferry

5 miles

This is a fun and exciting river paddle. You can enjoy both the SS Badger Ferry and the USS Cobia Submarine, then tour Manitowoc's urban area before the rural quiet beauty sets in. Something for everyone with no worries about wind velocity! You can paddle from the Manitowoc Marina to Manitou Park kayak launch for a 3.5-mile paddle, or all the way to South Rapid Road access for a 5-mile paddle. Double that if you plan on doing a there and back paddle.

We choose to rent Hobies and pedal from the Manitowoc Marina up to Manitou Park and back for a very enjoyable day. It is so much fun to have my son, Matthew, join me for the day. Quick lesson at the dock on how the Hobie works, and then we are on our way. Comfortable sitting and pedaling, nothing like I remember from the old pedal boats, where fifty feet of pedaling was exhausting! We became experts at steering with the rudder as we maneuvered out of the marina. To the right, in the harbor, is the YMCA baby beach, which would have been an alternative launch site if we had chosen to use our kayaks instead of renting the Hobies.

Then we look out the harbor and choose to float up for a view of the Manitowoc Lighthouse on the tip of the pier. The first Manitowoc lighthouse was built in 1839 and stood on shore on a hill. Then these parallel piers were built in 1873 and the first pier head lighthouse was completed, with a fog bell added in 1881. The old pier head lighthouse had been moved several times as the pier was extended and had become shaky, so it was razed in 1919, and the current steel lighthouse was built atop a concrete boathouse. The first story is the power room, and the second story housed the light keeper's office with a desk and chair, shower and bathroom. The round diaphone fog signal room is the third floor, and at the very top, the fourth layer, is the lantern room which had a fifth order Fresnel lens. This cool wedding cake looking lighthouse now has an electronic fog horn and an automated light as the Fresnel lens was removed in 2002 for safe keeping and it is at the Maritime Museum just up river.

After our quick peek at the lighthouse, we cross the harbor because the SS Badger Ferry was so obviously calling us! Toot, toot! The SS Badger arrives in Manitowoc at 11:30 am and stays until 1:30 pm—your best opportunity to check out this legend of the lake. She is a national historic treasure as the largest lake crossing passenger service on the Great Lakes and has provided an authentic steamship experience for over 60 years. She is also the only coal fired steamship in operation in the US with 7000 horsepower, with her coal ash off loaded and used to make cement. The SS Badger is big. Really big, massive, especially as we look up to her! We crane our heads way up to her bow, a hundred feet high, which is seven stories high! She is also kind of fat (sorry sweety), her girth is an obese 60 feet, but overall pretty slim when you consider she is 400 feet long.

We high tail out of there as it was getting close to her departure time and we don't want to deal with her bulk and her wake. So off we head up river past the Welcome to Manitowoc wall, and past the old Budweiser plant with her humongous six pack towers—thirsty

anyone? Hey, yeah, time for a sip of water. Hey, this is easy, I didn't have to put the paddle down to chug some fluids!

Just a thousand more feet along the north side of the river wall, the Maritime Museum beckoned us with her nautical port hole windows. This is a great place to learn about Wisconsin's Schooner Coast and commemorate the marine heritage of Manitowoc and Two Rivers. First up, the Native Americans were here, scooping out their canoes. Then the first European Americans settled in the Manitowoc area in 1820, and by 1847 the first schooner was built leading the Manitowoc shipbuilding industry. By World War II Manitowoc switched to constructing military vessels to assist the Navy's war effort. Enjoy all that the maritime museum has to offer: The Children's Waterways room, Wisconsin built boats, 1840's Wisconsin ship building, awesome authentic Lake Michigan lighthouse Fresnel lens, and the Great Lake 1911 steam engine.

From the river, we can't miss the Maritime Museum's star—The USS Cobia, a World War II submarine. 7000 men and women from the Manitowoc area built 28 submarines like the Cobia during World War II, working around the clock every day of the year. The Manitowoc submarines together sank 132 enemy ships. Four of the Manitowoc ships were lost at sea and are now on "eternal patrol". The USS Cobia herself sank 13 enemy vessels and was part of the attack of the Japanese convoy bound for Iwo Jima where she sank two vessels and was critical to the success in the US capturing Iwo Jima (remember the famous flag raising photo?). One sailor from the USS Cobia died during a running gun battle with two enemy ships, where the Cobia ultimately sank both of the vessels. She herself was almost sunk in 1945 when attacked by a Japanese minesweeper that blasted her into the sea floor—she escaped heavily damaged. Paddle past the USS Cobia slowly, touch her with kindness, and salute our veterans and especially those who gave all.

After the USS Cobia submarine, we head toward the bridges. On the right side of the river is a little park area named Manitowoc Shipbuilders Park, and on the other side of the river is Burger Boat Company Park, neither is accessible by kayak as there is a river wall. Above the skyline, the Manitowoc County Courthouse stands heads taller than the rest. She is historic, built in 1906 in the neoclassical style with columns and arches and her copper balustrade, now turned green. Her dome was originally glass, but several panes broke in a huge windstorm and are now replaced with shiny steel.

Pedal, you may paddle, under the 8th and then the 10th Street bridges. Both are bascule lift bridges with a fixed counterweight that balances the span through its upward swing. The twin bridges are "double leafed" opening up into an upward triangle. The 8th Street Bridge was built in 1926 and is historically important for its maritime use. The 10th Street Bridge is remotely operated by the bridge tender at the 8th Street Bridge since it is within eyesight.

After the bridges, it feels like we are heading to a cement wall, but never fear, the river does an odd right turn around a peninsula. This interesting industrial area has huge garage doors, stacks of giant wedding band rings, and oversized bulky "pipes". This is the Broadwind industrial plant where wind energy towers are manufactured. So, the pipes, are actually pieces of the wind towers that will be stacked up about 325 feet high on site to support the 115-foot long blades to drive the wind power.

At the bend in the river, across from the wind tower plant, is Riverview Park with steep slopes up to the park but offers appealing greenery with St. Paul Lutheran Church's steeple poking up over the trees. At the park, turn sharp left. On the west side is the Burger Boat Company, and the blue hammock for the yachts they build— wonder if they build kayak yachts?

Go under the "upstream" train trestle swing bridge and end up almost where we started after all the turns. Here is where Matthew floats past a beautiful blue heron, who kindly takes off to share his incredible blue splendor 5 1/2-foot flapping wing span. The river becomes shallower and quieter (probably better for the blue heron's fishing). On the left bank, the 19th Street river access slopes down to the river with Holy Family Memorial Hospital high on the shore.

Take the next crook in the river and go under the 21st Street Bridge with Riverview Park on the port side contributing tree green vistas. Then we enjoy the plate girder Canadian National Railway Bridge as the train track again crosses the river. Evergreen Cemetery is on the starboard side and Henry Schuette Park on the left, port side. You can explore either side of the 1,200-foot tall greenery island, with Manitou Park Conservancy area on the north side of the island and Henry Schuette Park continuing on the south side of the island.

Another train trestle bridge crosses the river and the island. It was completed in 1908 and sits 80 feet above the water, hence its name— High Trestle Bridge. We meet a gaggle of geese who high tail away splashing in their lift off as they gain in flight. There is kayak/canoe launch ramp located at the lower side of the river at Manitou Park which is on the northern starboard right side. We have traveled approximately three and a half miles upriver.

Henry Schuette Park continues on the steeper south shoreline around the peninsula with six miles of hiking trails, much of it a portion of the Ice Age Trail that meanders through Wisconsin for over a thousand miles (and we thought kayaking 300 miles to Chicago was an expedition!). The Ice Age Trail begins in Pottawatomi State Park in Door County by the bay of Green Bay and travels south through Manitowoc and then down deep into southern Wisconsin before heading north again and finally west to Interstate State Park in St Croix Falls on the Wisconsin and Minnesota border.

We continue paddling around the Henry Schuette Park peninsula to explore the other uninhabited islands. First comes a baby island, then a larger triangle shaped island that is 1400 feet long. Both sides of the triangle island offer green space but stay to the left side of the island to enjoy parkland and as the Ice Age Trail footpath emerges out of the forest, there is an access landing by a parking area before the Broadway Street Bridge with a small park shelter and benches.

Two more skinny islands head under the Broadway Street Bridge and there is another twist in the river as it heads up to South Rapids Road Bridge. As the name suggests, you may find a wee bit of white water depending on the depth of the river and the season. On the right north side of the river there is a small access road that offers a small craft launch path.

From the Manitowoc Marina, we have pedaled 4.5 miles upriver. As we head back down river, we are offered the opportunity to explore the other side of the islands we missed on the paddle up the river. Going down river with the current, should have made heading back a breeze. Yup, nope. . .now we are pedaling against the wind, with the wind and the current fighting it out. What the heck, we add paddling to our pedaling with some success!

Enjoy our river in rewind with different angles and views, we are happy to count our bridges backwards and wave again to the folks touring the USS Cobia. Back to the marina we go, with tired legs. Whew! I've built up arm strength with paddling, but the Hobies seemed to challenge new muscles. Please don't tell me that we are biking the Mariner's Trail tomorrow. . .

Logistics:

Manitowoc Marina boat ramp, Manitowoc:
44.0955, -87.6502. 425 Maritime Drive.
Fee for launching and Hobie kayak rentals. Restroom in the Marina.

YMCA beach in the Manitowoc River Harbor:
44.0951, -87.6611. 395 S. Maritime Drive, Manitowoc.
YMCA parking lot. May be possible to launch at the beach for free.

SS Badger Ferry dock and public harbor access, Manitowoc:
44.0892, -87.6510. 900 S. Lakeview Drive.
Park by the south pier for beach access.

19th Street Manitowoc River Access, Manitowoc:
44.0958, -87.6724. 650 S. 19th Street.
You may park curbside. Carry your watercraft around the back of the little brick building. No fee, no restrooms.

Manitou Park Boat and kayak launch, Manitowoc:
44.1041, -87.6862. 3000 Michigan Avenue.
A sign designates the park. Parking area, restrooms, and a shelter.

Henry Schuette Park Manitowoc River Access, Manitowoc:
44.0983, -87.6926. Clay Pit Road in Henry Schuette Park. Road opens to a picnic area and off-street parking, there is a little Ice Age Trail sign designating access to the river. No restrooms in this area.

South Rapids Road Manitowoc River Access, Manitowoc:
44.0957, -87.7010. 109 N. Rapids Road.
Off road parking. Carry kayaks to the river. No restrooms, no fees.

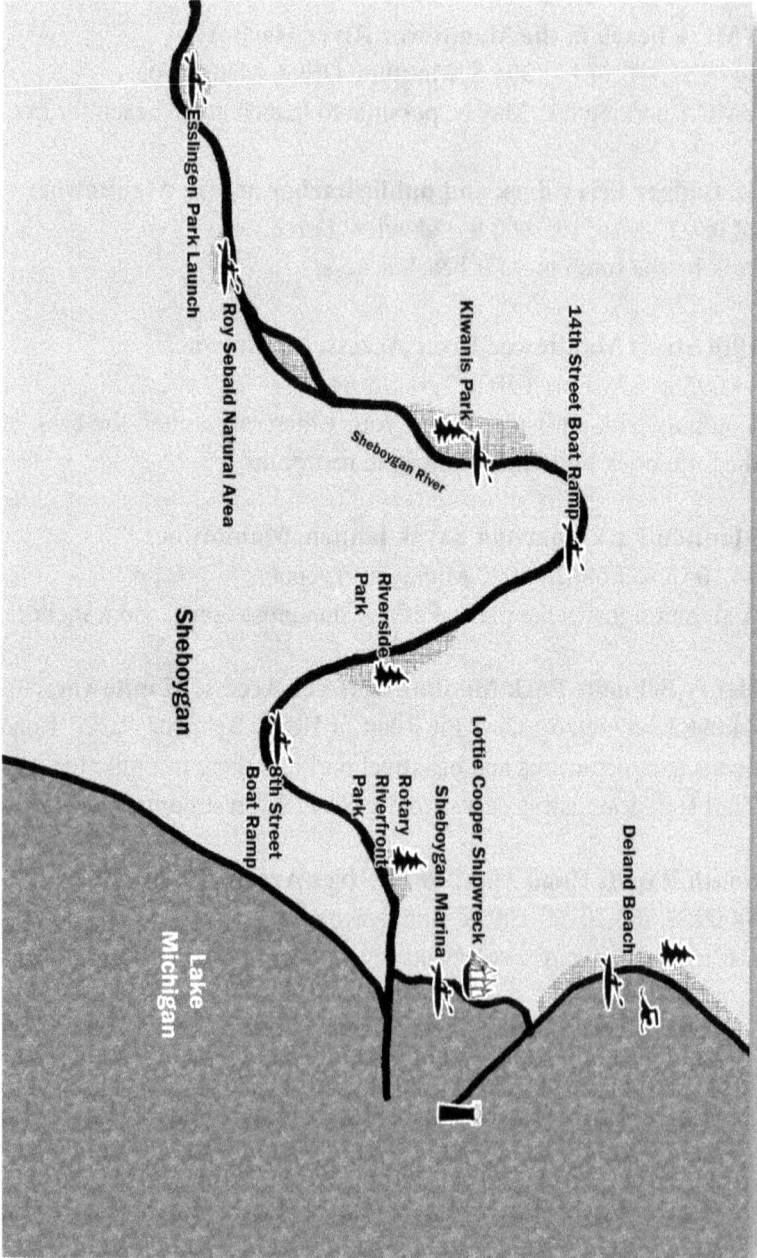

River Paddle

Sheboygan River Paddle

With Nature to the Riverfront Boardwalk

5 miles

So. . .we took our own advice. We knew it was going to be a windy day. But just in case, we drive to the lakeshore to be sure, maybe, just maybe, we could paddle the lake. Now, it is not a good sign when the surf boarders are showing up at the beach. Yeah, the white caps were hitting the beach hard. Some paddlers really enjoy the challenge of big surf—but these are huge! So. . .we decide to take our own advice. If you don't feel comfortable with the lake, Mother Nature offers an alternative—the Sheboygan River!

The Sheboygan River is long. It starts in obscurity somewhere between Fond du Lac and Plymouth, over 25 miles inland! She twists and turn and just about curly cues for 80 miles before reaching Lake Michigan. The river is navigable from St Cloud (no, not Minnesota) to the lake. She is wishy, washy, though. She can be wide for recreation kayaks and canoes, then switches after dams and waterfalls to fast running and narrow, with ripples and small rapids.

We launch at Esslingen Park canoe launch in Sheboygan. Our plan was to paddle upriver through the famous Kohler American Club, Black Wolf Run Golf Course, as close as we could get to the first dam six miles upstream. Then we would turn around and paddle down river to the harbor entrance on Lake Michigan five miles to the protected marina boat ramps.

Easy put in at the park with Rick remarking about the strong current. Yup, our plan got off to a great start, not even a third of a mile into our journey, we realize the flaw in our float plan. We literally cannot paddle upriver through the first riffles. Chris and I "race", neither of us actually moving forward at all. When we start laughing, we lose ground. Group decision, accept our folly, and have a leisurely float down river through Sheboygan.

Rick thinks we can literally float on the current down river and just lay back and snooze. Not so, with the strong wind fighting the current we do need to actually get some exercise. The Esslingen Park shoreline is dotted with parakeet green flowing grasses. While on the opposite bank, is calico greenery with hanging tree branches reaching down to the water to start our paddle. Across the river from Esslingen Park is Sheboygan's Lutheran High School and the University of Sheboygan campus.

Our first bridge to pass under is Indiana Avenue directly followed by South Taylor Drive bridge. Next to the second overpass is a small brown arched bridge that is part of the Taylor Drive Pathway, which is a multiuse trail starting south at Crocker Avenue and following the road north to Taylor Park for two and a half miles.

On the north side of the river, hidden by the boundary of trees is the Sheboygan Lakers Ice Hockey Center which offers adult and youth hockey in season. It is also the home to Splatterhaus, Sheboygan's October Haunted House. The south side of the river is Roy Sebald Sheboygan River Natural Area with a public shoreline scattered with colorful wild flowers and another kayak/canoe launch access.

Our first railroad bridge is the Wildwood Park Rail Bridge. The Union Pacific Railroad Bridge sits atop a stone stacked stair base and is constructed with quadruple-intersected dark chocolate brown lattice trusses. The span is about 160 feet long and was built in 1906 making it over 100 years old, and still in use!

Looking towards the north shore is the Wildwood Park baseball complex. Wildwood has three baseball diamonds and is the home to youth baseball and the Sheboygan A's semi-professional baseball team. Here, inspiring professional baseball players compete, and is a feeder program for the minor leagues. Batter up, play ball!

The river widens and we are confronted with a collection of islands. There are eight clustered islands with the longest one, Wildwood Island, being almost a thousand feet long. The islands are big enough to be wooded and grass covered. These islands, along with the rest of natural areas in Sheboygan are part of a bird habitat project. Nesting boxes have been erected for bluebirds, wrens, chickadees, kestrels, and screech owls. Heron rookeries and an osprey platform have been created. As if on cue, ducks migrate away from us to hide in the edges of the twigs and logs on the points of the islands.

We choose the right channel, and shadow the Sheboygan River's south shore, where our Union Pacific train track trails for almost 3/4 of a mile. It is hidden behind the leafy green trees gracefully arching down to the river surface. Rick starts weaving in, out, and under the twigs and branches, with the rest of us following the leader.

We meet a fellow paddler up river, looking like Dorothy from the Wizard of Oz fame, with a hat on his head and Toto in a basket on his bow. Actually, he is a local paddler who knows the river well. His canine companion "leads the way" and he just follows!

As we say goodbye to our new friend, we float under the New Jersey Avenue concrete bridge and then spy the curious River Park Railroad Bridge. On the sides of the river, it starts out as a burnt umber plated girder with the deck on top. Then the construction of the bridge switches to crisscross lattice trusses over the river. It sits on stone stratum bases that are fronted by curved points. The train rides the track on top of the bridge.

After the train bridge, a wonderful smell wafts through the air— hotdogs, hamburgers, popcorn and cotton candy. . .yum! The Kiwanis Park is on our left shore and there is a volleyball tournament going on. Someone bring us some food! We save our appetite and paddle past this picturesque park. The half mile of park river bank is lined by graceful willow trees, with the dainty leaves swaying down to the top of the waterway. At the north end of the

park is an open river bank for easy boat launching or stopping for a rest break, and is our only opportunity for a pit stop, restroom break.

Soon after the food smells from Kiwanis Park, comes the scent of coffee drifting to our nostrils. The Glas Coffeehouse is on the south bank with perfect steps providing access from the river's edge. Shall we stop for a quick cup of coffee? Such temptations!

As the river cork screws with an impeccable U turn, we stroke under the new 14th Street Bridge with its pedestrian and bike path under the north side of bridge. At the tip of the U on the south side, are the docks of Sheboygan's Boat Doctor, who does boat repairs. Next to the Boat Doctor dock slips is the public 14th Street boat launch. No dock or restrooms, but is free to use.

Immediately, we go under a skinny old railroad bridge. This is the Sheboygan Riverwalk Bridge and is part of the Shoreland 400 Rail Trail that starts at North Ave and travels nearly two miles south to the charming olde Train Depot at Pennsylvania Avenue. The girder bridge was once a swing bridge, with dark taupe deck plating. It is now refurbished and open to pedestrians.

The wonderful Water Street Park is next, on the north shore, with a rock and stone wall barrier. It is aptly named, as it has a children's playground and a clover shaped area with primary colored painted arches which are a fun looking splash pad for the nippers.

On the west side of the river are some private docks, while on the east side is the historic Garton Toy Factory, now converted into apartments. The toy factory made wheeled toys for almost a century. They introduced the iron velocipede, a forerunner of the modern tricycle. They were famous for pedal cars, sleds, and children wagons—painted with "Garton red" as wagons still are.

While the south shore is urbanized, the Riverwalk continues on the north shore past the Sheboygan Outboard Club, strap on a motor and join their fun? The trail continues into Boat Island Park. This park has a staging area with a vibrantly decorated half wall, park benches, and white replica vintage gas lamp lights.

In the middle of the river is Goat Island. Historically, a hermit raised goats on the island. The goats are long gone, but have been replaced by boats, hence its new name, Boat Island. The downriver tip of the island has a delightful metal bird sculpture and a lantern tower.

From here, we race some ducks down river and under the Pennsylvania Avenue Bridge. This bridge is a stringer bridge, with parallel steel beams supporting the road decking.

The south side of the river has private boat slips, while the north side is home lined on top of the steep river bank. Rockline Company is on the south shore, specializing in paper pulp and wet wipes, you know, we are in Wisconsin, America's #1 papermaker! Looking to the north shore, is a beautiful deep juniper green tree climbing hillside. Topping the crest of the hill, sits Sheboygan's Theater Company. The theater offers community plays, a small dinner theater, and theater in the park for children.

A church dome with an ornamented cross on its peak peeps out above the trees. Next door to the church is Sheboygan's Military Heritage Museum which prospers respect for the military and sacrifices made by our brave heroes. The 8th Street boat launch is in front of the Military Museum. This is a free boat launch with a dock, but no restrooms. Does have a nice little picnic area and is the beginning of the blue rail Riverfront boardwalk.

Across the river, is the first of many restaurants fronting the river with beautiful outdoor seating areas. The colorful umbrellas are a delight. Off this restaurant dock, is Eos, the local surf shop which does rentals for kayaks, SUP's, and surf boards—perfect for today.

We near the 8th Street Bridge, a bascule drawbridge with two counterweight leaves that pivot upwards for large boats. Just honk your horn —did you bring one?—and they'll open the bridge. From here, we catch a glimpse of Sheboygan's round-a-bout, with its cool sail art work symbolizing Sheboygan as the "Spirit of the Lake".

With that lake spirit, the south pier boardwalk is parking for the Mega Yachts. So much fun to check out the yacht names such as Bubba Grumpy, Happy Hooker, and High rollers. . .like the double meanings? Then there are the numerous charter fishing boats, just a sample includes— Slammin Salmon, Sea Dog, Fin Chaser, and of course Fish Tales. Give a try at Great Lake fishing for salmon or trout, we'll be over for supper. . .

As the river cruises north again, the west wall is flanked by commercial fishing boats. Unique boats with little port holes, huge bows and sliding side doors on the port side. From the side doors below the wheel house, the nets will hang over the side and are pulled up onto a picking table. The steel hulls of the fishing boats are super sturdy to break ice and roll over waves. The commercial fishing companies' fish for chub and whitefish. If you see a cluster of orange flags on Lake Michigan by Sheboygan, these are trap nets, which can be 25 to 150 feet deep and be a quarter mile long.

Again, wonderful smells are fanning from the numerous restaurants lining the boardwalk, German, English, Italian restaurants, fish shops, and sandwich or pizza shops. How dare they entice us as our hunger has set in! Choices, choices. . .it is a beautiful sunny day, so outside eating is desired.

Over on our left port side, is a beautiful bloomin' green park with an open sided shelter and rounded outcropping dock. Rotary Riverside Park offers a possible take out spot with a tall wall, if needed due to high seas in the harbor. Yup, it is time to notice that inside the harbor walls, are two-foot white caps. . .and we need to go around the corner before we get to the safe harbor of the marina.

As we get close to the US coast guard station, three long boat toots sound out—making me jump! They are just alerting us that the coast guard boat is backing out of their dock. As I wonder if they are heading out for a rescue and say a quick prayer, Chris chooses to

skirt up against the impending waves. The Coast Guard crew eyes us up, they seem to be trying to decide if we plan on heading out of harbor, and we may soon be their rescue. We smile, and reassure them, we have no plans to tackle the huge waves out on the lake.

Honestly, after the end of the north Riverwalk pier, we only have a thousand feet of rough surf to turn north into the marina entrance. We give the huge stone pile walls a wide berth to avoid a crash, and enter the much quieter marina. Today, there are no pleasure boats, so the boat launch is unusually quiet.

Rick heads out to retrieve the car and boat trailer on his scooter, as the girls pack up and dry our water splashed cockpits. Then it is time to explore. South of the boat ramps, is the Youth Sailing and the U.S. Sailing Centers, and the Sheboygan Yacht Club. Across from the boat ramps, is a fish cleaning station and rest rooms, ahh, I feel so much better. A beautiful marina store and lookout tower fronts the boat slips. Great opportunity to check out the harbor and the giant waves splashing over the north pier. The pier is safely closed today, no walking out to the lighthouse today. Yeah, this was the reason, we didn't paddle the lake, good choice.

Sheboygan has a history of great waves; it is considered the #1 spot for freshwater surfing. Yes, surfing, on a surfboard. When the winds come from the west southwest, or there is a nor'easter such as today, astonishing waves can be sculpted. The surfers were out in force today as we headed for dinner on the river near the harbor. Even the kiteboarders gave up on the lake's whirling grandeur, and play in the harbor waves. Such an impressive show, as they twirl and soar up in the air ten to twenty feet. We are royally entertained!

Logistics:

Esslingen Park, Sheboygan:
43.7406, -87.7508. 3200 County Highway PP/Indiana Avenue. Small parking lot, Wayside sign & park sign. No fee, no restrooms.

Roy Sebald Sheboygan River Natural Area, Sheboygan:
43.7409, -87.7428. 2797 County Highway PP/Indiana Avenue. Unmarked gravel parking area. No fee, no restrooms.

Kiwanis Park, Sheboygan:
43.7536, -87.7258. 1071 Kiwanis Park Road. Grassy bank to launch kayaks by the parking lot. No fee, restrooms by playground.

14th Street boat launch, Sheboygan:
43.7548, -87.7216. 1318 Niagara Avenue. Gravel parking area by river. Gentle boat launch into river. No fee, no restrooms.

8th Street boat launch, Sheboygan:
43.7451, -87.7136. Corner of South 8th Street and Riverfront Drive. Blue sign, parking area. Tiny shelter, fee to launch, no rest room.

Sheboygan Marina public boat ramps:
43.7515, -87.030. Corner of Broughton Drive and New York Avenue. Marina parking lot. Fee to launch, Restrooms available.

Kayak Wisconsin, Lake Michigan Water Trail

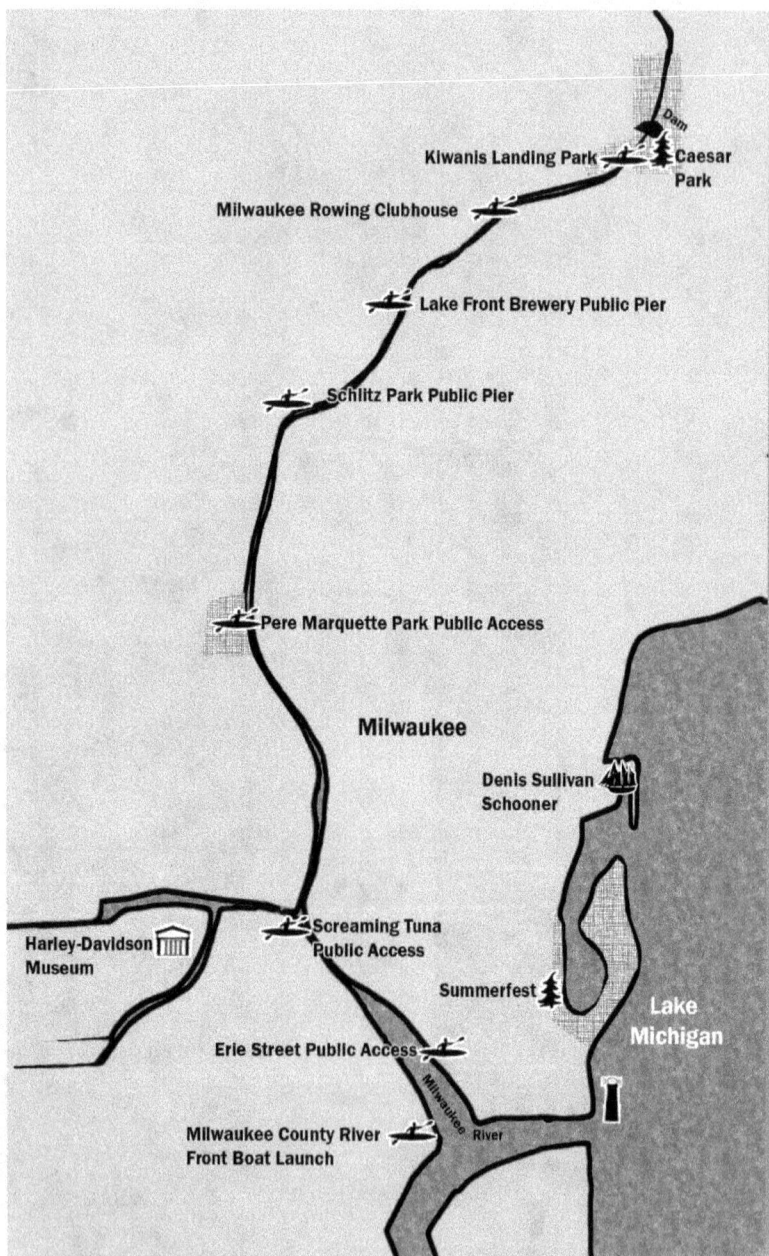

River Paddle

The Milwaukee River

With Milwaukee's RiverWalk

8 miles

Milwaukee, the city that beer built. . .but wait, what brought those German settlers to Milwaukee to make the beer? Water! Besides America's Third Coast of Lake Michigan, Milwaukee has three rivers that converge near the shoreline. Paddling Milwaukee gives a unique perspective of the RiverWalk along with green parks and the Harley Davidson Museum.

We launch at the river's boat launch at the west side of the Kinnickinnic and Milwaukee Rivers and paddle downtown and the RiverWalk for urban excitement to Kiwanis Park, before the dam. We've also paddled the river at night for an electrifying party atmosphere!

However, just over a half mile north of the boat landing, is the convergence of the Menomonee River, and paddling west offers a quiet park paddling opportunity. You can kayak for over 3.5 miles before returning back. Paddling the Menomonee River takes you past the Harley Davidson Museum—rrr rrr, just can't help oneself revving up the kayak engine as you paddle past. Then kayak past Marquette University, green space in a busy metropolitan area. Just past Marquette University is Menomonee City Lights Brewery. The river twists to the south and then west again. This is where on the south bank, The Mitchell Park Horticultural Conservancy Domes are located. With the three large glass cupulas filled with gorgeous gardens. Then on the south bank is Three Bridges Park, and the Hank Aaron Trail, which follows the Menomonee River. Lastly, paddle close to Miller Park, the Brewers Stadium where you'll get a glimpse of the brick arch facade and the arc of the retractable roof.

The third Milwaukee River is the Kinnickinnic River to the south. The new Harbor District is getting lots of attention and exciting growth. Paddle south from the Bruce Street Boat Ramp or Riverfront Launching Site as it says on its sign. After a little over a half mile you come to two small parks on each side of the river. The one on the east side is Kaszube Park, the smallest park in Milwaukee. It is an old historical site with a picnic table, a ship anchor and a few trees, and designates an old Polish fishing village on the peninsula on the east side of the river. Whereas, on the west side of the river is a very new park, Harbor View Park. Besides a water play area and a red lookout tower and slide, there is a canoe and kayak launch! Next, the big open water area is the Milwaukee Municipal Mooring Basin, a freight shipping vicinity. Turn southwest from here to continue on the Kinnickinnic River to discover Barnacle Buds, an outdoor dining seafood restaurant with a dock that you can tie up to. At about the 2-mile mark is Baran Park where the shoreline is green and leafy, but the river significantly narrows. It's about time to turn around and enjoy the river back to the confluence of the rivers.

Our story begins at the Riverfront Launching Site west of the Hoen Bridge at the confluence of the Milwaukee and Kinnickinnic Rivers. It's a very busy boat launch, as it is the only one on all three Milwaukee Rivers. We unload by the north patio and tree shade area, pack up the kayaks and then carry them to the slippery ramp to quickly enter and paddle away from the site. 'Hard to resist kayaking out and under the Hoen Bridge, just because it is a pretty bridge. And we might as well check out the red pierhead lighthouse before turning back to the rivers.

As we head toward the Milwaukee River, we are overtaken by a mega yacht, the Linda Lou. She is 197 feet long, and has four levels, with spacious windows. "Wow", is all we can say, wondering what celebrity she belongs to. However, she is a charter yacht—no fancy dancy superstar. For only $500,000 per week, you too can tour on her with her fourteen crew, and eleven of your special pals. The Linda Lou turns up the Kinnickinnic River, so we wave goodbye to head north on the Milwaukee River.

On the west bank of the Milwaukee River is Erie Street Plaza, a town square with brick patio, trees and bright yellow geometry shaped sitting pieces. The aptly named Sail Loft Restaurant with the riverfront deck is next. It's followed by Condos with lovely river views, and fronted by the Carefree Boat Club, whose membership grants unlimited usage of a variety of pontoon boats, speed boats, a sailboat, and kayaks and paddle boards! Between the two condo buildings is the Erie Street Pier, a public paddler friendly pier, meaning it has low access to the water. So, you can stop and tie up, or even launch here. On the west bank is Hansen Marina and boat slips. With all these options for boats on the river, this paddle is at a minimum an intermediate paddle.

Look ahead to avoid the old train bridge, sitting in the middle of the river. Abandoned now, this is a rare quadrangular lattice truss railroad bridge. At one time, it was known as the "400" bridge, since it was an instrumental part of the trains that ran from Chicago to

Minneapolis in 400 minutes! Midway along the bridge on the east shore is the Trestle Park. Built with exotic walnut ipe wood, which is strong and resistant to decay. The park has benches and planters with delightful views of the river. On shore are restored historic railway overhead signal lights, and green space to the north. The Riverwalk continues with Riverfront Pizzeria south of Trestle Park. On the east bank, are mid-rise, elegant contemporary apartments and loft condos with gorgeous balconies. Whereas, on the west shore, is Jerry's Docks and the Milwaukee Kayak Company. Here you can rent kayaks, canoes, and paddleboards, and skip all the loading and packing up of stuff.

We have come to our first bridge, the "what do you call it" bridge. The sign on it says the Broadway Bascule Bridge, however the streets that approach it are Pittsburgh Avenue and Young Street. What the heck? It is a newer two leaf bridge with counterweights on each side, and an open woven metal decking up on the street, so we can see the bottom of the cars going over us. The control tower is on the northwest side of the bridge and is a modern square tower with a curved east side and has a black rimmed top.

After the bridge, on the west bank is a series of apartment and condo buildings, all with nice lanais to sit outside and enjoy the river charm. Down the stairs from the Water Street Bridge is a public access dock amongst private docks. The one with a dolphin at the end of it, is the public one. On the east bank in the non-balcony building is the Milwaukee Institute of Art and Design. It is Wisconsin's only college of visual arts, where "passion meets purpose". The red brick building is again a condo building (the verandahs give it away), with Surg on the Water, a private event venue where weddings happen on the RiverWalk deck.

We have reached the Water Street Bridge, another bascule counterweight bridge with two leaves. The control tower is on the southeast corner, and looks like a match to the Broadway Bridge. We can see the Historic Third Ward sign over the road on the east side of the river. We have been paddling past the Third Ward since the mouth of the river. It designates this revitalized center of Milwaukee with historic architecture, and a creative culture with an expansion of condos, boutiques, the Milwaukee Public Market, and the Summerfest grounds.

There is a large condo building on the west bank at the convergence of the Milwaukee and the Menomonee Rivers. At the south end, is another public access dock, with some parking. The Screaming Tuna sushi restaurant is located here.

It is fun to head up the Menomonee River and under the railroad bridge. This rare "bobtail" swing truss bridge was built in 1904 and is still used today, including Amtrak, running from Chicago to St. Paul Minnesota. Motors rotate the bridge on a not quite center point, meaning it has to balance evenly to work.

Go under the Plankinton Avenue Bridge, another bascule bridge, and paddle to the intersection of the Menomonee River and the Menomonee River Canal to the Harley Davidson Museum. Going south on the canal, you will pass the Hillclimber statue and then a paddler friendly low access pier. At the Museum, you can see the oldest Harley known to exist, Elvis's Harley, and the Tsunami motorcycle—a cycle that floated 4000 miles from the Japan Tsunami. The museum has an experience gallery, where you can sit on motorcycles, and watch a video of motoring down the backroads of America. Milwaukee is home to Harley Davidson!

Back to the Milwaukee River, we head north again. There is greenery on the west bank. On the east bank are two public use docks. The Chicago Street dock has a semi-circle trellis with rectangular wooden benches. The dock steps down to the river for easy access, but only street parking here. Paddle past the Milwaukee Ale House with its huge beer vat hanging on the outside wall. It is located in a century old red brick structure where saddles and sails were once made. The boat slips out front are public, and the restaurant has outside sitting along the RiverWalk. The dock at the end of Buffalo Street is public. This deck offers a fish hook ramp tower for an overhead view of the river, and steps down to the dock for boat access. Next door in the huge arch window edifice, is the Black Swan, an elegant private venue.

The St Paul Avenue Bridge is a different type of bridge, it is a vertical lift bridge, where the entire road way lifts straight up for boats to pass under. The bridge tender house is on the south side of the bridge and is round in front with an angled full circle on its roof.

There is green space on both sides of the river after St Paul Avenue. On the west bank is a field of wild flowers and on the east side of the river is where Clearwater Kayak rents kayaks. There is a public access dock here also, but with street parking only. Across the street is the Milwaukee Public Market where a variety of locally owned food artisans sell their wares in an upbeat indoor market setting.

We then paddle under the noisy 794 Interstate bridges. The Clybourne Street Bridge is immediately after. It is another vertical lift bridge built in 1968, which is fun to see open, when on the water, if we are lucky! The bridgetender house is on the southwest corner with its steep triangle lime green roof and a bell tucked in the alcove.

Along the RiverWalk on the east side of the river, are lovely hanging baskets on replica cast iron posts. On the west side of the river under the parking garage with its circular slinky entrance are the three cruise boats for the Milwaukee Boat Line tours. They offer happy hour tours—naturally, this is Milwaukee! There is also a Gothic Great Lakes tour, and a spook-tacular tour. An attractive bright red fishing boat docks here also, with nautical round windows.

The Michigan Street Bridge is our third vertical lift bridge in Milwaukee—were they having a sale on them? This one has a U-shaped bridge tender house on the northwest side of the bridge. On the east side of the river is the black glass Chase Tower edifice, but it is the white historic structure on the west side of the river that catches our eye. The beautiful 1880's building was the Gimbels Department Store. Now entirely renovated inside, it is a multiuse building including the Marriott Residence Inn. They kept the outside historic with its row of colossal columns. There is an overhead walkway over the river that connects the historic building with the new glass structure.

Up comes the Wisconsin Avenue Bridge, the fourth vertical lift bridge, Milwaukee seems to love this type of bridge! The bridgetender house is on the south side of the bridge in the middle, and is a charming round tower with glass arched windows, then square upper windows and a birthday hat cone shaped green roof. As you paddle under the bridge, look for the Gertie the Duck statue on the north sidewalk piling. In 1945, during the ravages of WWII, a bridge tender discovered a duck nesting on the bridge's pilings. Gertie, and her ducklings became national news, featured in Life Magazine, and even had a book written about her!

On the east side of the river is a high-rise office building, with arched door entrances, tall arched windows, and on each side of the top there is a triangle roof line, with a taller central cupula topped with a flag. In the middle of the block is a round Bump out at Mason Street with steps down to the river for a public access spot, albeit with only street parking. Next up, is the 1909 City Hall ruddy red brick building, with renovated apartments. The RiverWalk curves out a bit with its green metal railing with square window boxes. Here stands the bronze "Fonz", doing his trademark double thumbs up. The Fonz was a character from the Happy Days tv show, which was set in 1950's Milwaukee. Go ahead, I know you want to do it, give him your double thumbs up and say "ayyy" to celebrate the Fonz and this great urban paddle! Behind the Fonz statue is a Chinese restaurant, and then the Safehouse Restaurant. The entrance is in the alley, with the door marked "International Exports", you enter into a hallway and need to know the password to gain entrance, or do some silly antics, which all in the bar can watch! The walls are covered in spy games, and you can do a scavenger hunt for some international spy intrigue fun.

On the west side of the river is the Riverside Theater. Built in 1928 for vaudeville acts, the historic structure is stunning inside with its ornate light fixtures, red velvet walls, and the original elevator. And then there is the music entertainment shows you can see while marveling at the stunning architecture. The Riverside's wall on the river has lovely waves and fish swimming above us. Between the next two old time Milwaukee buildings, is an alley and on the RiverWalk is another public access stair to the river for us kayakers. The Rock Bottom Restaurant and craft brewery is in the vivid white building with outside patio seating. There is another public access located here, but it is high pier.

The Wells Street Bridge is next. Want to guess how this moveable bridge works? Yes, again, it is a vertical lift bridge—were they cheaper by the dozen? This bridge has tan brick pilings and a bridge tender house with white ornamental cornice molding. But this is where it happens. Only in Wisconsin, maybe, only in Milwaukee, the king of beers city. On our night paddle, a party goer tosses us a can of beer! What do we do with a can of beer while paddling? Save it! Wouldn't want to open it anyway after it had been tossed. . .

Up first on the east side of the river is an old orange red brick building. The name at the top says "Milwaukee Electric Railway and Light Co." Built in 1899, this was a power generating plant for their electric street cars! Neoclassical Revival architecture is highlighted with large arched windows. Now converted into the Milwaukee Repertory Theater that entertains with world class professional theater productions. The white washed attached building is part of the Milwaukee Center with theaters. The RiverWalk has pretty arched metal work for climbing vines. The post-modern Milwaukee Center Office Tower completes the block with red brick and a peaked roof tower.

After the Wells Street Bridge on the west side of the river are several antique buildings. The 1897 "Cawker Building" with its bow oversized windows are condos above a bistro and beer garden with outside seating on the deck of the RiverWalk. The whitish building has boring rectangle windows on the river side, but on the street side its character has triple three arched windows. On the west RiverWalk is a rectangle of arches, with another public access semi-circular steps down to the river, with street parking only. This dock is framed by a mermaid arch, actually the Acqua Grylli, a mythical female gatekeeper. Pretty cool!

We paddle up to the Kilbourn Avenue Bridge. It is not a vertical lift bridge! It is the most architecturally significant of the Milwaukee Bridges. It is a double leaf bascule drawbridge with counter weights to lift each span. And it is old, built in 1929, with four limestone bridge tender houses! Each is a square tower with windows near the top, with lavish horizontal cornices and stepped pyramid roofs. Flanked by urn shaped balustrade railings.

Looking to the east, is the open-air covered Peck Pavilion, a band stand shell with a mature grove of chestnut trees behind. There are long straight steps to the river's edge with a wave metal railing. The ultra-moderne Todd Wehr Theater finishes the block with an intimate theater. Behind is the Marcus Performing Arts Center with an elegant large theater and home to the Milwaukee Symphony Orchestra and the Milwaukee Ballet Company.

After the Kilbourn Avenue Bridge, on the west side of the river is Pere Marquette Park. Truly, a green oasis, with sun drenched lawns, shade trees, and picnic areas. The chain link scalloped rail along the river leads to the center Gazebo, right next to the river. It offers curved steps to the river's edge, another public access spot with a great location for a rest break. The aptly named park, is because Father Marquette actually camped here on this location in 1674.

We have arrived at Milwaukee's oldest bascule bridge, the State Street Bridge. Erected in 1924, in the Milwaukee type, double leaf span bridge with simply charming copper clad octagonal bridge tender houses with two opposite side longer than the ends. On the west side of the river is Usinger Sausage—brightly titled in yellow at the top of the building. Now, when you stop at Pere Marquette Park for a rest break, half the group needs to jog over to Usinger's

for some protein packed beef sticks! And next door in the red brick building with arched windows at top, is a Cheese Mart. Grab some fresh cheese curds. Sausage and cheese curds, now I am powered to paddle on! In front of the west side buildings are the yachts for Edelweiss Cruises. They also have European style canal vessels for great views. Edelweiss offers skyline, concert, dinner, or historic cruises. On the east side of the river is Rojahn and Maloney, a florist, in a modern structure. Shall we stop for a bouquet of flowers for our kayaks? Dominating the skyline behind the flower shop, is a modern high-rise office building with curved windows at the top.

The new Highland Avenue bicycle and pedestrian bridge is up next. Built in the newer vertical lift style, with green metal railings and the RiverWalk hanging harp lights. The bridge culminates in a small park next to Rojahn and Maloney's on the east side of the river. The greenery continues in front of the gray condos lined up on the east side, but the RiverWalk only continues across the bridge to the west side of the river.   The Ale Asylum Riverhouse brewery and restaurant is here with a large covered patio for eating right on the RiverWalk.

Right before the next bridge on the east bank, is the Harp Irish Pub and a public access dock, down the steps from the bridge. We have come to the new Juneau Avenue Bridge. This is the location of Milwaukee's Bridge Wars in the 1840's when Juneautown on the east side, and Kilbourntown on the west side, fought over where and whether any bridge should be built over the river. They actually rammed and demolished each other's bridges, until finally they agreed to incorporate into Milwaukee. The Bridge Wars continue? The Juneau Bridge is the winning newer type bridge with a vertical lift. There is square bridge tender house on the northeast corner with angled corners and a big flat top roof. On the west side of the river with the walkway, is the Aloft boutique hotel with a modern vibrant jive. The east side loses with just a parking lot.

The Knapp Street Bridge is another new vertical lift bridge that allows for wide river channels. It is considered tower-less, but on the southwest corner is a square tower with green glass. The RiverWalk continues on the west bank with the red brick Spectrum structure with arched windows. They offer pleasant green space with trees and grass on their north side. The glass fronted construction is Manpower's Global Corporate Headquarters with 30 flags flying along the RiverWalk—one each for country Manpower does business with. We attempt to name all the countries belonging to the flags. . . we fail, we did not even accomplish a 50% score.

The exquisite bascule leaf Cherry Street Bridge is next. Erected in 1940 with the two Bridgetender houses built in a divine Art Deco style. They are built with stainless steel and glass with shiny bells. As we paddle at night, they glow gorgeously! On the east bank of the river are renovated office buildings followed by luxury apartments with balconies. The Schlitz Park office community in a central business district, is on the west bank and the RiverWalk endures with a lovely tree lined trail with overflowing flower boxes. There is a nice dock for public access, but with only street parking.

East Pleasant Street Bridge, is a newer vertical lift bridge. It has clean lines and a pleasing bridge tender house that somewhat mimic's the Wisconsin Avenue bridge we paddled past earlier. This one is D shaped, with the round side on the pilings coming up from the river and the flat side along the sidewalk. The Pleasant Street bridge has the arched windows on top with a green roof. On the west side of the river is the Brewers Hill District with several apartment buildings aptly named, such as the Beerline, and the Brewers Point Apartments. In the middle, at the end of Vine Street is a public access dock on the river, with quiet street parking. Right before our next bridge, is Lakefront Brewery in an old renovated coal power plant. It too offers a paddler friendly low height public access dock. On the east river bank are red brick apartments with balconies alternately stacked. A lovely tree lined river side walk, is followed by green space land.

The Holton Street bridge may be the most unique bridge in Milwaukee. Erected in 1926, with metal trusses, it was a bascule span that no longer opens. It is tall. So tall, they added a pedestrian and bike path, a marsupial bridge, under the main overpass. And, there is a Swing Park under the bridge on the east side of the river, with recycled tire swings hanging from the bridge underside, and a soft sandy floor. Along the east bank metal wall are cream-colored brick luxury apartment buildings, and some river condos that sit higher up on the pebble hill bank. Along the RiverWalk on the west bank, are a row of apartment buildings with balconies, and townhouses. Halfway to the next bridge is a dock. This belongs to the Milwaukee Rowing Clubhouse and they are sharing their paddler friendly low pier with us. Please share nicely, and let them come and go first—and pretty please close the gate.

We have paddled to our last bridge, the new Humboldt Avenue bridge. The bridge is a white stone stationary bridge with a gentle arc and arch window railings, and no need for a bridge tender tower. High up on the east river bank sit houses hidden by hillside shrubs and trees. Then the Riverview Apartment tower rises up high. It is a ten-pointed sunburst tower. Caesar Park begins before the dam and green parkway continues for almost eight miles after the dam following the Milwaukee River with the Oak Leaf bike trail.

Our goal, is Kiwanis Landing, the park on the west bank. There is a paddler friendly riverbank ramp launch site in the park, with street parking. The River Revitalization Foundation is located here with the mission to create urban parkway, with public accesses, and to improve water quality. We are grateful to them for the river we have enjoyed today and especially for this park and a chance to stretch! Parks continue for miles after the dam on this side of the river, along with the Beerline bike trail. Time to rest and relax on the river bank, snack a little bit more, before heading back towards downtown.

As you head back down river, look for all the art sculptures along the RiverWalk. The Milwaukee RiverWalk is loaded with artwork! After our nighttime paddle, back at the boat launch on the convergence of the rivers, as we are unloading, Milwaukee celebrates with us! Summerfest has an incredible night show of fireworks. We hardly need flashlights at all to unload the boats, as we ooh and aah with delight at the sparkles and booms!

Logistics:

Milwaukee County Boat Launch (only one on the rivers):
43.0249, -87.9040. 600 S. Water Street.
Fee, port-a-potty. Very busy boat ramp with limited parking.

Kinnickinnic River Harbor View Plaza Kayak Launch:
43.0170, -87.9029. 600 E. Greenfield Avenue. No restrooms.

Menominee River kayak launches:
Emmber Lane Public Boat Launch Dock:
43.03294, -87.92912. Emmber Lane, northwest of bridge.
Street parking northwest of Menominee River bridge or in the "Keep Greater Milwaukee Beautiful" lot, sidewalk to dock.

Three Bridges Park (three possible launch sites):
43.0247, -87.9594 **Village Passage, on Canal Street**
43.0266, -87.9548. **S. 33rd Court.** Stairs to north bank launch, or go over the pedestrian bridge to the Hank Aaron Trail, turn right and follow the curve to boat ramp on south side of river.

Milwaukee River Kayak Launch docks:

Erie Street Pier, east side of river (Paddler friendly low pier):
43.0272, -87.9034. 581 E Erie St. Street parking, no restrooms/fee.

Waterfront Condo Public Access dock, west side of river:
43.0309, -87.9099. 130 S. Waters St. Be careful of the dolphin statue at end of pier. Street parking only, no restrooms or fee.

Chicago Street Pier, east side of the river:
43.0376, -87.9101. Corner of Water Street and Chicago Street. Street parking only, no restrooms, no fee.

Milwaukee Ale House Public Access, east side of the river:
43.0337, -87.9099. Corner of Water Street and Buffalo Street. Street parking only, but may off load at end of Buffalo Street. High pier, no restrooms, no fee.

Riverwalk Park, St Paul Avenue, east side of the river:
43.0353, -87.9096. Corner of Water Street and St Paul Avenue, east of bridge. Street parking, low pier, but must cross under the Riverwalk supports. Clearwater Kayaks rents kayaks here.

Plankinton Alley Public Access dock, west side of the river:
43.0395, -87.9199. 720 N. Plankinton Avenue. Street parking only, but may drop off at end of alley. No restrooms/no fee.

Mason Street Public Access Pier, east side of the river:
43.0398, -87.9103. Corner of Water Street and Mason Street. Street parking only, no restroom, no fee.

Rock Bottom Brewery Public Access, west side of the river:
43.0398, -87.9112. 740 N. Plankinton Ave. Lot or street parking, but difficult to load at this location. High pier, no restroom, no fee.

Plankinton Alley Public Access, west side of the river:
43.0409, -87.9122. 820 N. Plankinton Avenue.
Street parking only, but may drop off in alley. No restrooms, no fee.

Pere Marquette Park Public Access Pier, west side of the river:
43.0405, -87.9133. 898 N. Plankinton Avenue. Street parking only, no restroom, no fee, but there is a shelter and picnic areas.

Harp Irish Pub Public Access Pier, east side of the river:
43.0455, -87.9130. 113 E. Juneau Avenue. The Harp Irish Pub is on the southeast side of the Juneau Avenue Bridge. Street parking only, and that is limited. No restroom, no fee.

Schlitz Park Public Access Pier, west side of the river:
43.0494, -87.9107. Schlitz Park. You cannot park in the parking lot, please find street parking only. No restroom/no fee.

Trostel Square Condos Public Access pier, west side of the river:
43.0597, -87.9068. 525 E Vine Street. Dock is at end of street. Street parking, no restroom, no fee.

Lakefront Brewery Public Access Pier, west side of river (Paddler friendly low pier):
43.0545, -87.9049. 1872 N. Commerce Street. Low pier with retrofit, drop off boats, park on street please. No restroom, no fee.

Milwaukee Rowing Club Boathouse Public Pier, west side of river (Paddler friendly low pier):
43.0566, -87.9016. 1990 N. Commerce Street. Street parking. Please give rowers priority for launching and take out, and please close the safety gate! No restrooms, no fee.

Kiwanis Landing Canoe and Kayak Ramp, west side of river (Paddler friendly ramp):
43.0573, -87.8969. 2135 N. Riverboat Road. From Water Street. Path to river ramp launch. Street parking only, no restrooms, no fee.

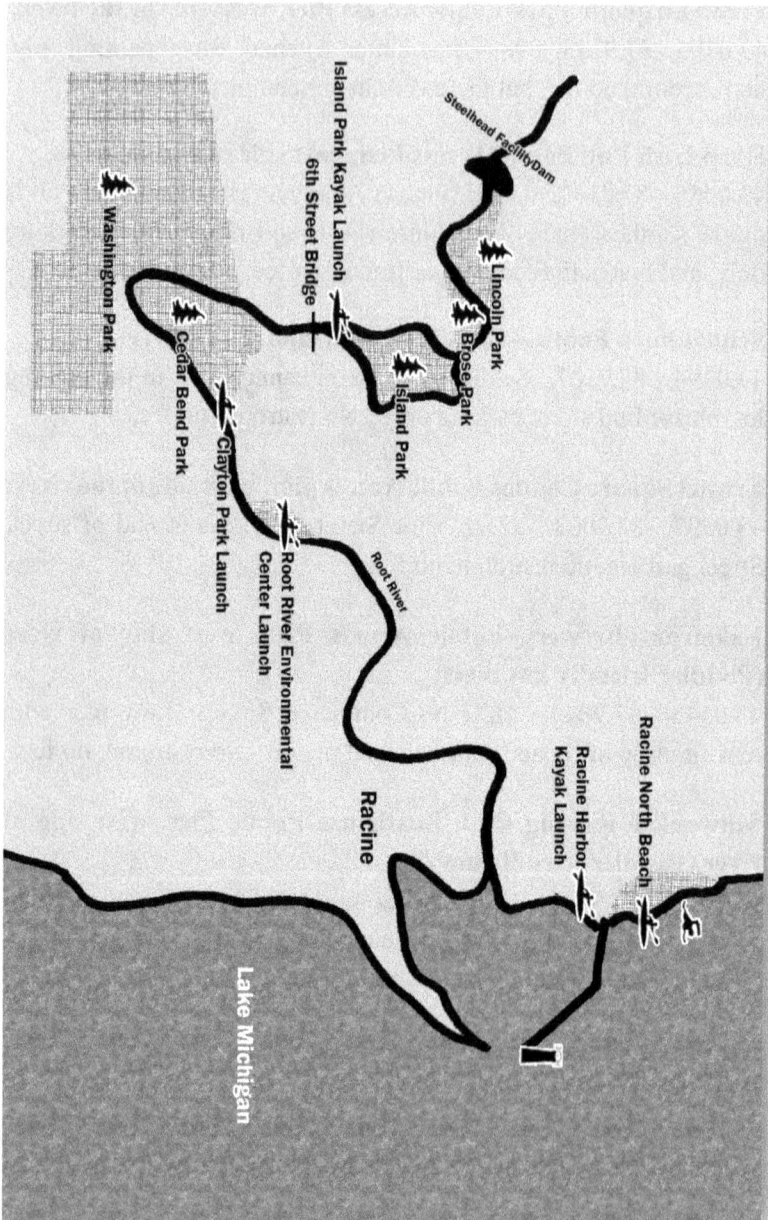

River Paddle

Root River Paddle

Racine

With Bridges and Parks

8 miles

Bridges, there are lots of pretty bridges in Racine over the Root River. Some new, some really old, all unique and interesting. Take a scenic tour around Island Park, and then head east toward the Yacht Clubs and city happenings!

Girls day out! Sister weekend! Thrilled and energized to spend the weekend with my sis Becky and explore the rivers in southeast Wisconsin. We launch in Racine in Clayton Park on the north shore of the Root River at their natural kayak launch. Then we head west through lots of parkland and paddle around Island Park, and head back to Clayton Park for our picnic lunch. This was a 3-mile paddle, you could add on and continue west on the river at the top of Island Park for a 4-mile tour. In the afternoon, we kayak east toward downtown, and the Yacht Clubs and parties on the shorelines. You can paddle into the harbor where there is a nice kayak launch, have a rest break, and then head back to Clayton Park for a 5-mile paddle.

A lovely early autumn day, as we pull into Clayton Park. Bright blue sky. Perfect. Except for the high water of the river covering the path for the Root River Parkway, and the end of the kayak launch. Clayton Park is a 6-acre neighborhood park that offers a playground, tennis courts, and is in an environmental corridor of wetlands. Ya' think? We slip and slide a bit in waterlogged mud as we gingerly try to get into the kayaks without wiping out in muck. Rinse our flipflops off in the river, along with our feet, as we settle into the kayaks. "Which way should we go first?" Becky asks. I recommend going west, upriver, the hard way first. "Good idea", but it wasn't even hard to paddle upriver—"this is a breeze!"

Clayton Park evolves into Cedar Bend Park, a natural area along the U curve in the river. We come to our first bridge! It is a suspension bridge with a lovely basket woven wood strip railing, and towers on each side to hold the cables. The Washington Park Golf course is on both sides of the river with its nine holes. It is the oldest golf course in a city limit in all of Wisconsin. The park has woodlands along the fairways, and also a critical species habitat area.

Our first bridge is quickly followed by another bridge. This one is built on brick supports topped with a double arch red rustic brown metal railing. The bike trail bridge joins the Root River Parkway on both sides of the river. A pair of bikers cross the bridge as we paddle under. Bike, paddle, walk, lots of ways to enjoy the Root River!

We continue to paddle with serenity. The homes on the east side of the river are hidden by a tree lined shore, and the west side of the river is a forest with the bike trail through it. Several families of ducks join us, flocks when in flight, and a "paddling" when they are swimming on the river. How appropriate! We have something in common. They skirt away from us as we near them, as we gently whisper to them that we mean no harm.

Soon we can see the acclaimed most beautiful bridge in all of Racine, the 6th Street bridge. It is truly the most unique bridge I have ever seen, and I have paddled under quite a few now. . . From our view on the river, this is an astonishing art deco, moderne style architecture with terra cotta ornamentation. First, we see the curved arch of the overpass and the open arches within open arches on the sides of the bridge. Then we notice the main center decoration—bilateral artistic eagles holding a shield between them. But as we get close, and float under this open-spandrel, concrete barrel-arch bridge, we notice the gargoyle like faces that are the channels for storm water off the roadway pavement. What are these faces? Bulldogs, like Becky offers, or fish faces that I suggest? The literature describes them as Neptune-like faces, the Roman God of Water. I still think we should mix Becky and my descriptions, and call them bullhead fish faces.

Whatever, this bridge, is for sure, a historic bridge. Built in 1928, and designed by the renowned architect, Charles S. Whitney, it is one of the most architecturally significant concrete bridges—and definitely a Racine jewel. As we float under it, the smooth upper belly reflects the water patterns as it shimmers and sparkles. . .a natural firework display!

We are still ohhing and ahhing over the 6th Street Bridge when we come to a fork in our road, err. . .paddle. We have come to Island Park, an actual island. To the left is the Horlick Drive bridge, the one over Root Creek, on the west side of Island Park. This beautiful bridge is a replacement and was built in 2004. They did a nice job giving the new bridge some character with her church window arch concrete railing.

We choose to go the right and paddle up the wider Root River. The park island shoreline is tree lined with a grassy plain in the middle. On the east side of the river is a row of well-kept homes, all built in the early 1900's and have a wonderful view of the river and the park. The river is narrower now, with gorgeous trees, including willows, sweeping down to the river surface. We come to another charming pedestrian and bike trail bridge of the Root River Pathway. This one has wooden posts and spindle railings.

Next up is the second Horlick Drive bridge. . .looks a lot like the first. Except this one has two arches since the Root River is wider than Root Creek. The bridge is also called the Liberty Street Bridge, maybe to distinguish the two of them? It again is a concrete closed spandrel arch bridge, and was built with the parapet wall pointed arch window boxes in her railings and has gorgeous globe street lamps.

We come to another decision. Continue west on the river, or do a sharp turn and continue circling the Island Park on Root Creek? If you travel further on the Root River, you can enjoy Brose Park and Lincoln Park for about a half mile, until you come to the dam for the Steelhead Facility. There is a fish ladder here and an underwater viewing station. The rivers in Wisconsin are too warm and the level of the water fluctuates too much to sustain Lake Michigan salmon and trout populations. At the Steelhead Facility, men play match makers and manually harvest eggs and sperm, introduce them to each other, and then send the fertilized eggs to fish hatcheries in Wisconsin. This Steelhead Facility helps the population of chinook and Coho salmon, and brown and rainbow (or steelhead) trout for Lake Michigan fisherman.

A sharp right turn at the intersection of the Root River, allows us to continue orbiting around Island Park. Root Creek twists and turns around the irregular shape of the island. Island Park offers baseball diamonds, a playground, tennis courts, and a shelter and picnic areas. About half way down the west side of the park, is yet another foot bridge for the Root River Pathway. Another exceptional design, this one is a stunning natural stone look bridge. We appreciate that they didn't do cookie cutter pedestrian bridges, and instead made them all unique!

We come to several low-lying tree trunks, so much so, I can't actually tell which is the trunk and which side is the branches. Is it possible this tree has a trunk on each side of the river? Or is it probable that there are two trees with a tangle of branches over the river?

As we approach the pointy south end of the island again, on the southwest side of the point, is a grassy entrance for another kayak launch. Several teams of ducks are using the kayak launch today. One group chooses to out swim us and head across the river, but that is where I am. So, they turn to go down river with us. Becky is busy chatting with the second flock of ducks resting on the shore. "Umm, Becky, you are about to run over the family of ducks"—as she then takes emergency maneuvers to avoid a duck crash!

We get to float under the other Horlick Street Bridge, as we leave Island Park and head back to Clayton Park. We wave at several groups of bikers sightseeing on the Root River Pathway. And meet up with a trio of kayakers heading the opposite direction we are, enjoying the river too!

Back at Clayton Park, we slide up on the bank and pull out a tarp for a picnic blanket. Quiet park for a picnic along the shore. Becky pulls her boat up on the grass, I tuck mine in under the bank. Becky jumped up during our lunch to grab my boat, as it has chosen to float away to explore the river on its own! Thanks Sis!

In the afternoon, we choose to paddle down river and head to the harbor. Just downstream, is the Memorial Drive Bridge. Two large arches over the river, and each concrete arch has ten arches along its length—that's twenty arches total. The arches are open throughout the width of the bridge, giving it a nice airy lacy look. Built in 1936, it actually has another arch on north side of the river for a road tunnel, now the Root River Pathway.

Immediately after this, is a railroad bridge. Although it is brown and rusty, it is actually quite unique. The railroad bridge was built in 1908 and is a double intersected deck truss. It rests on a one round stone and metal pier. This means, the bridge swung open on its center pivot, which is quite rare and historically significant. Rare, because, it takes great engineering to make this work, one miscalculation with one side heavier than the other and it doesn't swing and pivot, but tilts and falls. . .hopefully, not while we are paddling under it! Alright, they don't actually open it anymore anyway—so we are all safe.

On the left, now west side of the bridge is a kayak launch for the Root River Environmental Center. Free for the public to use, but with a caveat, there is a steep hill to carry or roll kayaks down to the boat ramp from the parking lot. They do also rent kayaks and canoes, for an easy way to explore the river. The Root River Environmental Center is a partnership with the University of

Wisconsin–Parkside and the city of Racine. Their mission is to promote appreciation and stewardship of the Root River, along with education and research.

Right after the Environmental Center, is another 6th Street Bridge. This one, new and boring from the river, but with some fun mosaics on the railings along the roadway. After the bridge is a wooded shoreline with industrial areas on both sides of the river. We cross under an old abandoned pedestrian suspension bridge. All metal and chain link, it would be ugly, except for the exquisite green vines taking over the bridge from both sides, trying to hold hands in the middle, giving it a lovely look!

The Marquette Street bridge has minimal personality. Old docks are on the south side of the river, but on the north side of the river is the Fifth Avenue Yacht Club, with pleasant landscaped lawns, a private boat ramp, and docks lined with motor boats. It is by the bank of the Fifth Street Yacht Club, that the three masted top sail schooner, the J.V. Taylor, was abandoned and sunk, and parts of her may still be buried under the river. The schooner was built in Winneconne Wisconsin in 1867.

The northwest curve of the river has the Root River Parkway joining us above the shoreline, with a very old boardwalk dock system lining the river's edge. The southeast side of the river has some docks with motor boats and a park like shoreline with benches above.

Then on the west side of the river is the Boat House of Racine, where they specialize in service and repair of motor and sail boats, and have slip rentals and storage. Followed by the Harbor Lite Yacht

Club whose mission includes yachting, cruising, and seamanship for pleasure and recreation. There is a party going on today—the Carboard Boat Races! We have impeccable timing to choose kayaking down a river filled with cardboard boats! We get to groove with music at the club as we paddle past.

The Yacht Club is located at the State Street Bridge, a single bascule bridge with a brick control tower on the southeast corner. More motor boats line the docks after the bridge. Our Top Ten favs are: Lake roamer, Just Had To, Fish Whisperer, Euphoria, Always Dreaming, Making Memories, Fire Escape Chicago, Irish Wake, and the winner is: Unauthorized Purchase! Who thinks up these names? My Pgymy kit boat, made just for me, a tiny lady, is the Day Tripper. Becky has a transitional kayak that I'll name Bluefin, because it's blue with a rudder!

We've come to our last bridge, the Main Street Bridge. This one is a double leaf, meaning both sides open up into a V shape, bascule bridge. Its drawbridge grid is painted pretty Lake Michigan turquoise. It has two control towers with brown window rooms and topped with matching turquoise roofs.

Just a third of a mile of the river is left, past more boat docks, with the Root River Pathway now on the south side of the river along the river wall. There are condo buildings behind the shore path. Once we come to the harbor, look straight ahead to notice the Racine Lighthouse. It is a small red square light tower on stilts. This style was typical for old time pier light houses. The old design pierhead lighthouses usually were wood, but this one is now covered in steel plating to protect it from the weather. The lantern room is hexagonal, and originally had a fourth order Fresnel lens, but now is only lit by floodlights at night.

We turn north, a left turn for us, to go to the Lake Michigan Pathway Water Trail kayak launch for a rest break. Then it is time to do a U turn and enjoy the river back again to Clayton Park. A fun paddle in Southeast Wisconsin and a revitalized Racine!

Logistics:

Clayton Park shoreline kayak launch, Racine:
42.7230, -87.8025. 1843 Clayton Avenue.
Parking lot. Free to launch, no restrooms.

Island Park shoreline kayak launch, Racine:
42.7274, -87.8058. 500 Horlick Drive. Kayak launch is at the southwest corner of the island. Street parking, no fee, restrooms available in the shelter on the northeast side of the island.

Root River Environmental Center, Racine:
42.7245, -87.7959. 1301 W. 6th Street. No fee to launch, restrooms! Long carry to river downhill. Kayak/canoe rentals.

Racine Harbor, the Lake Michigan Pathway Kayak launch:
42.7367, -87.7786. 1 Barker Street, Racine. At the end of the road, what looks like private area for the RYC (Racine Yacht Club), there is public access to follow the Lake Michigan Pathway road around the Club 560 feet to a whole new parking area! Nice kayak launch made just for us in the Racine Harbor! No fee, no restrooms.

Kayak Wisconsin, Lake Michigan Water Trail

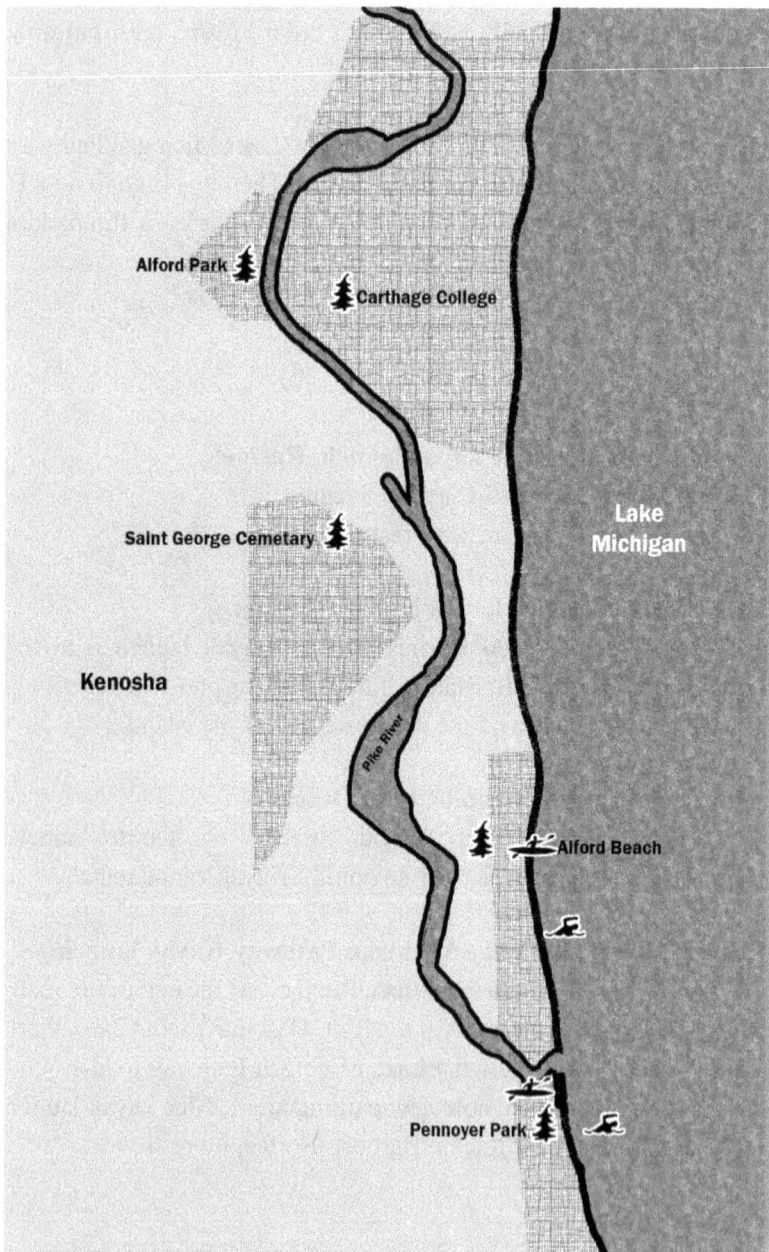

River Paddle

Pike River Paddle

Kenosha

With natural beauty

3 miles

Short but sweet. Nonetheless, very enjoyable quiet paddle in a natural area. There were many birds, especially herons, that must not see too many intrusions on their privacy, as they were always surprised and skittish to see us!

The Pike River runs about 15 miles from its mouth at Lake Michigan in Kenosha, west through Kenosha county. The river level can switch from shallow to high water, making it a guessing game how far you can paddle. The Pike River often has high shoreline banks with downed trees and low bridges that cross it. So, if you are willing to portage, you can travel a nice distance through Kenosha County. We paddled only three miles, so we obviously have an aversion to portaging!

Sisters weekend! A get-a-way to Southeast Wisconsin to explore the rivers. We were hesitating at kayaking today, "It's too cold, it's too windy", but maybe it'll be warmer and not windy once we are down on the river. We arrive at Pennoyer Park in Kenosha, and check out the river. Yup, quiet. "Eww, there is quite a current". We can handle it. "Will we get under the first bridge?", as we stare west at the river. "I think it is deceiving", I say with more bravado than certainty. We could always paddle out on the lake if we don't fit under the bridge. "This could be a really short paddle. . ." as we decide to give it a go.

Becky and I launch at Pennoyer Park in Kenosha at the mouth of the Pike River. Popular spot for fishing in the river, and also casting into Lake Michigan. It is an easy, peasy short carry down to the river's edge. This is the same spot that Rick and I launched to tackle Lake Michigan on a very windy wavy day to head to Illinois. Today, the lake is much calmer with only one footers wracking the shoreline. But, when Rick and I launched, we skirted up in the quiet river and then paddled through huge three-foot surf out into the lake. Today, there is mostly a sand dam with only a trickle of the river making it into Lake Michigan—even with high river water!

"Oh, this is nice" as Becky and I settle into our kayaks and head upstream, without any difficulty. We have no problem fitting under the first bridge, going under Sheridan Road/Alford Park Drive. A

pretty white cement bridge with pointed arch church windows railings. The Pike River Bike Trail crosses the river here also. The bike trail is a ten-mile trail following Lake Michigan, then through the Historic District of Kenosha, and then along Lake Michigan again, before turning west to rejoin and follow along the Pike River.

After we go under the bridge, the river opens up a bit with a marshy area along the Alford Park Drive. Although there is a busy road just to the east of us along Alford Park and Lake Michigan, we are in our own sequestered nature area. We see gaggles of geese, teams of ducks, and herons. Lots of herons. In the trees on the shoreline, less than ten feet above us, or along the marshy shorelines. As soon as I stop paddling to quietly pull out my camera, they flutter away. Shucks, shucks, aww shucks again.

"I'm glad we paddled today", Becky whispers. We are watching a small blueish bird dive bomb into the river, obviously fishing. "What is it?" I ask, "a blue jay?" Becky responds, but blue jays don't fish do they?

On the west side of the river, the shore opens up into a grassy plain above the river bank, with three flags flying, the U.S. flag, the Wisconsin flag, and a vertical half and half yellow and white flag. We can't tell what the flag is, it's not for Kenosha County, is it the cemetery's flag? We are at Saint George Cemetery, calm and peaceful.

A large down tree is blocking the middle of the river, "Can we get around it?" Becky asks. Yup, there is room on either side to traverse. Then, another living tree is traipsing across the river, "Is

this the end of our paddle?" we wonder. Nope, room to squish around that tree too. "Maybe this is a far as we can go" as two trees are hanging down into the water, but they too have left a natural door between them for us to paddle through.

The river narrows, as we pass by several homes. A rowboat, and several kayaks line the shore, ahh, we aren't the only ones who paddle the river. A gentleman is mowing his lawn, a large, long, yard. . .skip the lawn care and come paddle the river with us! Next, a home is perched high up the steep river bank. The bluff is covered in rock gardens, and a dog is climbing amongst the boulders and flowers just like a Billy goat. His Mom is gardening, balancing on the bluff precipitous.

The appealing natural shoreline continues. An old six-foot-high tree stump is on the river's edge. The tree stump is topped with new troll doll hair greenery, a bushy mass surrounding it's top. A whispering willow tree is creating ripples on the water surface as its soft supple branches just tickle the river.

We float under Alford Park Drive again, a matching white cement bridge with the church window railings. I'm pretty sure, no one even notices us enjoying the river, as they speed over the bridge. Not even sure if they know a river is next to them! Another Pike River Trail bridge crosses the river. Red wrought iron arched railing bridge across the river. And now, like on cue, a pair of bikers cross the bridge! With a clackity clank as they go over the wooden deck, we wave them on. Just another way to enjoy this pleasant river.

Now we are in the grounds of Carthage College. Founded in 1847, it is an arts and sciences school, with over fifty majors and minors. Lake Michigan and the Pike River offers students an abundance of research opportunities. And the Pike River is a wildlife arboretum on campus. We are excited to tour the college from our unique perspective.

But. . .we come to the red bridge. It is only one foot above the river today, with a log jam on the other side of the bridge. "Want to portage?" I ask, as we look up at the bushy banks. Groups of Carthage red wearing students cross the bridge. There obviously is going to be a game in the stadium to the west of us. One cluster of noisy students notice us, "Any sharks in there?".

Since we don't relish getting wet and muddy attempting to portage with crowds of young adults cheering us on, we choose to turn around and head back to Pennoyer Park. A gentle float back to the beginning, giving us time to search out more herons.

When we arrive back at the mouth of the river, we decide to check out if we can get through to Lake Michigan. Mounds of sand at the mouth, with only a narrow channel today out to the lake. "I can squeeze through". "Umm, no, I can't, it is too shallow". But now the current is strong, "Opps, I might have to try to traverse it". I do manage to turn around without getting wedged in the little channel in front of a knot of fisherman, and we land back on the shore of the river at Pennoyer Park.

Still early in the afternoon, we get to spend the rest of the day exploring Kenosha! We check out the original Kenosha lighthouse on Simmons Island, the Kenosha North Pier Lighthouse, the new playground ship, and the refurbished Bath House on Simmons Island. Then over to Harbor Park, to enjoy the historic trolleys, and the Promenade Art Walk—Becky's favorite sculpture? Pig Strumming Guitar. And supper with a view at the Boat House Pub.

Logistics:

Pennoyer Park Pike River access, Kenosha:
42.6068, -87.8193. 3601 7th Avenue. Parking area to access the mouth of the Pike River. No fee, no restrooms.

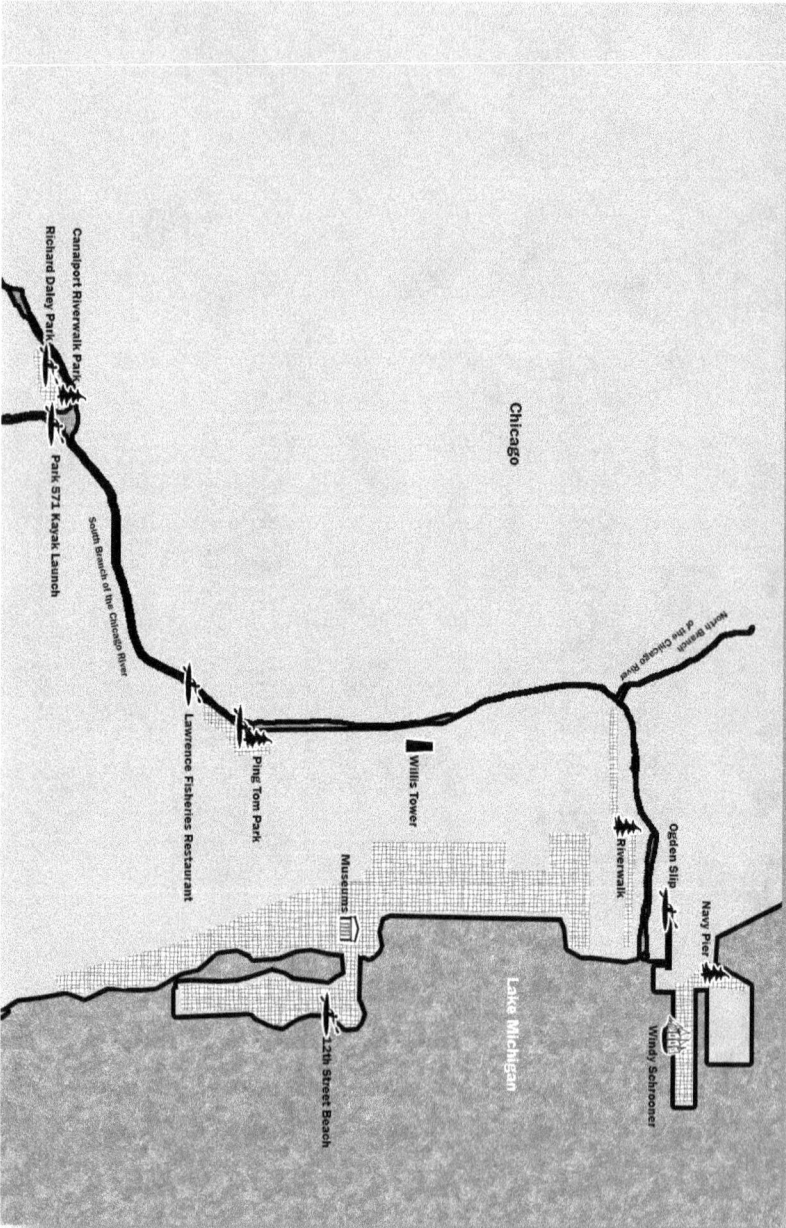

River Paddle

Chicago River Paddle

With Skyscrapers, Riverwalk and Navy Pier

9 miles

Chicago, Chicago, I'll show you around, I love it—as sung by Frank Sinatra. We'll show you around on this urban paddle, The Willis (Sears) Tower, the Riverwalk, then through the lock and enjoy Navy Pier. Chicago, Chicago, have the time of your life!

We paddle from Lawrence Fisheries dock on the south branch, east on the main Chicago River along the Riverwalk, through the lock, and into Lake Michigan to enjoy Navy Pier, then we turn around and enjoy it all again for a 9-mile paddle. Chicago, Chicago, I love it!

Other options include, launching at Richard Daley Park on the Chicago Ship Canal that converges with the South Branch of the Chicago River which is 3 miles from Lawrence Fisheries dock. There is the North branch and Goose Island you could explore also. Launching north at Clark Park and heading south on the north branch and circling back around Goose Island through the Chicago River canal and back to Clark Park is about a 9-mile paddle with a completely different view of Chicago.

The Chicago River is a bit tricky to kayak. Most of the shoreline is unforgiving metal walls, when boats whip by, their wake pushes to the shore, then the metal wall shoves it back and throws you right back into the river. You can get bounced around. Therefore, this paddle is designated an intermediate paddle. If you are unsure about your abilities, don't despair! REI does tours from Ping Tom Park, and Urban Kayaks does tours from downtown at The Cove on the Riverwalk, and Kayak Chicago starts their tours by North Avenue on the North Branch of the Chicago River by Goose Island.

If you put in at Richard Daley Park, there is a nice boat launch. This is not a river; you are actually putting into the Chicago Sanitary and Ship Canal with its interesting history. The original canal was completed in 1848. This newer and wider Chicago Ship Canal was completed in 1900 and is 28 miles long. Going from the Chicago River to the Des Plaines River, to the Illinois River, to the Mississippi River. Thus, connecting the Mississippi River to the Atlantic Ocean through the Great Lakes. This helped make Chicago become one of the fastest growing cities in America. Creating this canal is what reversed the direction of the Chicago River, making it now flow out of Lake Michigan rather than into the lake!

As you put into the Chicago Ship Canal at Richard Daley Park, just west is the Eight Track Bascule Train Trestle to explore. It is an unusual construction of four parallel double tracks and double leaf bridges. There are four bridges, side by side, and each have two tracks, which equals eight tracks (railroads, not a music tape). They are known as the "Scissors Bridges" because the counterweight machinery is not on the same side, so they open like a scissors!

Paddle east under the historic Western Avenue Bridge. This bridge has four huge Art Deco pillars and the original ornate bronze railings. After the bridge, on the north side of the canal is Domino Foods, maker of sugar, so take a sniff to see if you can smell the sweet smell of success!

The next bridge is the South Damen Avenue Bridge. On the south side of the river, after an eight pack of industrial silos, is the Canalport Riverwalk Park, with Bliss Point which offers fishing stations. Behind the Riverwalk is the Chicago Sun Times. Their early claim to fame was publishing the erroneous story that the O'Leary cow started the Chicago fire. Their new claim is to be the "hardest working paper in America".

Paddle under the South Ashland Avenue burgundy brown bridge. A very wide and rare pony truss bascule bridge. Traffic moves between the thick metal trusses up on the roadway, but the top is not joined together with cross beams. The bridge was built in 1938 with depression related funding. The two attractively decorated bridge tender buildings are eight sided with windows all around the top. The bridge is still in operation for boats, so just honk!

Immediately after the bridge is the confluence of the South Branch of the real Chicago River with Canal Origins Park. The park offers a continuation of walking paths. Across the river is Chicago Park #571—I guess Chicago has so many parks, they just started numbering them? But this park is special, because there is a floating dock for launching non-motorized boats (yup, that's us, folks) and a Boat House for rowers.

You have the opportunity, if you choose to explore the 1.25 miles of the South Branch of the Chicago River, a dead-end channel. It was made famous in Upton Sinclair's book "The Jungle". The river's nickname is Bubbly Creek. Aww, cute, yeah? Nope, the creek got its nickname from meat packing companies dumping entrails into the river, where the rotting animals fell to the bottom, decayed and the gases of the decomposing flesh bubbled the river.

Charming. . .supposedly, the creek still bubbles. However, it is a quiet paddling area, that is being cleaned and rescued. Now you can paddle down and enjoy living ducks, herons and turtles. You can paddle under the Stevenson Expressway, to the Chicago Maritime Museum. It tells the story of the Chicago waterways from when Jolliet and Father Marquette first paddled from the Mississippi River and portaged to the Chicago River in 1673. Then the story of making of Chicago the largest inland cargo port in the United States.

From Park #571 continue north on the South Branch of the Chicago River. Go under the newer Loomis Street Bridge, and past industrial areas and channels with areas of tree lined shores, and gardens. The next bridge is the bygone Halsted Street Bridge, which looks a lot like the South Ashland bridge. . .don't worry, you haven't gotten lost and paddled backwards. This bridge is a three-pony truss bridge, a rarity, since there are only three in all of Chicago.

Immediately after the notable bridge, is the contemporary Interstate 90/94 bridge. Smooshed between two old buildings is the West Cermak Road Bridge. It is the sole-survivor of Chicago's Scherzer rolling lift Bascule bridges. The dark red-brown steel double leaf bridge with the heavy cross trusses above the road bed has ornate railings and metal arches over the sidewalks. The two ends with the massive steel that curves up in the U shape are the rolling mechanism that lifts the two spans of the bridge. Before the bridge is the Hoyt building with elaborate Prairie style stone ornamentation, and on the other side of the river after the bridge, is the old Thompson and Taylor Spice building with contrasting white limestone details. These buildings are examples of Chicago's riverfront industrial pre-skyscrapers, constructed with the flatiron look to fit into the non-rectangular street pattern.

After the Cermak Road Bridge is a tree lined shore on the east side followed by a low linear dock. This is the dock of the Lawrence Fisheries on Canal Street in Chicago. They have made their dock available to the public for canoeing and kayaking. We park in their lot and carry our boats to the dock by the side of their building next to Canal Street. We thank them by returning after our paddle for a great fish dinner! Get hooked at Lawrence's Fish and Shrimp restaurant, Chicago's favorite fried fish and shrimp since 1950.

The Canal Street Bridge is the longest pony truss trunnion bascule bridge in Chicago. A pony truss bridge has no cross beams connecting the steel formation over the road and the cars drive between the trusses. A bascule bridge has a counter weight that continuously balances each leaf of the bridge. The Canal Street bridge is a trunnion bridge with its axle or counterweight on the river bank—the part that swings up. Got it? And it is the longest one in all of Chicago! And it is considered new. . .as it was built in 1949. The bridge used to be painted white but now is Chicago maroon.

Don't blink, because we don't want to miss the next landmark bridge! It is the Canal Street Train Bridge, or aka the Pennsylvania Railroad bridge. The two huge side towers lift the bridge vertically straight up in its entirety! Erected in 1915, it is the only one of its kind going across the Chicago River, and is the heaviest of any vertical lift bridge of any kind in the United States.

The east side of the river is Ping Tom Memorial Park. There is gorgeous green space above the metal wall with walking paths the full third of a mile along the river. We know we are in Chinatown when we paddle past this gem of a park, because the Pagoda has time honored Chinese roof tiles and ornamentation. There are ginkgo trees and bamboo in traditional Chinese gardens, and the entrance has four tall columns etched with Chinese Dragons. On the river front, by the pagoda is the Chicago water taxi stop for Chinatown. After the pagoda, there is a circular playground for kids.

Then float under the 18th Street Bridge, which is a single leaf truss bascule bridge with a polygonal arch, which is far less common than the double leaf spans we have been seeing. It is the newest historic bridge we've explored on the river.

Ping Tom Memorial Park resumes after the bridge. The Boat House has a public dock for non-motorized boats with restrooms. REI rents kayaks here! The park offers special events yearly, including Chinese Dragon Boat Races and the Chicago River Flatwater Classic canoe and kayak race. After the Boat House are steps to the water's edge from the walking path, right before the vivid red railed pedestrian path that extends over the river's edge.

St Charles Air Line Bridge is next. Looking like a large-scale erector set, it is another Strauss heel trunnion design with a counterweight that is not fixed and the bridge has a teasing tangle of trusses. The first span is still in use and operates for boaters, whereas the one sticking straight up in the air is now no longer in use.

The humongous array of train tracks on the bank of the river is a railroad yard, which loads box cars onto each train line. Then, we come to the Roosevelt Street Bridge. Another truss bascule bridge with see through road decking above us. Two beautiful circular bridgetender buildings with decorative ram heads on top. As the road heads east toward the museum complex on the lakeshore, there are towering obelisks, fluted lampposts, and sculptures. After the bridge, on the west bank is the at-risk iconic Art Moderne Union Power Station building. Built with Art Deco influences, it has parallel windows rising up to its two tall chimneys. On the east bank of the river is the S shaped River City Marina and apartments. The Chicago Lakefront Cruise line docks at the marina. Back on the west bank is a United States Post Office building complex.

We paddle under the Harrison Street Bridge, a new Chicago bascule bridge which continues the classic Chicago pony truss design with very few new upgrades. Immediately after this bridge is the Congress Parkway Bridge, painted white, with two double leaf bascule bridges. Interstate 290 terminates here as the roadway tunnels under the Old Post Office, crosses the river, and the busy interchange is known as the "Spaghetti Bowl".

We now have some of the best views of the Chicago Loop and the famous skyscrapers of Chicago! A high-rise condominium is right after Congress Parkway Bridge on the east side of the river. It looks like white Lego blocks are sticking out of the sides of the building and a white rectangle square frame at the top.

Paddling under the Van Buren Street Bridge, we can look up through the metal grate road decking. The double leaf bascule bridge was built with simplistic square bridgetender towers. On the west side of the river is an office building and on the east bank is a tad of green. But above the green, is the skyscraper that catches our eye. It is the 311 South Wacker Street post-modern building. The crowning jewel is the cylindrical translucent top with four smaller tubes, that glow at night, making it one of the most visible skyscrapers in the evening.

Float under the Jackson Boulevard Bridge, one of Chicago's oldest of the deck truss bascule bridges. It has an appealing graceful arch that we get to see from the river. This bridge is part of the Historic Route 66 that starts in Chicago. On the west side of the river is Union Station tower and grand hall. Union Station is the third busiest station of the national railroad hubs. On the east side is an office building with a triangle top, then the Willis Tower. This is the second tallest skyscraper in the United States. With 108 floors, and the signature black aluminum and bronze tinted windows, it has a step back design, with the floors getting smaller as it rises up. The Observation deck is on the 103rd floor with "the ledge", glass balconies with transparent floors where you can look out at four states and the sparkling blue of Lake Michigan!

The Adam Street Bridge is next, a true deck truss bridge with the trusses completely below the road. Due to the busy city area, the trunnion and counterweights on the sides are not identical to each other. The two bridge tender houses are limestone with exquisite ornate roofs. The attractive landscaped Riverside Plaza is on the west side of the river.

Head under the Monroe Street Bridge, the first Chicago Bridge to have a smooth curved pony truss design. It is also unique because they couldn't put the counterweight under the roadway due to underground train tracks from Union Station, so the west side of the bridge has a heavier cast iron weight. The bridge tender towers are lovely with enchanting roof toppers. The Riverside Plaza walkway continues on the west bank with trees peeking out above the white waving reeds railing. There is a midrange skyscraper building on the west bank, with the taller Heller International building behind it. The Heller skyscraper is the tallest building west of the Chicago

River, and is noted for the rectangular step up turret on the southeast corner which is illuminated white at night. While on the east bank of the river is the Chicago Mercantile Exchange building with its twin towers. Both towers with fun zig-zag corners, intentionally curve outward to hold the exchange ceiling between them aloft.

The Madison Street Bridge was built in 1922 and is the first bridge to use rail height trusses. There are trusses above and below the roadway with the trusses on the roadway 3 feet tall and separates pedestrians from vehicles. The limestone bridge tender houses have pretty roof lines with a bird statue perched on the tippy top. On the west bank is one of the Chicago River Taxi stops in front of the Riverside Plaza art deco building. It was also one of the first buildings constructed over an underground railroad. Across the river is the Civic Opera Building, built in 1929 in the shape of a throne, so that it's owner's spirit could sit on his throne and watch the growth of Chicago after his death. The Lyric Opera House is in a traditional European style with an international reputation. The Madison Street Bridge is also known as the Lyric Opera Bridge.

Paddle onward to the Washington Boulevard Bridge. Initially, there was a tunnel under the river here for wagons and pedestrians. The tunnel served as an escape route to flee the city during the Great Chicago Fire in 1871. However, boats would scrape the roof of the tunnel. Therefore, the present bridge was constructed in 1891, making it the oldest Chicago River Bridge. The bridge tender houses are unique in mauve and green, with interesting ornamentation and molded copper sheeting. The riverside plaza walkway continues on the west bank with two levels with trees and garden pots. Then the Boeing International Building soars above. As we look way up, we see the modern clock tower. The steel trusses on the shorter portion of the building is needed to support the building over the railroad tracks underneath. Looking east, we see two office buildings, one with a pyramid on top that it lighted with flood lights inside at night.

The Randolph Street Bridge is a box girder bridge with hollow beams, and the single square nondescript bridge tender house. The Riverside plaza walkway has ended on the west side of the river. But, look east! First is a high ratio window line glass office building, and then the Great Lakes Building—a repurposed warehouse covered in green vines. But here is where the Chicago Riverwalk begins on the east side of the river with The Riverbank, a promenade of public lawn and gardens down to the shoreline of the confluence of the rivers!

Stop and enjoy the massive Lake Street Bridge, one of the finest and most impressive fixed trunnion bascule bridges in Chicago. A double decker bridge, it carries trains on the upper deck and cars and people on the lower deck. The first river crossing was here in 1829, a ferry which cost 6 ¼ cents! The bridge tender houses feature extravagant Beaux-Arts architecture in the French Neoclassical style with ornamental details and two sloped mansard roofs.

We have come to a parting of the ways—the North Branch of the Chicago River, or the main channel of the Chicago River. In the center is Wolf Point. We choose to follow the main river east on the along the Riverwalk. As we paddle around the corner, buildings are reflected on the curved glass of the 333 Wacker Street building. This building was featured in Ferris Buellers Day Off movie. The high-rise office building is a reflection of the curve of the Chicago River with blue green glass that mimics the color of the river.

As we around the corner of the river, we paddle under one of the prettiest bridges in Chicago—the Franklin Street Bridge. The bridge has its original railings with flowers in the panels. The Bridge Tender houses rise above and are topped with fancy crowns. On the now south bank of the river, is an office building, with brilliantly lit top hats on each corner. The Riverwalk continues with The Jetty, a series of piers and floating gardens. Folks can fish from the piers. But, do not miss the Merchandise Mart on the north bank of the river. The amazing huge retail mall, built in the Art Deco norm with limestone, terra-cotta, and bronze, with decorative V shaped chevrons. Topped with green octagonal pyramids on the four corner towers, and the huge central tower. The north side Riverwalk is lined with Art Deco obelisks, with the eight tallest ones capped with big bronze heads of merchandizing pioneers. David Letterman nicknamed them the "Pez Hall of Fame" and name survives!

Up comes another massive bridge, a non-identical twin to the Lake Street Bridge—the Wells Street Bridge. This bridge connects the north side of Chicago with the Chicago Loop. The double decker carries trains on the top and pedestrians and vehicles on the bottom. The bridge tender houses are posh with fancy flumes on the roofs. On the north bank is a short building with glass cubes on the top. Then a waterfront public garden along the river. Across the river at street level are concrete flower baskets along the decorative spindle railings. On the Riverwalk, the Water Plaza has a zero-depth pool and a floating walkway with bubbling and jumping water fountains.

Float under the lovely La Salle Street Bridge, a single deck double leaf bascule bridge. The two ends of the trusses up on the road have charming top chord curves. There are four bridge tender towers to mark the Gateway to the Chicago Loop's financial district. The houses are lofty, with concave decorative corners. The tops are lavishly adorned in the Beaux Arts style with two-sloped mansard roofs and large shields on the sides. The pedestrian roadway railings are also richly embellished with flowing flowers in the center of each railing. This bridge is a beau!

Just after the LaSalle Street Bridge is where a terrible disaster happened in 1915. The S.S. Eastland capsized while docked. I'm sure you've heard of it, right? It happened only 3 years after the Titanic disaster. The "speed queen of the Great Lakes", the S.S. Eastland was at dock, loading people planning an all-day adventure across Lake Michigan. However, after 2,572 passengers boarded, with many on the upper deck to wave at family and friends, the ship started listing and in less than 2 minutes collapsed on her side. The poor passengers in the lower decks were crushed by furniture and drowned trying to escape—many of them women with heavy skirts.

The folks on the upper decks were thrown into the water. Part of the blame, falls on the Titanic—honest. After that disaster, all ships needed to be retrofitted with lifeboats and life jackets, which made the boat top heavy. . . and disaster awaited. 844 people died that day. Unlike the unfortunate souls, the ship was salvaged, renamed (I wonder why?) and used as a gun-boat in World War II.

The north bank of the river is completely dominated by the Reid Murdoch building, a Chicago Landmark. Look up at its classic clocktower. There is a river walk above the metal shoreline with flower boxes, single globe lampposts and a water taxi stop. On the south bank, is a limestone and granite mid-skyscraper, topped with an arched sun beacon which glows at night. Next door is the sleek glass One Illinois Center. Built as a series of columns of glass it creates a unified reflective façade. The sidewalk of Wacker Drive is a gorgeous assemble of short obelisks with globed lights with white steps leading down to rivers edge—The River Theater. This interface of geometrics with a sloped wheelchair ramp down to bank of the river, offers stairs and terraces. The River Theater poses an urban oasis with trees growing from the steps.

Next on our tour, is the Clark Street Bridge which is similar to the La Salle Street Bridge with the eye-catching pony truss bascule double leaf design. The first bridge here was a floating bridge in 1840 that was destroyed in an icy flood. Chicagoans tried again with a swing bridge that was destroyed in the Chicago Fire. This bridge, built in 1929 with metal riveted trusses, survives nicely. The bridge tender towers are beautiful with curved embellished roofs. On the north side is a modern riverfront glass structure, followed by the Westin Hotel with angled windows to give spectacular city views. On the south bank is the post-modern architectural glass and columns of white granite with the top floor a Greek triangular pediment gable. Wacker Drive is nice with baluster railings and cement flower pots. Below the sidewalk is The Cove, part of the Riverwalk. The Cove has a gentle slope down to the river's edge, where you can tie up your kayaks and enjoy part of the Riverwalk.

Paddle on after The Cove, to the Dearborn Street Bridge. The Dearborn Bridge has the same pony lattice and lace trusses that had worked so well for Chicago for decades. Float under the bridge to see the single bridge tender house on the south east corner in a sleek modern design. On the north bank, are the two Marina City cylindrical towers, a Chicago iconic landmark. Constructed in the 1960's, the mid-century modernism "corncob" towers, actually had the inspiration of petals on a sunflower with curved patios. At river level, Marina City, does have a marina, then several stories of restaurants. Looking to the south bank, there is a postmodern office building, then the Renaissance Hotel. Wacker Street carries on the fetching concrete rail with hanging flower baskets and ornate flower beds to separate walkers from cars. Stairs down to the Riverwalk with benches, and the City Winery patio. Motor boats and kayaks can tie up at river's edge at The Marina portion of the Riverwalk.

Up comes the State Street Bridge. Completed in 1949. . .it took a long time to construct due to steel shortages during World War II. It is one of the widest of the pony truss bridges with eight lanes of traffic and the bridge has three pony truss guardrails. The Bridge Tender houses are Art Deco with limestone walls and a flat roof and ornamentation around the windows. On the north side of the river is a modernist structure of black anodized aluminum exterior with floor to ceiling windows. There is a plaza on street level with tree and flower gardens. At rivers edge is a living wall topped with bright flowers. Looking south, the modernist office building is clad in white marble. In contrast, its neighbor is the olde Jewelers Building. Built in 1926 in a wedding cake design with a dome on top. The building used to have a car elevator—yup, that is not a typo—a car elevator, that brought cars up to the 40th floor! The Jewelers Building is an Art Deco design with decorative towers on the four corners which initially stored water for fire suppression. On the northeast corner is the Father Time ornate clock. Wacker Drive sidewalk continues with decorative garden planters filled with trees and flowers. A statue of Washington is in Heald Square. Down the steps brings us to the Riverwalk with a sloped green grass hill, and steps with plateaus of green lawn with a railing along the river. The whole plaza is lighted by ornate glowing globes. On the river is the Vietnam Memorial, with a flowing fountain and the names of 2,900 Illinois servicemen who paid the ultimate price of their life in the Vietnam War. Chicago Remembers.

Quickly, we are at the North Wabash Avenue Bridge, designated the "most beautiful steel bridge" when it was built, with delicate railings. The bridge tender houses are lavish with the two sloped roofs. On the north bank, soars the immense Trump Tower. It is a hotel condo mix and is the second tallest skyscraper in Chicago. The Trump Tower copies the Willis Tower in its stacked design. It is the world's tallest reinforced concrete structure concealed with glass and steel. The glossy exterior reflects the nearby Chicago skyline, and is unmistakable since TRUMP is stamped on the exterior in enormous letters. In contrast to the glass tower, is the luminous white terra-cotta historic landmark Wrigley building next door. The two towers were completed in 1924 as a headquarters for the chewing gum company. Fabricated in the French Renaissance architecture, the towers are not twins. The tower closest to the river is topped with the four-sided clock tower. Each clock is 20 feet in diameter, and the clock tower is capped with a Greek cupula. The Wrigley Building, the "Gateway to the Magnificent Mile" glows at night with floodlights. From the water, there are two levels of pedestrian paths in a green park, with steps, tree planters, a water garden and one of Chicago River taxi stops.

Sweeping over to the south bank, is the Wyndham Grand Hotel with its glass penthouse ballroom and terrace at the top. In the middle is the landmark Mather Tower. The terracotta Neo-Gothic tower is the skinniest skyscraper in the city. At the top is an octagonal turret topped with a golden crown. At the corner of Michigan Avenue is the London Guarantee Building. Created in a classical revival Beaux Arts style with columns at the front entrance, huge columns near the top and a cupula with ringed columns with a dome top perched on the pinnacle. This historic building, is located where the original shore of Lake Michigan was and where Fort Dearborn once stood. Paddling on the river, this side of the river is the pretty side, with large trees, old fashioned globe lights, and pretty umbrellas by the Riverwalk Café. At the east end of the Riverwalk, before the next bridge is the McCormick Bridgehouse and Museum. As we enter at river level we are in the belly of the beast and get to see the massive gears that lift the bridge up. Climb to the top of the bridgetender house, and see what the bridge tender gets to look at all day—360 degrees of river and the city!

We are at the Michigan Avenue, Du Sable Bridge. Erected in 1920, it is a world-famous moveable bridge, and a wonderful work of art. It is another double decker bridge, but in this case, the lower level is not for trains but for a service road. The bridge is actually two side by side bridges that could be lifted independently of each other.

There are four baroque Beaux Art Parisian bridgetender houses, capped with decorative temples. There are bas relief sculptures on each of the bridge towers. On the north side of the river is the River Esplanade with several levels of walkways, down by the river's edge, with arched walkways under the building. Next door is the University of Chicago Gleacher Center. After the tour boat dock for Shoreline Sightseeing is a pretty X crossed railing on the River Esplanade with diamond decorated pillars with square decorative lights, and green trees and shrubbery behind. On the south side of the river, is an art deco skyscraper. It has a marble base, topped by patterned limestone bands and glass. The next building is the sleek One Illinois Center in an international style with panes of glass in a series of columns, and then the Hyatt Regency with tall vertical pillars of windows. The final skyscraper is the Columbus Plaza, with six stacked window cubes. At the south side river level are several cruise lines.   The Chicago First Lady Cruises which specializes in Chicago Architecture Cruises and the Skyline Cruise line, which offers urban adventures and night cruises. Behind the tour boats is a Beer and Cider garden, followed by a Café and Wine bar with shelter under broadening tree cover with bistro tables.

We have now paddled to the newest and widest of the Chicago River bridges, the Columbus Drive Bridge. It is a basic box girder bridge with hollow beams instead of trusses.   It was built to allow pedestrian walkways under the bridge continuing the Riverwalk. The one bridge tender tower follows the modern design of the bridge. The building on the north bank with the round corner turrets is the Sheraton Grande Hotel, in a post-modern design. Next an apartment building rotated on a diamond to maximize views of Lake Michigan and the Chicago River. Followed by a condominium complex of two towers of stone, brick and green glass overlooking the river. Down at river level by us, we look up at the continuation of the River Esplanade with the asterisk railings and pillars with a diamond motif and square lights on top. The Esplanade is lined with green trees with the Centennial Fountain. A fabulous fountain with water flowing down an arc of steps with a water veil that we can walk inside behind. And, fairly important to mention. . .is the water cannon, the "Big Squirt" that shoots out an arch of water over the river almost to the south bank of the river. Tourists come on the hour, to see if the water cannon hits any wayward boaters. . .

After the Columbus Drive Bridge on the south shore, we have glass building after glass buildings. Please don't throw stones. . . Each are unique geometric shapes, first a long narrow rectangle office building, then the triangular contemporary luxury Swissotel. Next up is a rectangular modern apartment building, followed by an ellipse shaped condominiums high-rise. Lastly, is a rectangle with curved front and back with floor to ceiling windows. Towering behind the first two glass buildings is the Radisson Blu Aqua, a hotel skyscraper with an undulated, curvy, flowy façade. The Riverwalk, below Lower Wacker Drive, is a parkland area with grass and trees. Urban Kayaks with lime green kayaks, is located here with rentals for experienced kayakers and tours for beginners. Island Party Hut offers a deck with blue umbrellas and picnic tables by the shoreline.

We've come to our last Chicago River bridge, the Lake Shore Drive Bridge, another Strauss bascule bridge. It carries one of the heaviest traffic for a moveable bridge in the world. There are actually two bridges, the double leaf bridge over the Chicago River and the smaller fixed bridge over the Ogden Slip. The Lake Shore Drive bridge has a lower deck, now a secondary vehicle road. The Lake Shore Drive Bridge is a Massive Gateway to Chicago!

Once past the Lake Shore Drive Bridge, the river opens up. To the north is the DuSable peninsula, a former industrial site that is awaiting rehabilitation for a park. On the east shore is Polk Brothers Park, the entry to Navy Pier. The park has lawns for art and culture events, and a large programmable water fountain that can imitate flocks of birds, schools of fish, and Lake Michigan waves! It is water playground for kids and is color lighted at night. The golden skyscraper is a condominium shaped like a 3 edged triangular boomerang. We turn west and go down the Ogden Slip and back under the Lake Shore Drive Bridge. Both sides of the Ogden Slip have a river promenade. The north side historical brick and timber building is lofts, whereas on the south side are townhouses. The Chicago Line cruise ships dock is on the north side. At the end of the slip are steps up from the water. We can stop here if in need of a stretch and rest break. Probably not a great launch site as parking may be difficult. Paddling down into the Ogden Slip and back adds three quarters of a mile to our paddle.

We paddle straight, towards the Chicago Harbor Lock. On the south side, we pass the Chicago Marine Safety Station. It is a unique white Cape Cod style structure with a green roof. This is a Coast Guard Station that shares the building with the Chicago Police. Might be a good idea to be on our best behavior. . .

We love locks! It is in our family DNA, our family history. Our grandfather was a lock master on the Fox River in Appleton. My grandpa would let me, a skinny small child, help him turn the lock gate, which was done by hand, I'm sure I was a great help! The Chicago Harbor Lock was built to control the water level in the Chicago River. The lock is 600 feet long, 80 feet wide and 22 feet deep. We are sharing the lock with a very large Navy ship that takes up the whole one side of the lock. . .puts an added dimension into our busy lock tour. We need to stay at least 50 feet away from the stoplight on the control tower on the north wall, and make sure the lock master can see us. If you are not sure, you can call the lock master on channel 16. All of us must wear our PFD to be in the lock. When the lock opens, a horn will sound and the stoplight will turn to green. I know that means go, but it is safest to let the motor boats (and the very large Navy ship) to enter first. Then paddle as fast as possible into the lock. Find a hanging rope to hang onto. The lock master keeps telling me to hold the rope, I need a bull horn to answer back that "I can't reach it". I finally find a strand long enough to hold and then the lock master is happy. For safety, we do need to hold the rope, or hold onto another boat that is holding a rope. The lock closes and the gate in front opens just a couple of feet to change the water level. When the gate in front fully opens, a horn again blows. Stay put and let the boats exit first for our safety, then we paddle with a purpose to leave the lock. Once out, we keep paddling past all the waiting boats to enter the lock. It takes about 15 minutes for the full cycle of the Chicago Harbor Lock.

And then we've done it! We've paddled the Chicago River! Time to explore Navy Pier!

Logistics:

Richard Daley Park, Chicago:
41.8370, -87.6866. 3150 S. Western Avenue. Nice parking lot, and easy boat launch, however no restrooms available.

Chicago Park No. 571 Floating Boat launch dock, Chicago:
41.8440, -87.6635. 2828 S. Eleanor Street. Restrooms, no fee.

Lawrence Fish and Shrimp Restaurant and Fishery, Chicago:
41.8542, -87.6389. 2120 S. Canal Street. Private dock that is offered for public use. Please park to the back of the parking lot, and thank them by enjoying the restaurant!

Ping Tom Memorial Park, Chinatown Chicago:
41.8589, -87.6341. 300 W 19th Street. 1000-foot carry into the park and to the Boathouse. Restrooms. Rei does rent kayaks.

Ogden Slip steps, possible launch site, Chicago:
41.8903, -87.6174. 433 N. McClurg Court.
Street parking only, good luck.

It actually might be easiest to just rent kayaks if you only want to do the downtown skyscraper area:

Rei at Ping Tom Park:
REI Boathouse: 43.8582, -87.6346, 300 W. 19th Street. Cement steps to river access.

Urban Kayaks Boat Rental or Tours, Chicago Riverwalk:
41.888, -87.61751. 435 E. Chicago Riverwalk. Located between the Columbus Drive Bridge and Lake Shore Drive Bridge on the south side of the river.

Kayak Chicago Boat Rentals or Tours, Chicago:
41.9091, -87.6580. 1220 W. LeMoyne Street. Kayak Chicago is at the end of the street by the river.

About the Author

Babs Malchow Smith

I have an easy propensity to saying yes to just about any adventure one of my brothers dream up. I am married to my husband, Mike, who indulges me and lets my West wind flow, whereas, he steers clear and likes to stay well grounded. I am an occupational therapist by trade, so although I am not the most skillful paddler, I am handy at the end of the day when any muscle aches flare up.

Thank you for reading my book. If you enjoyed it, won't you please take a moment to leave me a review at your favorite retailer?

Connect with me:

Babs_daykayaking@yahoo.com

Enjoy the paddles!

Babs Smith

With Special Thanks

Rick and Chris Malchow, My paddling partners:

My brother Rick, is our fearless leader, giving us a gentle push off when launching, and guides us safely into shore in rough terrain. Rick is a powerful dynamic paddler who can outdistance us at any time. My special sister-in-law, Chris, with her easy laugh, helps Rick from overstressing on planning details. She is natural paddler with a smooth, easy, efficient stroke.

Ryan Malchow, Graphic Design:

Ryan, Rick and Chris's son, has a B. A. in Marketing and Visual Arts, which is a great asset to me. He's an artist who enjoys creative pursuits.

Gerry LaBonte, Editing:

Gerry and his wife Ann are great friends who love sailing and canoeing. Thanks for making this book have correct spelling and grammar, and for teaching me what em-dashes and ellipses are!

www.ingramcontent.com/pod-product-compliance
Lightning Source LLC
Chambersburg PA
CBHW062151270326
41930CB00009B/1503